12-26-62

CZECHOSLOVAK NATIONAL INCOME AND PRODUCT
1947–1948 AND 1955–1956

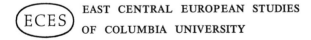

EAST CENTRAL EUROPEAN STUDIES
OF COLUMBIA UNIVERSITY

CZECHOSLOVAK NATIONAL INCOME AND PRODUCT 1947-1948 AND 1955-1956

By THAD PAUL ALTON

AND

VACLAV HOLESOVSKY, GREGOR LAZARCIK
PAUL D. SIVAK, ALEXEJ WYNNYCZUK

COLUMBIA UNIVERSITY PRESS 1962

NEW YORK AND LONDON

EAST CENTRAL EUROPEAN STUDIES
OF COLUMBIA UNIVERSITY

The East Central European Studies, a companion series to the Studies of the Russian Institute, comprise scholarly books prepared under the auspices of the Program on East Central Europe of Columbia University or through other divisions of the University. The publication of these studies is designed to enlarge our understanding of an important region of the world, which, because of its relative inaccessibility in recent years as well as because of the linguistic problems it presents, has been somewhat neglected in serious academic study. The faculty of the Program on East Central Europe, without necessarily endorsing the conclusions reached by the authors, believe that these studies contribute substantially to knowledge of the area and should serve to stimulate further inquiry and research.

PREFACE

IN RECENT YEARS the Soviet economy has been the subject of numerous studies by Western scholars, but the Soviet-type economies in East Central Europe—East Germany, Poland, Czechoslovakia, Hungary, Rumania, Bulgaria, and Albania—have been largely neglected. With a population equal to forty-five percent of that of the USSR and a national product roughly of the same order of magnitude, this area is an important element in the world economy. Although an increasing amount of economic information is being published by these countries, unfortunately the concepts in which some of the data are reported and the peculiarities of the underlying price systems in which the values are expressed require a separate analysis to be comprehended by Western students. The present volume, as part of a larger study of the structure and growth of these economies carried on by the Research Project on National Income in East Central Europe, is directed toward filling this gap in our knowledge.

At the outset of the study a cooperative effort by Paul Sivak, Gregor Lazarcik, and myself was aimed at showing the structure of the gross national product of Czechoslovakia in 1947–48 by sectors of origin and by final uses. Paul Sivak left the project after completing a draft of the national accounts for these years. Subsequently Vaclav Holesovsky and Alexej Wynnyczuk joined the research team, and the study was expanded to cover the years 1955–56.

All members of the research group contributed to the study in terms of drafting portions of it and commenting on the work of their colleagues. In general, Gregor Lazarcik was primarily responsible for the estimates pertaining to the agricultural sector for all the years considered, and he contributed as well to other aspects, notably to estimates of employment and wage and salary incomes. Vaclav Holesovsky and Alexej Wynnyczuk did the basic research on most of the nonagricultural estimates for 1955–56, and the former adapted the draft of the 1947–48 accounts for inclusion with the 1955–56 study in a single volume. I am responsible for the design of the study, its immediate substantive supervision, consultation on various estimates, the section on factor cost adjustments, and the final assembly of the study.

Students of the Soviet economy are familiar with the kinds of problems we faced in this work. The lack of direct information in some instances had to be bridged by deductions from related data, and in a few instances informed guesses were necessary. In all cases we tried to keep in mind reasonable limits for our estimates and to give our sources, methodology, and impressions of reliability for the figures.

The authors are indebted to Professor Abram Bergson for his work on the Soviet national income, which showed the need and the possibility for this kind of work. We are happy to acknowledge also our debt to him and to Professor Harold Barger for reading and commenting upon drafts of our study. Dr. Maurice Ernst and Professor Boris P. Pesek afforded us numerous helpful consultations on problems of research and analysis. Finally, our thanks are due to many others for help in libraries, typing, statistical computations, and other assistance. The authors alone are responsible for any shortcomings in the work.

THAD PAUL ALTON

New York, N. Y.
July, 1962

CONTENTS

TABLES

CZECHOSLOVAK NATIONAL INCOME
AND PRODUCT
1947–1948 AND 1955–1956

I. INTRODUCTION

OUR AIM in the present study is to show the structure of the Czechoslovak economy in quantitative terms for four post-war years, 1947–48 and 1955–56. By dividing the economy into a small number of decision-making sectors and recording transactions between them in regard to production, consumption, and wealth formation, we are able to derive the familiar national income aggregates in a consistent manner. The inter-related accounts insure that the requirements of consistency are faced.

Our final results show, first, the gross national product and its composition by sectors of origin and by categories of final use at the actual transaction prices, and, second, the gross national product and again its composition at estimated factor cost. Both representations are of interest. The first, besides being a steppingstone to the second, facilitates an understanding of monetary phenomena, showing the articulation of the economic system in the financial values actually experienced; the second seeks to revalue the components of economic activity from market prices to factor cost, thus making possible an appreciation of the importance of the various sectors of production and final use in terms of resources consumed. For many Western economies the structure at market prices is reasonably close to that at factor cost; thus, no revaluation may be required. However, in the case of the Soviet-type economies, even a very superficial acquaintance with the price system shows serious divergencies from factor cost caused primarily by the incidence of very high indirect taxes almost exclusively on consumer goods and services and by failure to account adequately for capital costs. This is not a matter of slight divergence; our adjustment in 1955, for example, shows personal consumption declining from 55.0 percent of gross national product at market prices to 44.4 percent at factor cost.

Those who are familiar with the task of constructing national accounts well know the necessity of making estimates from related data to fill gaps in information. Sometimes we have had to settle for something much less than the ideal in order to complete particular estimates; at all stages, however, we have tried to show our methodology in full and to give our sources, and, where appropriate, to point out shortcomings.

Despite certain limitations stemming from lack of information, the study seems justified on the following grounds: (1) for the years 1947–48, it supplies an independent alternative to the Czechoslovak estimates; (2) for the years 1955–56, it fills a gap created by the failure of Czechoslovak agencies to publish their estimates; (3) for all years, it furnishes national accounts constructed in keeping with methodology and concepts generally understood in the West; and, finally, (4) it provides an objective basis for a number of further inquiries concerning the structure, performance, and orientation of the Czechoslovak economy. Among these inquiries we consider the allocation of resources to sectors of production and to final uses and the sources of finance for gross investment and various collective expenditures. Our findings should also be of interest in connection with future studies of growth of the Czechoslovak economy.

Official Czechoslovak national income concepts for the years 1947–48 agreed in many respects with those used in our study; still there were important differences, and not enough was indicated on the level of detailed procedures. By 1955–56, however, the Soviet national income concept referring to material production and excluding services considered non-productive had been established, and, to complicate matters further, no national income aggregates in current prices have been published for the years since the Communist *coup d'état* in 1948. The index of national income in constant prices and the percentage composition of national income in current prices, which are published without supporting information, leave many questions unanswered. Our study, therefore, is the only detailed construction of Czechoslovak national accounts available at the moment this is written.

ECONOMIC SETTING

The two periods covered by our study are separated in time by the turbulent years of the First Five-Year Plan (1949–53). Thus, the two sets of national product estimates provide a picture of economic structure before and after the transformation of the economy from a mixed ownership system with relatively few centrally established priorities to a system with preponderant state ownership and with highly centralized planning and control covering the major sectors of production.

In the "mixed economy" as it emerged from the first wave of postwar nationalization measures, socialized industry employed about 80 percent of the industrial labor force. The second wave of nationalization in 1948 raised this to 95 percent. Agriculture, with the insignificant exception of state farms, remained private. In the same period, despite a large segment of industry under state ownership, the central regulation of the economy did not go much beyond price fixing and the corollary subsidies, rationing, control of foreign trade, and the enunciation of comparatively general policies aimed at recovery of production to prewar levels.

By 1955–56, industry was 100 percent nationalized; state farms and peasant collective farms, together comprising socialized agriculture, accounted for slightly over 40 percent of the land under exploitation; and private handicrafts and service trades had dwindled from about 460,000 employees in 1948 to less than 30,000 in 1956.[1]

In the meantime the Soviet model of highly centralized economic planning and control had been progressively installed. Two banks, the State Bank and the Investment Bank, accounted

[1] State Statistical Office, *Statistická ročenka*, 1957, pp. 117, 180.

for practically all business enterprise loans, leaving the small residual activities and personal savings deposits to the state savings banks. Financial control was tightened over the socialized enterprises by a system of financial transfers linking them to the state budget. The planning of production, at first extremely detailed in the assignment of production goals, later became somewhat less detailed, with emphasis on products of the highest priority. Labor legislation became stricter in an attempt to combat absenteeism and poor discipline. A drastic monetary reform (1953) destroyed a large part of the money at the disposal of the population and, together with other measures, succeeded in stabilizing prices.

The years of the First Five-Year Plan witnessed heavy pressures for increasing industrial production, frequent changes in the production priorities, overly ambitious investment projects, planning errors and poor coordination of economic activities, and increasing pressures on the population, all of which resulted in considerable waste and disorganization.[2] Inventories increased sharply as a consequence of unstable supply and marketing relationships.[3]

With lessened rigor following Stalin's death, Czechoslovakia, along with other satellite countries, was permitted to take a biennium, 1954–55, to correct some of the disproportions brought about by the forced draft industrialization of the earlier years. This respite was followed by the Second Five-Year Plan in 1956. Thus, the second period covered by our accounts, namely, 1955–56, covers a year of readjustment and a year of renewed pressure for expansion.

[2] For example, a resolution on the reorganization of planning, July 4 and 5, 1952, stated: "Output targets of cooperating branches were not properly harmonized at the level of the state plans; as a consequence, output programs of plants were frequently changed, sales of products and the supply of plants with raw materials and intermediate products got into difficulties." See *Rudé právo,* October 14, 1952.

[3] *Rudé právo,* May 6, 1954, indicates that inventories almost doubled between 1950 and 1953. The issue for January 1, 1953, witnesses the poor correspondence of plans to the actual demands: "Unfortunately, for some articles we have twice as many orders as we are able to satisfy according to plan, while for others we have orders covering only one tenth [of the planned output]."

The economic policies pursued by the government in 1955–56 can be summarized as follows:

1. There was continued pressure for expanding production by mobilizing the resources still available, for example, unemployed women, and by more intensive use of the resources already employed.

2. Investment, which had been allowed to slow down in the period of readjustment, 1954–55, regained emphasis: an index derived from official figures in constant prices shows a decline from 100 in 1953 to 97 in 1954, followed by an increase to 106 in 1955 and 113 in 1956.[4]

3. Purchasing power of the urban population was kept firmly in bounds.

4. Farmers were allowed to increase their income by selling a larger share of their produce at the higher above-quota prices, and a smaller share as compulsory deliveries at the low state procurement prices. The drive for collectivization was resumed in 1956. Although the collective farms received preferential treatment over private farms, agriculture as a whole apparently was allowed to recuperate somewhat from the lean years of 1950–53.

An event of particular interest for national income accounting was the revaluation of fixed capital as of the beginning of 1955 in terms of replacement cost based on July, 1954, prices. This was followed in 1956 by sharply increased depreciation allowances to conform more closely to actual capital consumption in current prices. The low allowances in the years before the revision raised the question of the validity of the net national product estimates.

NOTE ON SOURCES

Sources of statistical information are far from fully satisfactory for either 1947–48 or 1955–56; yet, when the data are taken together within the constraints imposed by our system of accounts, it is possible to derive the major economic aggregates with a fair degree of reliability. One disadvantage of the available data is that they are found mostly in condensed, secondary

[4] State Statistical Office, *Statistická ročenka,* 1957, p. 71.

sources, namely, in the various publications of the State Statistical Office. Two important exceptions are: (1) the executed state budgets as given in the full closing accounts for 1947 and 1948, compiled by the Central Auditing Office, and (2) data on postwar agriculture based on continued observation of a sample of 494 farms from 1926 to 1947.

There would be no question of the intended reliability of the published data we used; however, there is often a lack of precision in defining the concepts used and in specifying their scope of coverage. Moreover, the procedure by which the published figures were derived is not made clear in many cases. We must differentiate, too, between statistics on lower levels and the more highly aggregated national statistics. Clearly, despite shortcomings in the statistics at the lower levels caused by personal inefficiency or motives of self-preservation or gain on the part of the reporting units, these statistics inevitably must be the starting point for economic analysis. But it is on the higher levels of aggregation, especially on the level of national income, that the official policy of withholding information or providing insufficient background for evaluation of the few published statistics is most apparent. Indeed, it is because national income data in current prices are lacking and because such few percentage composition figures as are published relate to the Soviet-type incomplete definition of national income and to a warped system of relative prices, that the present study is necessary.

Published information for 1955–56 is generally more systematic than that for 1947–48, possibly as a by-product of the more comprehensive state ownership and control in the later period. By contrast to the years chosen for our inquiry, the intervening years represent a veritable statistical vacuum. Still, despite a relative abundance of statistics, we found it necessary to piece together disparate bits of information gathered in periodicals and in the daily press, a technique familiar to researchers in Soviet studies. Information on the state budget in 1955–56 was truly sparse in comparison to the detail available for 1947–48. In both periods, however, military expenditures were available simply as single totals, without any breakdown. Because of this secrecy, our estimates must be regarded as rough approximations, and the possibility of disguised military expenditures under other categories of the state budget must be kept in mind.

PLAN OF THE STUDY

In Chapter II we describe our accounting framework, and we present sectoral and consolidated national accounts in current market prices. The accompanying text comments on each accounting entry with regard to content, sources, and reliability. Full supporting details are given in Appendixes A through F.

In Chapter III we show the distribution of gross national product by sectors of origin and final use at factor cost. Our adjustments to market prices are related, first, to our definition of a factor cost standard and, second, to divergencies from this standard identified in a survey of the current market prices. Detailed calculations carrying out the principles of the adjustment are given in Appendixes G and H.

Finally, in Chapter IV we discuss a few of the economic implications of our findings, particularly the sources of government and investment finance, the allocation of resources, and the relation of our results to Czechoslovak official estimates. Supporting calculations are presented in Appendix I.

II. SECTORAL AND CONSOLIDATED ACCOUNTS

ACCOUNTING FRAMEWORK

The system of national accounts used here is based on a classification of transactors into a limited number of categories, on a breakdown of economic activity into basic forms, and on identification of types of transactions.[1] We identify three domestic sectors—households, business enterprises, and government—and one foreign sector, to close the system. For many purposes in our calculations, we also treat agriculture as a separate sector, although it enters the enterprise sector at the level of our formal sectoral tables. For each sector we have set up three accounts corresponding to the functions of production, consumption, and capital formation, and within these accounts we identify various types of transactions as significant for economic analysis.

A number of basic identities is fundamental to the system of accounts. Thus, for example, total gross value added in production (net value added plus capital consumption) in the various sectors of a closed economy must equal consumption plus gross capital formation, and saving plus capital consumption allowances equal gross capital formation. In each account, of course, the sources of income must be balanced by the uses.

The household sector is taken to include all individuals who

[1] For a detailed discussion of this type of social accounting, see United Nations, *A System of National Accounts and Supporting Tables;* see also Organization for European Economic Cooperation, *A Standardized System of National Accounts* (1958 ed.). An earlier discussion and an example are given in the essay by Stone, "Functions and Criteria of a System of Social Accounting" in International Association for Research in Income and Wealth, *Income and Wealth.*

are normal residents and all private nonprofit organizations which are supported mainly by members' fees and dues and not established mainly to render services to enterprises or to serve as agencies of the government. We include domestic servants as producers also in the household sector, although it would be a simple matter to show all productive activity as belonging to the enterprise sector. Consolidation of the sectoral accounts does, of course, yield a single production account; the detail afforded by separate production accounts or by more detailed entries and supporting documentation in a single production account may be regarded as a matter of choice.[2]

Under the enterprise sector we include all firms and establishments producing goods for sale at a price intended to cover roughly the cost of production. This sector covers: private farms, retail shops, craftsmen, professional people, socialized or private chartered enterprises, cooperative enterprises, nonprofit institutions serving enterprises, the post office, transportation and communication services, trading and financial services, and miscellaneous government-owned service establishments, such as theaters, where the services are sold to the general public. All owners of dwellings, including owner-occupants, are included here in their capacity as landlords.

The government sector comprises all the agencies of general government, both central and local, except those which we put into the enterprise sector because of their sales to the public. Services falling in the government sector are those which are organized for, but normally not sold to, the community, for example, public administration, education, defense, and social security arrangements, regardless of whether they are supported by the government budget or operate on extrabudgetary funds.

The "rest-of-the-world," or foreign, sector closes the system by accounting for the external transactions of the economy.

We provide three accounts for each sector, as follows:

(1) A production account shows the revenues and expenditures connected with the sector's productive activity. On the re-

---

[2] It is recognized that the distinction between domestic services, which we show in the household production account, and other services, which are included in the enterprise sector account, is more or less arbitrary.

ceivable side of this account appear the receipts from sales, government subsidies to production, and the value of the physical change in stocks. The payable side records the charges against the product of the sector, namely, purchases from other sectors, indirect taxes, capital consumption allowances, and the net value added by factors of production. In a formal sense the net value added corresponds to factor incomes generated in the sector, that is, compensation of employees, net rent, interest, and profit; but in a more fundamental sense we must inquire as to whether indirect taxes in Czechoslovakia can be treated conventionally as nonfactor charges or whether they comprise factor rewards.[3]

(2) The appropriation account shows the consumption activity of the sector. Its receivable items include the value added by the sector transferred from its production account, as well as all current income from other sectors, whether these represent payments for services rendered or current transfers. The payable items show the distribution of the total current income receipts to various uses: income payments, direct taxes, expenditures on current final consumption, transfers, and saving.

(3) The capital account brings together all the transactions related to additions to wealth. Its receivables include the saving of the sector, capital consumption allowances transferred from the sector's production account, where applicable, and capital transfers and loans from other sectors; its payables show the allocation of the total capital resources to gross investment in the sector or loans and transfers to other sectors.

As already indicated above by way of examples of payable and receivable items, the types of transactions recorded in the accounts are intended to introduce further distinctions in the structure of the economy beyond the differentiation introduced by the division into major sectors and sets of accounts. Besides the basic types of transactions reflecting on the one hand goods and services and on the other purely financial transfers, depending on the desired detail, transactions can be identified by subsectors as transactors and by subcategories for commodities, services, and transfers.

[3] See Chapter III.

In general we have tried to record transactions as flows of payables and receivables relating to the economic activity of the given year, and these do not necessarily correspond to actual payments and receipts. In many cases, however, the information on which we relied offered no basis for establishing the distinction.

Upon consolidating the sectoral accounts described above over the whole economy and rearranging some entries, we derive at once the familiar national aggregate, the gross national product, from the production accounts, national income and net national product from the appropriation accounts, and a reconciliation of saving and investment from the capital accounts.

We present below in Tables 1 to 5, subdivided into sections A, B, and C to correspond to production, appropriation, and capital formation, our sectoral and consolidated accounts in current market prices for the years 1947–48 and 1955–56. Comments on individual entries will follow the tables.

TABLE 1 A

HOUSEHOLD SECTOR PRODUCTION ACCOUNT

(*Million crowns*)

	1947	1948	1955	1956
RECEIVABLE				
1. Sales to household sector appropriation account				
A. Domestic services	1,189	1,289	360	374
B. Services of nonprofit organizations	849	1,022	60	61
Total receivable	2,038	2,311	420	435
PAYABLE				
2. Current purchases by nonprofit organizations	200	239	14	14
3. Value added by sector	1,838	2,072	406	421
A. Wages of domestic servants				
(1) Money wages	707	770	157	163
(2) Wages in kind	434	467	156	162
B. Wages and salaries of employees of nonprofit organizations	612	718	42	43
C. Social security contributions for:				
(1) Domestic servants	48	52	47	49
(2) Employees of nonprofit organizations	37	65	4	4
Total payable	2,038	2,311	420	435

TABLE 1 B

HOUSEHOLD SECTOR APPROPRIATION ACCOUNT

(*Million crowns*)

	1947	1948	1955	1956
RECEIVABLE				
1. Value added by sector	1,838	2,072	406	421
2. Income from other sectors	203,289	221,751	95,870	102,460
A. Enterprise sector	155,180	169,205	71,676	76,537
(1) Cash income	129,862	143,023	65,288	69,230
a. Wages and salaries	101,609	115,423	54,024	57,561
b. Entrepreneurial income	18,053	15,000	1,200	1,100
c. Income of farmers	9,800	12,300	7,300	7,600
d. Income from forestry	400	300	64	69
e. Director's fund	0	0	500	600
f. Other cash income	0	0	2,200	2,300
(2) Income in kind	19,662	20,274	5,845	6,150
a. Wages and salaries in kind	4,200	4,600	145	150
b. Income in kind of farmers	14,462	14,674	5,700	6,000
c. Income in kind in trades and professions	1,000	1,000	0	0
(3) Cash and imputed net rental income	5,213	5,293	0	0
a. Cash	3,008	3,062	0	0
b. Imputed	1,505	1,531	0	0
c. Farm rents	700	700	0	0
(4) Interest	433	615	1	25
(5) Imputed wages	0	0	542	1,132
B. Government sector	48,109	52,546	24,194	25,923
(1) Cash wages and salaries	22,009	23,146	9,418	10,090
(2) Income in kind (military subsistence and clothing)	1,000	1,000	850	700
(3) Transfer payments	25,100	28,400	13,491	14,576
(4) Imputed wages (for unpaid labor on community improvement projects)			435	557
Total receivable	205,127	223,823	96,276	102,881
PAYABLE				
3. Purchases of goods and services; payments to government	200,304	211,476	94,037	97,646
A. Purchases from the household sector	2,038	2,311	420	435
(1) Domestic services	1,189	1,289	360	374
(2) Services of nonprofit organizations	849	1,022	60	61
B. Purchases from the enterprise sector	177,022	184,014	82,812	85,784
(1) Cash purchases	153,900	160,400	75,513	78,297
a. Retail trade purchases of goods	130,500 *	129,000 *	63,793	65,808

TABLE 1 B (continued)

	1947	1948	1955	1956
b. Farm market purchases			1,100	1,200
c. Purchases of services	19,200	27,100	9,513	10,115
d. Gross cash rentals	4,200	4,300	1,107	1,174
(2) Imputed purchases	23,122	23,614	7,299	7,487
a. Wages and salaries in kind	4,200	4,600	145	150
b. Income in kind of farmers	14,462	14,674	5,700	6,000
c. Income in kind in trades and professions	1,000	1,000	0	0
d. Imputed rentals	2,100	2,150	554	587
e. Military subsistence and clothing	1,000	1,000	850	700
f. Gifts from abroad	360	190	50	50
C. Payments to the government sector	21,244	25,151	10,805	11,427
(1) Dues to quasi-governmental organizations	1,100	1,500	670	740
(2) Direct taxes	12,437	11,928	8,203	8,834
(3) Social security contributions	5,985	9,817	351	353
(4) Other payments	1,722	1,906	1,146	943
(5) Imputed tax			435	557
4. Saving	4,823	12,347	2,239	5,235
Total payable	205,127	223,823	96,276	102,881

* Includes a and b.

TABLE 1 C
HOUSEHOLD SECTOR CAPITAL ACCOUNT
(*Million crowns*)

	1947	1948	1955	1956
RECEIVABLE				
1. Saving	4,823	12,347	2,239	5,235
2. Transfers from the foreign sector	360	190	50	50
3. Borrowing from the government sector (net)	1,098		694	625
Total receivable	6,281	12,537	2,983	5,910
PAYABLE				
4. Lending and capital transfers to other sectors				
A. To the enterprise sector	6,201	878	2,983	5,910
B. To the government sector (net)		11,104		
C. To the foreign sector	80	555		
Total payable	6,281	12,537	2,983	5,910

TABLE 2 A

ENTERPRISE SECTOR PRODUCTION ACCOUNT

(*Million crowns*)

	1947	1948	1955	1956
RECEIVABLE				
1. Sales to other accounts	257,959	290,186	150,437	155,263
A. Sales to the household sector production account	200	239	14	14
B. Sales to the household sector appropriation account	177,022	184,014	82,812	85,784
(1) Cash sales of goods and services	153,900	160,400	75,513	78,297
(2) Imputed sales of goods and services	23,122	23,614	7,299	7,487
C. Sales to the government sector production account	20,373	21,653	20,323	16,373
D. Sales to the government sector capital account	8,985	11,603	2,835	3,314
E. Sales to the enterprise sector capital account	22,453	34,938	28,391	30,856
F. Sales to the foreign sector production account	28,926	37,739	16,062	18,922
2. Inventory changes	− 7,434	4,733	4,235	11,556
A. Agriculture ⎫ B. Other branches ⎭	− 7,434	4,733	4,235	11,556
3. Subsidy receipts	6,576	6,144	6,406	7,687
Total receivable	257,101	301,063	161,078	174,506
PAYABLE				
4. Purchases from the foreign sector	32,469	39,304	15,353	17,218
5. Indirect taxes	42,630	46,106	45,428	46,724
6. Capital consumption allowances	14,000	14,500	6,012	10,835
7. Value added by sector	168,002	201,153	94,285	99,729
A. Compensation of employees	105,809	120,023	56,911	61,143
B. Income of self-employed	42,406	55,159	15,765	16,021
C. Social security contributions	8,385	12,481	5,573	5,938
D. Profits	5,746	7,582	16,035	16,602
E. Rents and interest	5,656	5,908	1	25
Total payable	257,101	301,063	161,078	174,506

TABLE 2 B

ENTERPRISE SECTOR APPROPRIATION ACCOUNT

(*Million crowns*)

	1947	1948	1955	1956
RECEIVABLE				
1. Value added by sector	168,002	201,153	94,285	99,729
2. Current transfers from the government sector	4,058	4,354		
Total receivable	172,060	205,507	94,285	99,729
PAYABLE				
3. Payments to other sectors	173,154	193,394	91,187	96,950
A. Payments to the household sector	155,180	169,205	71,676	76,537
(1) Cash payments	129,862	143,023	65,288	69,230
a. Wages and salaries	101,609	115,423	54,024	57,561
b. Entrepreneurial income	18,053	15,000	1,200	1,100
c. Income of farmers	9,800	12,300	7,300	7,600
d. Income from forestry	400	300	64	69
e. Director's fund	0	0	500	600
f. Other cash income	0	0	2,200	2,300
(2) Payments in kind	19,662	20,274	5,845	6,150
a. Wages and salaries in kind	4,200	4,600	145	150
b. Income in kind of farmers	14,462	14,674	5,700	6,000
c. Income in kind in trades and professions	1,000	1,000	0	0
(3) Cash and imputed net rental income	5,213	5,293	0	0
a. Cash	3,008	3,062	0	0
b. Imputed	1,505	1,531	0	0
c. Farm rents	700	700	0	0
(4) Interest	443	615	1	25
(5) Imputed wages	0	0	542	1,132
B. Payments to the government sector	17,974	24,189	19,511	20,413
(1) Social security contributions	8,385	12,481	5,573	5,938
(2) Direct taxes	7,867	9,802	13,938	14,475
(3) Other payments	1,722	1,906	0	0
4. Income retained by the sector	− 1,094	12,113	3,098	2,779
A. Farm investment in kind and changes in inventories of farm products	− 5,262	6,949	1,113	844
B. Other	4,168	5,164	1,985	1,935
Total payable	172,060	205,507	94,285	99,729

TABLE 2 C

ENTERPRISE SECTOR CAPITAL ACCOUNT

(*Million crowns*)

	1947	1948	1955	1956
RECEIVABLE				
1. Earnings retained by the sector	− 1,094	12,113	3,098	2,779
2. Capital consumption allowances	14,000	14,500	6,012	10,835
3. Borrowing and capital transfers from the household sector	6,201	878	2,983	5,910
4. Capital transfers from the government sector				
A. Fixed capital financing	6,408 *	5,252 *	16,264	15,031
B. Working capital financing			5,355	10,947
5. Borrowing from the government sector (net)		6,928		
Total receivable	25,515	39,691	33,712	45,502
PAYABLE				
6. Gross investment by the enterprise sector				
A. Additions to fixed capital (including capital repairs)	22,453	34,938	28,391	30,856
B. Inventory changes	− 7,434	4,733	4,235	11,556
7. Lending to the government sector (net)	10,496		1,086	3,090
Total payable	25,515	39,691	33,712	45,502

    * Includes A and B.

TABLE 3 A

GOVERNMENT SECTOR PRODUCTION ACCOUNT

(*Million crowns*)

	1947	1948	1955	1956
RECEIVABLE				
1. Imputed sales of government services to the government sector appropriation account	47,469	50,314	31,450	28,085
2. Imputed sales to the government sector capital account			435	557
Total receivable	47,469	50,314	31,885	28,642
PAYABLE				
3. Purchases of goods and services on current account	20,521	21,946	20,373	16,423
A. From the enterprise sector	20,373	21,653	20,323	16,373
B. From the foreign sector	148	293	50	50
4. Value added by sector	26,948	28,368	11,512	12,219
A. Compensation of employees	22,009	23,146	9,418	10,090
B. Military subsistence and clothing	1,000	1,000	850	700
C. Social security contributions	3,939	4,222	809	872
D. Imputed wages			435	557
Total payable	47,469	50,314	31,885	28,642

TABLE 3 B

GOVERNMENT SECTOR APPROPRIATION ACCOUNT

(*Million crowns*)

	1947	1948	1955	1956
RECEIVABLE				
1. Income from other accounts				
A. From the household sector				
appropriation account	21,244	25,151	10,805	11,427
(1) Dues to quasi-governmental organizations	1,100	1,500	670	740
(2) Direct taxes	12,437	11,928	8,203	8,834
(3) Social security contributions	5,985	9,817	351	353
(4) Other payments	1,722	1,906	1,146	943
(5) Imputed tax (unpaid labor in community improvement projects)			435	557
B. From the enterprise sector production account: indirect taxes	42,630	46,106	45,428	46,724
C. From the enterprise sector appropriation account	17,974	24,189	19,511	20,413
(1) Social security contributions	8,385	12,481	5,573	5,938
(2) Direct taxes	7,867	9,802	13,938	14,475
(3) Transfers	1,722	1,906	0	0
D. From the government sector production account: social security contributions	3,939	4,222	809	872
Total receivable	85,787	99,668	76,553	79,436
PAYABLE				
2. Imputed purchases from the government sector production account	47,469	50,314	31,450	28,085
3. Transfers to other accounts	35,734	38,898	19,897	22,263
A. Transfers to the household sector appropriation account	25,100	28,400	13,491	14,576
B. Subsidies to the enterprise sector production account	6,576	6,144	6,406	7,687
C. Interest payments to the enterprise sector	4,058	4,354		
4. Saving	2,584	10,456	25,206	29,088
Total payable	85,787	99,668	76,553	79,436

TABLE 3 C

GOVERNMENT SECTOR CAPITAL ACCOUNT

(*Million crowns*)

	1947	1948	1955	1956
RECEIVABLE				
1. Saving	2,584	10,456	25,206	29,088
2. Capital transfers from the foreign sector	610	351		
3. Borrowing from other sectors				
A. From the household sector (net)		11,104		
B. From the enterprise sector (net)	10,496		1,086	3,090
C. From the foreign sector	3,857	2,399		
4. Gold sales to the foreign sector		217		
Total receivable	17,547	24,527	26,292	32,178
PAYABLE				
5. Government sector investment				
A. Capital purchases from the enterprise sector	8,985	11,603	2,835	3,314
B. Gold purchases from the foreign sector	187			
C. Value of imputed wages in community improvement projects			435	557
6. Capital transfers to other sectors				
A. To the enterprise sector				
(1) Fixed capital	6,408 *	5,252 *	16,264	15,031
(2) Working capital			5,355	10,947
B. To the foreign sector	404	308		90
7. Lending to other sectors				
A. To the household sector (net)	1,098		694	625
B. To the enterprise sector (net)		6,928		
C. To the foreign sector	465	436	709	1,614
Total payable	17,547	24,527	26,292	32,178

* Includes (1) and (2).

TABLE 4 A

FOREIGN SECTOR PRODUCTION ACCOUNT

(*Million crowns*)

	1947	1948	1955	1956
RECEIVABLE				
1. Imports of goods and services	32,809	39,905	15,403	17,268
A. By the enterprise sector	32,469	39,304	15,353	17,218
B. By the government sector	340	601	50	50
2. Balance on production account			659	1,654
Total receivable	32,809	39,905	16,062	18,922
PAYABLE				
3. Exports of goods and services	29,118	38,047	16,062	18,922
A. By the enterprise sector	28,926	37,739	16,062	18,922
B. By the government sector	192	308		
4. Balance on production account	3,691	1,858		
Total payable	32,809	39,905	16,062	18,922

TABLE 4 B

FOREIGN SECTOR APPROPRIATION ACCOUNT

(*Million crowns*)

	1947	1948	1955	1956
RECEIVABLE				
1. Balance on production account	3,691	1,858		
2. Surplus of nation on current account			659	1,654
Total receivable	3,691	1,858	659	1,654
PAYABLE				
3. Balance on production account			659	1,654
4. Deficit of nation on current account	3,691	1,858		
Total payable	3,691	1,858	659	1,654

TABLE 4 C

FOREIGN SECTOR CAPITAL ACCOUNT

(*Million crowns*)

	1947	1948	1955	1956
RECEIVABLE				
1. Deficit of nation on current account	3,691	1,858		
2. Transfers from other sectors	472	758		90
A. From the household sector	68	450		
B. From the government sector	404	308		90
3. Borrowing from other sectors	477	541	709	1,614
A. From the household sector	12	105		
B. From the government sector	465	436	709	1,614
4. Gold purchases by the government sector	187			
Total receivable	4,827	3,157	709	1,704

TABLE 4 C (continued)

	1947	1948	1955	1956
PAYABLE				
5. Surplus of nation on current account			659	1,654
6. Transfers to other sectors	970	541	50	50
A. To the household sector	360	190	50	50
B. To the government sector	610	351		
7. Lending to the government sector	3,857	2,399		
8. Gold sales by the government sector		217		
Total payable	4,827	3,157	709	1,704

TABLE 5 A

CONSOLIDATED PRODUCTION ACCOUNT

(*Million crowns*)

	1947	1948	1955	1956
RECEIVABLE				
1. Value of domestic services produced by household sector	2,038	2,311	420	435
2. Sales by enterprise sector	208,460	230,555	114,038	119,954
A. To household appropriation account	177,022	184,014	82,812	85,784
B. To government capital account	8,985	11,603	2,835	3,314
C. To enterprise capital account	22,453	34,938	28,391	30,856
3. Inventory changes	− 7,434	4,733	4,235	11,556
4. Value of government services including unpaid labor in government investment	47,469	50,314	31,885	28,642
5. Foreign sector balance on production account	− 3,691	− 1,858	659	1,654
Gross national product	246,842	286,055	151,237	162,241
PAYABLE				
6. Indirect taxes less subsidies	36,054	39,962	39,022	39,037
7. Capital consumption allowances	14,000	14,500	6,012	10,835
8. National income	196,788	231,593	106,203	112,369
A. Compensation of employees	130,571	146,124	67,969	72,858
B. Income of self-employed	42,406	55,159	15,765	16,021
C. Social security contributions	12,409	16,820	6,433	6,863
D. Profits	5,746	7,582	16,035	16,602
E. Rents and interest	5,656	5,908	1	25
Gross national product	246,842	286,055	151,237	162,241

TABLE 5 B
CONSOLIDATED APPROPRIATION ACCOUNT
(*Million crowns*)

	1947	1948	1955	1956
RECEIVABLE				
1. National income	196,788	231,593	106,203	112,369
A. Value added by household sector	1,838	2,072	406	421
B. Value added by enterprise sector	168,002	201,153	94,285	99,729
C. Value added by government sector	26,948	28,368	11,512	12,219
2. Indirect taxes less subsidies	36,054	39,962	39,022	39,037
Net national product	232,842	271,555	145,225	151,406
PAYABLE				
3. Household consumption	179,060	186,325	83,232	86,219
A. Services produced by household sector	2,038	2,311	420	435
B. Purchases from enterprise sector	177,022	184,014	82,812	85,784
(1) Cash purchases	153,900	160,400	75,513	78,297
(2) Imputed purchases	23,122	23,614	7,299	7,487
4. Value of government services	47,469	50,314	31,450	28,085
5. Savings	6,313	34,916	30,543	37,102
A. By households	4,823	12,347	2,239	5,235
B. By enterprises	− 1,094	12,113	3,098	2,779
C. By government	2,584	10,456	25,206	29,088
Net national product	232,842	271,555	145,225	151,406

TABLE 5 C
CONSOLIDATED CAPITAL ACCOUNT
(*Million crowns*)

	1947	1948	1955	1956
RECEIVABLE				
1. Saving				
A. By households	4,823	12,347	2,239	5,235
B. By enterprises	− 1,094	12,113	3,098	2,779
C. By government	2,584	10,456	25,206	29,088
2. Capital consumption allowances	14,000	14,500	6,012	10,835
Total receivable	20,313	49,416	36,555	47,937
PAYABLE				
3. Gross domestic investment				
A. By enterprises	15,019	39,671	32,626	42,412
B. By government	8,985	11,603	3,270	3,871
4. Net foreign investment	− 3,691	− 1,858	659	1,654
Total payable	20,313	49,416	36,555	47,937

We shall comment briefly on the individual entries in the sectoral accounts, covering in the order shown in the tables, first, the receivable and, next, the payable items, outlining their content and the general methods by which they were derived, as well as our best judgment of their degree of reliability. For a detailed explanation of the estimating procedures and sources we refer the reader to Appendixes A–F.

HOUSEHOLD SECTOR PRODUCTION ACCOUNT (TABLE 1 A)

The value of services produced by the household sector for use within the sector consists of two parts: the value of services supplied by domestic servants, and the value of services supplied by nonprofit organizations serving households.

The entries on the receivable side represent imputed transactions, a formal "sale" of the value of services to the household sector appropriation account. Viewed from the monetary side, the transaction amounts to a formal accounting flow in the opposite direction: funds received as incomes from other sectors on the household sector appropriation account are paid into the production account to serve as a source of finance for the production of paid services taking place within the household sector.

Domestic services (item 1.A). Data on employment and money compensation of domestic servants in 1947 and 1948 were fully adequate, but employment in 1955 and 1956 had to be roughly estimated on the basis of a rate of decline presumed to have taken place since 1948, while wage rates could be gauged by the new wage scale decreed in 1956. In estimating compensation in kind we relied on analogies with similar data for groups as close to domestic servants as we could find. Social security rates paid by households as employers of domestic servants were available.

Services of nonprofit organizations (item 1.B). The value of these services comprises current purchases from enterprises, wages and salaries, and social security contributions. The aggregate value was built up starting from estimates of wages and salaries, based on adequate data for 1947 and 1948, and on a rough guess for 1955 and 1956; current purchases were assumed to be in the same proportion to the wage and salary bill as in the central administration; social security rates applicable to wages and salaries are reasonably adequate estimates based on various sources.

Current purchases by nonprofit organizations (item 2). These are singled out from the total value of the services supplied by nonprofit organizations, as consisting of purchases from the enterprise sector.

Value added by sector (item 3). Components of the value added, namely, wages and salaries and social security contributions, are explained above in the notes to the receivable side. The value added is transferred as a whole to the household appropriation account receivable side for eventual allocation. The detailed breakdown seeks only to show the composition of value added by types of factor returns, used later in consolidation of all production accounts; hence the detailed items have no formal counterparts on any other account.

HOUSEHOLD SECTOR APPROPRIATION ACCOUNT (TABLE 1 B)

This account lists all incomes of households on the receivable side and their expenditure on the payable side. All entries are estimated independently except for the balancing item, saving, which cannot be estimated directly mainly because of the difficulty in measuring changes in cash balances of the population. As a residual, saving includes the statistical discrepancy. Imputed income (in kind) appears on each side: as income received on the receivable side, and as a corresponding imputed purchase on the payable side. The entry of imputed wages received from the government sector represents the value of labor supplied by households without compensation on various public investment projects; the corresponding entry on the payable side is the imputed tax, that is, a tax paid "in kind," in the form of labor, which is the formal treatment we chose for this type of transaction.

Value added by sector (item 1). This entry, transferred from the household sector production account, represents incomes received in exchange for services produced within the household sector.

Wages and salaries (item 2.A.(1)a). This item includes money compensations paid to hired employees in agricultural and nonagricultural enterprises. The calculation of the individual components summed up in the entries is explained in detail in Appendix E. In general, the data on employment and earnings were superior to any other group of data available, both in scope and quality. There may be a slight understatement in the 1947 and 1948 data because of extralegal payments of the so-called "black wages" that went unrecorded. Among the wage categories in 1955 and 1956, only average rates in the private sector of agriculture and of the private nonagricultural branches had to be estimated by analogy with other occupations. Understatement of total wages because of missing wage payments, made above and outside the so-called "wage fund," is probably insignificant and seems much smaller than in 1947 and 1948, despite the play given these payments in the Czechoslovak press.

Entrepreneurial income (item 2.A.(1)b). This entry represents private business profits, reduced, in 1955 and 1956, to incomes of private craftsmen and tradesmen, physicians, and other professional personnel. The 1947 estimate is relatively the most reliable of the four years, being based on data for income tax purposes. The 1948 estimate, based on the first one, suffers from our ignorance of changes in economic variables that occurred in 1948. The 1955 and 1956 figures are rough estimates and probably are on the low side.

Income of farmers (item 2.A.(1)c). The 1947 and 1948 data are from official sources. The 1955 and 1956 figures were calculated from official income and employment data; the results were found consistent with our independent calculation based on comprehensive estimates of gross sales and cash production costs.

Income from forestry (item 2.A.(1)d). The 1947 and 1948 data were found in a United Nations publication and are apparently based on government supplied figures. They are taken to represent income from privately owned forests. The 1955 and 1956 estimates are derived from total value added in forestry, on the assumption that the private sector's share was the same as its known share in total gross output of forestry.

Director's fund (item 2.A.(1)e). This is a rough estimate of disbursements to persons from the so-called "director's fund" of socialized enterprises. This fund (designated, beginning in 1957, as the "workers' enterprise fund") was financed from profit allocations or from state subsidies (in the case of deficit enterprises). We found it convenient to treat these payments as comparable to wages, although, formally, part of them represent distributed profits.

Other cash income (item 2.A.(1)f). This includes an estimate of cash compensations to persons not on regular payrolls (the so-called "nonpersonal fund," that is, compensation for services, fees to consultants, lecturers, and authors of literary contributions) and various rewards or supplements not included in the wage bill (scholarships paid by enterprises, one-time cash bonuses, and so forth). The magnitude of the nonpersonal fund payments was estimated on the basis of Polish data; the rest is a rough approximation.

Wages and salaries in kind (item 2.A.(2)a). For 1947 and 1948 we made separate estimates of compensation in kind in industry, agriculture, industrial crafts and trades, and trade and services. For 1955 and 1956 we based our estimates on official data for industry and took other branches into account merely by upward rounding. Compensation in kind became less and less significant in the 1950s as a result of reduced employment in private enterprises (especially in agriculture) and of the hard drive against wages in kind in the socialized sector.

Income in kind of farmers (item 2.A.(2)b). The 1947 and 1948 estimates are based on the results of a 1946 sample study conducted in the Czech lands. The 1955 and 1956 estimates are derived from data concerning the year 1957. Our estimates are all in terms of current prices received by farmers.

Income in kind in trades and professions (item 2.A.(2)c). For 1947 and 1948 we used official data. For 1955 and 1956 this category of income was considered too small to warrant uncertain estimates for which no reliable data were available.

Cash and imputed net rental income (item 2.A.(3)a and b). The 1947 and 1948 estimates represent the residual of gross rentals, after subtraction of the estimated maintenance cost and taxes on housing. Gross cash rentals were obtained from published data, whereas gross imputed rentals were estimated on the basis of the prewar ratio between the two, as calculated by Miloš Stádník, the principal national income specialist in Czechoslovakia, before the country's switch to Soviet concepts in national income statistics. The estimated maintenance cost and taxes were allocated proportionately between the cash and the imputed values.

Net cash and imputed rentals in 1955 and 1956 were set equal to zero. We arrived at this decision by comparing the estimated gross rentals with payments charged against them. The two were almost in balance. In reality, given the low average level of controlled rents and the high cost of providing housing services, net rents after depreciation—which we do not impute here—would be negative.

Farms rents (item 2.A.(3)c). These were obtained from a United Nations publication, based on a communication submitted by the State Planning Office. Leasing of agricultural land was abolished in 1949. The nominal payments to collective farmers for their collectivized land, a type of income that may qualify as farm rent, have been negligible and are presumably included in the cash income of farmers.

Interest (item 2.A.(4)). The 1947 and 1948 figures refer only to interest on savings deposits. The 1955 and 1956 figures represent the net balance of interest on savings deposits and an estimate of interest on consumer credit. We do not make the complicated imputations usually considered for banking services. Checking accounts have been unimportant in Czechoslovakia, and banking services rendered to households are therefore insignificant.

Imputed wages (item 2.A.(5)). This represents the value of unpaid labor supplied by households for private housing construction, that is, as if sold to the enterprise sector. The private builder appears here in a double function: as part of the household sector he furnishes labor to himself in his role as a business enterprise. This imputed transaction is recorded in several entries as follows: (1) the value of imputed wages first appears among the enterprise sector production account receivables in the sales to the enterprise sector capital account; (2) as part of value added in the enterprise production account payables it is transferred to the enterprise sector appropriation account; (3) the value of these imputed wages is then transferred from the latter account to the household sector appropriation account as income received, where it appears as the present entry; (4) the same value next appears in household savings, which are transferred to the household sector capital account receivables; (5) finally, this value appears as a capital account transfer from the household sector to the enterprise sector, where it is one of the sources of financing the private housing construction that appears in full value among the enterprise capital outlays.

Cash wages and salaries (item 2.B.(1)). This item, established with precision for 1947–48 from detailed state budget closing accounts, at least as far as civilian employees are concerned, had to be estimated in 1955–56 from rather poorly defined data on employment categories and from corresponding average wages, or their approximations. Wages paid in the "quasi-governmental organizations" were taken from data pertaining to the official category of "social organizations" (trade unions, political parties, and so forth). Since some of the state cultural establishments are essentially business firms, and thus belong to the enterprise sector, the wage bill in the employment category "education and culture" was split between the government sector and the enterprise sector. The wage bill in "education and culture" was further reduced by the estimated wages of religious associations classified as belonging to the household sector.

Cash emoluments of the military and security personnel are understandably rough estimates based on assorted data having the degree of unreliability usual in such matters.

Military subsistence in kind (item 2.B.(2)). This item is an approximation of government expenditures for standard food, footwear, and clothing furnished to military personnel. The average cost of these items was estimated for 1947 and 1948 according to the per capita value of civilian purchases of staples believed to enter military subsistence; for 1955 and 1956 it was approximated as the average per capita food and clothing expenditures in working families. The estimated number of recipients is subject to the same reservation as noted above in connection with cash income of military personnel.

Transfer payments (item 2.B.(3)). These transfers include social security benefits, pensions to retired employees of state enterprises and administration employees, and miscellaneous unspecified transfers. For 1947 and 1948 we used data from official sources. For 1955 and 1956 the data pertaining to payments within the "national social security" scheme were taken from official statistics (the bulk of pensions and allowances and social security benefits); other minor categories were estimated on the basis of scattered information. The transfer figures for 1955 and 1956 include a specific cash transfer for the purpose of financing religious associations. Religious organizations were financially attached to the government budget. Since we included them in the household sector, it was necessary to show a corresponding transfer of funds from the government to the household sector.

Imputed wages (item 2.B.(4)). This item belongs to the chain of accounting entries recording the value of labor supplied without compensation by households to the government sector on various community improvement projects in 1955 and 1956. The treatment is analogous to the case where cash wages of government employees engaged in government capital construction would be financed from a specific household tax covering these wages exactly. Our imputations show:

1. Imputed wages paid from the government sector production account to the household sector appropriation account (the present entry)

2. The same value received by the government sector production account from an imputed sale to the government sector capital account payable where it enters the value of government investment

3. A payment from the household sector appropriation account equal to the value of unpaid labor (recorded as imputed tax, or corvée) to the government sector appropriation account

4. The same value on the latter account passing through

government savings to the government sector capital account receivables, where it figures as a source of capital finance, matching the corresponding value of unpaid labor embodied in the value of government investment (see 2 above)

Purchases from the household sector (item 3.A). See comments to the entries on the household sector production account.

Retail trade purchases of goods (item 3.B.(1)a). For 1947 and 1948 we used official estimates. For 1955 and 1956 our estimates were derived from the officially given total value of retail sales, including sales in restaurants and catering enterprises, by subtracting estimated nonhousehold purchases. The latter comprised 20 percent of total retail sales in 1955 and 23 percent in 1956.[4] Our estimate reflects the following partial estimates of purchases in the retail trade network made for purposes other than household consumption:

1. Agricultural purchases of current production materials
2. Agricultural purchases on capital account
3. Retail trade purchases made from per diem and travel allowances of the enterprise and government sectors
4. Purchases for individual housing construction
5. Purchases of tools and materials by independent handicrafts
6. Purchases by the government and socialized enterprises

The last item, constituting about one half of the total nonhousehold retail purchases, was based on the official estimate for the year 1957 adjusted roughly to 1955 and 1956, taking account of pertinent legislation that changed from restrictive measures on such purchases, in force until 1955, to permissive ones in 1956, and back to restrictive in 1957.

Farm market purchases (item 3.B.(1)b). For 1947 and 1948 these purchases were assumed to be included in the official estimate of consumer cash purchases used in the preceding entry. For 1955 and 1956, estimates were made on the basis of some percentage data in the press and on a reconstruction of pertinent

[4] This is a comparatively high share. Bergson and Heymann, *Soviet National Income and Product, 1940–48*, p. 144, estimate purchases by what they call "institutional buyers" in the USSR in 1940 at 7.5 percent and in 1944 and 1948 at 5 percent of total retail sales.

aggregates in absolute terms. In Czechoslovakia, farm market purchases play a minor role, in contrast to other East European countries.

Purchases of services (item 3.B.(1)c). For 1947 and 1948, we used official figures reduced by our estimate of dues to "quasi-governmental organizations," which they include. For 1955 and 1956, we converted an official percentage breakdown of services furnished to the population by the socialized and cooperative sector into absolute figures, using the known sales figures of socialized and cooperative barber shops, which were assumed, in contrast to other categories of services, to belong entirely to household consumption. The resulting total was adjusted for purchases from the private enterprises by adding estimates of services bought from handicrafts and private health services and subtracting rental payments. The totals for 1955 and 1956, showing a negligible difference, were finally adjusted in order to reconcile them with the official growth figure of expenditures for services.

Gross cash rentals (item 3.B.(1)d). See our comments above on cash and imputed net rental income (p. 25).

Imputed purchases (item 3.B.(2)). See the comments above (pp. 25 and 27) on identical entries on the receivable side of this account: wages and salaries in kind; income in kind of farmers; income in kind of trades and professions; imputed rentals; and military subsistence and clothing. Gifts from abroad refer to gift parcels, the value of which was available for 1947–48 from balance of payments estimates and was assumed to be about the same magnitude in 1955–56.

Dues to quasi-governmental organizations (item 3.C.(1)). In the case of trade unions and the Communist Party, our estimates are based on membership figures and estimated average dues. For the remaining organizations the figures are orders of magnitude set in probable proportion to the trade-union and Party figures.

Direct taxes (item 3.C.(2)). For 1947 and 1948, we used official data on personal direct taxes paid to the central government and a rough estimate of those paid to local administrations. The 1955 and 1956 figures are from the reconstructed state budgets (see Appendix E). Direct taxes paid by the household sector represent mainly the wage tax (in 1947 and 1948 also the income tax and the small rent tax); they do not include the agricultural tax, handicraft tax, and house tax.

Social security contributions (item 3.C.(3)). For 1947 and 1948, these include (1) social security contributions paid by the household sector in its role of employer of domestic servants and of employees of nonprofit organizations serving households, and (2) those directly paid by the members of the household sector as employees. During this period, social security contributions were paid partly by employers and partly by the employees themselves. For 1955 and 1956, the first category continues to exist, whereas contributions by wage earners under this title disappear. Instead, according to official interpretation, wage earners contribute for this purpose through the wage tax. The 1955 and 1956 figures in Table 1 B represent an estimate of social security contributions by farmers (private and collective) and by self-employed persons. In 1947–48 comparable outlays would be made for nongovernment insurance.

Other payments (item 3.C.(4)). We based our very rough estimates for 1947–48 on the sum of diverse payments (fees to the central government, revenue fines, and estimated unspecified revenues of the local governments), which we allocated, in arbitrary proportions, between the household and enterprise sectors. The 1955 and 1956 figures include some items having the nature of income taxes (tax on literary and artistic activity and tax on personal incomes, neither of which is itemized in the official budget figures), various minor revenues, and a portion of the budget income called "other revenues." These "other revenues" were divided between the household and enterprise sectors somewhat arbitrarily in the ratio of specified "revenues from the socialized sector" and "revenues from the population" (according to the official breakdown of the state budget).

Imputed tax (item 3.C.(5)). See the comments above to imputed wages received from the government sector.

Saving (item 4). This is the balancing entry between receivables and payables, and as such it absorbs errors of estimation of other items in the account.

HOUSEHOLD SECTOR CAPITAL ACCOUNT (TABLE 1 C)

Household sector savings, transferred from the appropriation account, and capital transfers and borrowing from other sectors comprise the receivables of this account; lending and transfers to other sectors exhaust the household sector capital resources. The entries in the household sector capital account could not all be specifically traced; hence some transfers between sectors were assumed. Upon consolidation, however, these transfers cancel out, leaving the gross investment and saving of the economy unaffected.

Transfers from the foreign sector (item 2). This is an estimate of the value of private gifts and remittances from abroad.

Borrowing from the government sector (item 3). This is an imputed item balancing the account. Upon consolidation of the sectoral capital accounts such entries cancel out.

Lending and capital transfers to the enterprise sector (item 4). The main items in this entry are transfers of funds to the enterprise sector for financing private building construction (treated as enterprise sector activity), repayment of debt, changes in savings deposits, and the excess of insurance premiums paid over the counter payment of insurance claims.

For 1947 and 1948, we assumed that practically no housing construction was directly financed from household sector resources. This seems reasonable in view of the postwar method of financing housing construction by credits and subsidies.[5] Besides, the original data do not permit a breakdown of housing construction between private and other. Debt payment was ignored because of lack of data and the small scale of personal credit operations in Czechoslovakia.

For 1955 and 1956, our data include both types of transfers. In estimating the value of household sector resources spent

[5] General Secretariat of the Economic Council, *Průběh plnění hospodářského plánu*, 1947, p. 208.

on private housing construction, we subtracted from the given total value of private construction the amount of state loans assumed to have been spent entirely on material purchases. As explained before,[6] the household sector appears here supplying household savings to the enterprise sector to meet the cost of private housing construction, which is treated as falling entirely in the enterprise sector. The expenditure for housing construction, both in labor and in cash, is a result of an involved calculation by means of which the total value of investment in private housing given in official sources was broken down into the requisite parts. Payment of debts in 1955 and 1956 represents net repayment, that is, net change (reduction) in loans outstanding.

Our estimates relating to savings deposits and insurance are based on published banking data and government statistics.

Lending and capital transfers to the government sector (*item 4.B*). This is a balancing entry that represents an imputed transaction explained in the introductory paragraph to the household sector capital accounts.

Lending and capital transfers to the foreign sector (*item 4.C*). These are private gifts and remittances sent abroad in 1947 and 1948. In 1955 and 1956, these transfers were assumed to have been negligible.

ENTERPRISE SECTOR PRODUCTION ACCOUNT (TABLE 2 A)

The receivable items of this account show the sector's annual gross value added (that is, including capital consumption) in terms of sales to other accounts, value of inventory changes, and subsidies from the government; on the payable side the total receivables are allocated to purchases from other sectors, indirect taxes, and production charges against the gross value added. Net inventory changes may be regarded as a sale to the enterprise sector capital account analogous to sales of fixed capital. In both cases the funds to finance these sales come from savings originating in the enterprise sector or put at its disposal by other

[6] See above, pp. 26–27.

sectors. Subsidies, coming from the government sector as a current transaction, cover the outlays on the payable side insofar as the other receivables are insufficient. Among the payables, the production charges against the product originating in the sector include capital consumption allowances and rewards to factors of production: profit, interest, rent, and compensation of employees, including social security contributions.

Sales to household sector production account (*item 1.A*). See comments above to the household sector accounts under *Services of non-profit organizations* (p. 22).

Cash sales of goods and services to the household sector appropriation account (*item 1.B.(1)*). See comments above to the following entries of the household sector appropriation account comprising the present entry: retail trade purchases of goods, farm market purchases, purchases of services, and gross cash rentals (pp. 29–30).

Imputed sales of goods and services to the household sector appropriation account (*item 1.B.(2)*). See the comments to the following entries in the household sector appropriation account, which comprise the present entry: wages and salaries in kind, income in kind of farmers, income in kind in trades and professions, imputed rentals, and military subsistence and clothing, and gifts from abroad (pp. 25, 27, 30).

Sales to the government sector production account (*item 1.C*). These are sales of materials and services required for current operations of the central and local governments and of the quasi-governmental organizations. Included are estimates of military purchases treated wholly as purchases on current account. For the years 1947–48 two additional items were included separately: payments by the government for the cost of management of the state debt (other than interest), and current purchases by social security institutions (counted as part of the government sector, despite their business firm character in 1947 and part of 1948). Data for estimating purchases by the central government in 1947–48 were found in reliable detail in the official closing accounts to the state budget; estimates for 1955–56 are based on state budget data, rearranged and broken down into categories geared to our accounts (see Appendix F). The

1955–56 figures cover military purchases and purchases by local administrations. Military purchases for 1947–48 were estimated separately from total military expenditures by subtracting estimates of other outlays. Local government purchases in 1947–48 were obtained as estimates forming part of a reconstructed balance of revenues and outlays of local administrations.

Sales to the government sector capital account (*item 1.D*). This entry covers a number of expenditures identifiable as capital outlays of the government sector. For 1947–48 we included the small outlays spent on the reconstruction of Lidice and Ležáky, but these very probably did not yet reach the stage of actual housing construction. We disregarded capital expenditures of quasi-governmental organizations since they were insignificant.

Our 1955–56 estimates were derived as the sum of the officially given investment categories which we identified as belonging to the government sector, minus the value of labor supplied without compensation by households on public investment projects, plus the estimated value of capital repairs in government proper.

Sales to the enterprise sector capital account (*item 1.E*). The estimates represent the value of completed additions to fixed capital, capital repairs, and investment in kind in private agriculture. The value of new fixed capital includes the labor supplied by the household sector in private housing construction, which is recorded as "imputed wages" on the payable side. Data for 1955–56 were generally adequate; farm investment in kind was estimated on the basis of 1955 data obtained from a sample inquiry in fifty-one agricultural collectives. The original 1947 and 1948 data apparently refer to investment outlays undifferentiated with respect to completion and presumably excluding capital repairs. The data were used as found on the assumption that unfinished investments, which should be subtracted (as an element in inventories), and capital repairs, which should be added, cancel out, as suggested by 1948 data.[7]

Sales to the foreign sector production account (*item 1.F*). The 1947–48 figures represent exports of goods and services as given in a publication by the International Monetary Fund.

[7] See State Statistical Office, *Statistická ročenka*, 1959, pp. 107, 115, 132.

The 1955–56 figures are based on official export data in current prices, f. o. b., presumably in foreign exchange crowns. Export prices in terms of foreign exchange crowns are on balance most probably below the purchasing prices in domestic crowns paid by state export companies to their suppliers. Taking a foreign exchange crown as equal to a domestic crown in their calculations, the foreign trade enterprises suffer a loss on exports; this is made up, on one hand, by probable profits on imports, arising from the difference between prices in domestic and foreign exchange crowns, and, on the other hand, by state subsidies. To insure consistency, we converted the official figures to domestic crowns.[8]

Inventory changes (*item 2*). For 1947 and 1948, inventory changes were estimated as the balancing residual of the account. The bulk of the change seems to have been contributed by farm inventories: by their sudden depletion in 1947, a year of extraordinary drought, and by their reconstitution in 1948. Inventory changes in 1955 were approximated from an estimate of "accumulation" by subtracting from it net addition to fixed capital, which is the other component of "accumulation." Changes in inventories thus derived include additions to state reserves. Inventory changes in 1956 were again estimated as the balancing residual.

Subsidy receipts (*item 3*). The 1947 and 1948 estimates were obtained as the sum of various budget expenditures answering the description of subsidies. The 1955 estimate was obtained as a residual in the production account, and, to obtain the 1956 estimate, we raised the 1955 figure by an amount corresponding roughly to the effect upon business losses of increased production and increased production costs due mainly to the steeply raised rates of depreciation. We made rough estimates, or used available data referring to the period 1956–57, for some of the most important subsidized branches (machine tractor stations, agriculture, factory canteens, socialized housing, and coal industry). The sum of these partial estimates was of a similar order of magnitude as the rough over-all estimates we used in

[8] See below, p. 45.

the accounts. Insofar as the latter estimates may seem too low, for example, with respect to the unknown but probably considerable foreign trade subsidies, it should be borne in mind that part of what might be called subsidies may be included in the not too clearly defined category of transfers of working capital.

Purchases from the foreign sector (*item 4*). See the comments above to sales to the foreign sector production account, p. 36.

Indirect taxes (*item 5*). The 1947 and 1948 figures, which are sums of several types of indirect taxes, include net proceeds from the state tobacco and other monopolies and an arbitrary share of other undefined government revenues. The bulk of the 1955 and 1956 figures is represented by the turnover or sales tax of the Soviet type. In all years the house tax was treated as an indirect tax, the rationale being that the tax was levied on the basis of housing property and not on the basis of returns to this property.

Capital consumption allowances (*item 6*). This is an estimate of bookkeeping depreciation allowances, not of the value of fixed capital actually consumed. It does not contain imputations for those sectors of the economy that, to our knowledge, operated without actually charging depreciation. We did not attempt to adjust the bookkeeping depreciation charges for the years 1947, 1948, and 1955, when they were known to be set far below a realistic rate in the sense of the current cost of replacement of wear and tear, not to speak of obsolescence. The 1947 and 1948 estimates are based on the difference between the official estimates of gross and net investment.

The 1955 and 1956 estimates are based on published data on the results of a general revaluation of fixed capital in the economy during 1955. Depreciation rates used for 1955 were those prevalent in industry. The 1956 rates were those of all so-called "economic organizations." Thanks to the 1955 census of capital stock, the 1956 estimate is considerably closer to an economically meaningful concept of depreciation than those for the previous years.[9]

[9] Compare p. 148.

Value added by sector (item 7). This entry represents an independent estimate obtained by adding up the components of value added in the enterprise sector. These components are explained in the enterprise sector appropriation account. In the production accounts we show value added by types of factor rewards, with social security payments given separately, whereas in the appropriation accounts we detail the payments by receiving sector.

Enterprise Sector Appropriation Account (Table 2 B)

This account contains, as sources on the receivable side, value added by the enterprise sector plus income received from other sectors; on the payable side, these sources are allocated among the sectors, the part retained by the enterprise sector being transferred as savings to the enterprise sector capital account.

Value added by sector (item 1). See the remarks above on the enterprise production account.

Current transfers from the government sector (item 2). This entry represents interest payments on central and local government debts, payments taking place only in the years before 1953, when the entire state debt was repudiated. Interest payments to the household sector were disregarded because the bulk of the public debt was held by financial institutions.[10]

Payments to the household sector, (item 3.A). Comments to all entries under this heading appear above under the household sector appropriation account (pp. 23–27).

Social security contributions (item 3.B.(1)). These are contributions made by enterprises to the social security system, considered in all years as part of the government sector. Insofar as some enterprises had their own pension plans—this was the case in 1947–48 for state enterprises—we made an imputation showing direct payment to the government social security system and from there to the household sector (for pension recipients).

Direct taxes (item 3.B.(2)). The bulk of direct taxes in 1947–48 was made up of the tax on the self-employed (called

[10] Ministry of Finance, *Státní hospodaření za války a po revoluci*, p. 169.

the "general profits tax") and the agricultural tax. In addition, profits of state enterprises were included as a form of direct tax. Direct taxes in 1955–56 consist of analogous payments: handicraft tax, profit tax, tax on cooperatives, and agricultural tax. Sources were generally adequate.

Other payments (item 3.B.(3)). These cover miscellaneous payments to the government, the total being allocated between the household and the enterprise sectors.[11]

Farm investment in kind and inventory changes in agriculture (item 4.A). These entries represent that part of value added which does not take the form of a cash compensation of factors. See comments above to sales to the enterprise sector capital account and inventory changes in the enterprise sector production account (pp. 35, 36).

Other income retained by the sector (item 4.B). This is the balancing item in the enterprise sector appropriation account. Since private entrepreneurial money income after taxes has been transferred in its entirety to the household sector, the present item refers only to socialized enterprises.

ENTERPRISE SECTOR CAPITAL ACCOUNT (TABLE 2 C)

Earnings retained by the sector (item 1). This is a formal transfer from the enterprise sector appropriation account; see comments above.

Capital consumption allowances (item 2). See comment to the identical entry on enterprise sector production account, above (p. 37).

Borrowing from the household sector (item 3). See comment to lending to the enterprise sector in Table 1 C, above (p. 32).

Capital transfers from the government sector (item 4). The 1947 and 1948 figures represent the sums of budget expenditures having the character of capital transfers to the enterprise sector. In those two years no distinction can be made between transfers for fixed capital investment and those for working capital purposes; repayment of government debt is included here.

---

[11] See other payments on the household sector appropriation account, above, p. 31.

The 1955 and 1956 figures represent the sum of separate estimates of transfers for fixed capital investment and for additions
to working capital. The fixed capital transfers were calculated
on the basis of data on centrally planned capital construction
and the various sources of finance. The working capital transfers are estimates obtained as residuals in the reconstructed state
budgets (see Appendix F).

Borrowing from the government sector (net) (item 5). This
is the balancing item of the account for 1948.

*Additions to fixed capital (including capital repairs) (item
6.A).* See comment to sales to the enterprise sector capital account in Table 2 A, above (p. 35).

Inventory changes (item 6.B). See comment to inventory
changes in Table 2 A, above (p. 36).

Lending to the government sector (net) (item 7). This is
the balancing item of the account for the years 1947, 1955, and
1956.

GOVERNMENT SECTOR PRODUCTION ACCOUNT (TABLE 3 A)

This account formally resembles the enterprise sector production account, but it differs from it in substance in that the
revenues in the government account do not represent actual
sales but rather imputations showing the value of government
services as "sold" to the other government accounts. In this way
value added in government services formally enters the gross
national product tabulation, while the financing of the services
is shown in detail as transfers in the other government accounts.
The payable items on the production account represent current
personnel and material expenditures in providing government
services.

*Imputed sales of government services to the government
sector appropriation account (item 1).* We show current government services as "sold" to the appropriation account.

*Imputed sales to the government sector capital account (item
2).* This unusual entry, which concerns the value of imputed
wages for unpaid labor on community improvement projects, is

explained in comments to imputed wages in Table 1 B (see p. 28, transaction number 2).

Purchases of goods and services on current account from the enterprise sector (item 3.A). See sales to the government sector production account in comment to Table 2 A, above (p. 34).

Purchases of goods and services on current account from the foreign sector (item 3.B). This represents outlays for the maintenance of diplomatic missions abroad and for membership fees and contributions to international organizations.

Compensation of employees (item 4.A). See cash wages and salaries in comment to Table 1 B, above (p. 27).

Military subsistence and clothing (item 4.B). See military subsistence in kind in comments to Table 1 B, above (p. 27).

Social security contributions (item 4.C). This represents an intrasectoral transaction, a payment from the government sector production account to its appropriation account.

Imputed wages (item 4.D). See imputed wages in comments to Table 1 B, where the present entry is described in transaction number 1 (p. 28).

GOVERNMENT SECTOR APPROPRIATION ACCOUNT (TABLE 3 B)

This account shows, on the receivable side, current income from other sectors and social security contributions for government sector employees, an intrasectoral payment from the production account. On the payable side, it shows this income used to pay for government services (a formal transfer to the production account) and for transfers to other sectors, leaving saving as a residual.

Income from the household sector appropriation account (item 1.A). See dues to quasi-governmental organizations, direct taxes, social security contributions, other payments, and imputed tax, in comments to Table 1 B (pp. 30–31).

Income from the enterprise sector production account: indirect taxes (item 1.B). See indirect taxes in comments to Table 2 A (p. 37).

Income from the enterprise sector appropriation account (*item 1.C*). See social security contributions, direct taxes, and other payments, in comments to Table 2 B (pp. 38–39).

Income from the government sector production account: social security contributions (*item 1.D*). See social security contributions, in comments to Table 3 A (p. 41).

Imputed purchases from the government sector production account (*item 2*). See the corresponding imputed sales, in comments to Table 3 A (p. 40).

Transfers to the household sector appropriation account (*item 3.A*). See transfer payments in comments to Table 1 B (p. 28).

Subsidies to the enterprise production account (*item 3.B*). See subsidy receipts in comments to Table 2 A (p. 36).

Interest payments to the enterprise sector (*item 3.C*). See income from the government sector in comments to Table 2 B (p. 38).

Saving (*item 4*). This entry is the balancing item in the account; as such this residual reflects any errors in estimating the other entries.

GOVERNMENT SECTOR CAPITAL ACCOUNT (TABLE 3 C)

This account shows, among its receivables, the saving of the government sector and capital transfers and borrowing from other sectors and, among its payables, government investment and capital transfers and lending to other sectors. Because our information on capital transactions is incomplete, some of our entries reflecting capital transactions between domestic sectors have an arbitrary character, being assumed to bring the capital accounts into balance. Since, at the least, information on changes in cash balances held by sectors would be difficult to obtain, these changes in any event would have to be obtained as balancing residuals in the capital accounts. It seems proper to regard changes in cash balances as borrowing or lending between the government and other sectors, for the money in question simply represents claims against the government. We are on less justifiable footing insofar as other, possibly arbitrary, elements enter the flows shown between our sectoral capital accounts; however, in the consolidated capital account the borrowing, lending, and transfers cancel, leaving the statement of saving and investment unaffected.

Saving (item 1). This is a transfer from the government appropriation account.

Capital transfers from the foreign sector (item 2). These are reparations and long-term capital transactions under the title of "settlement of claims arising out of war damage."

Borrowing from the household sector (net) (item 3.A). This is the balancing item of the household sector capital account for 1948.

Borrowing from the enterprise sector (net) (item 3.B). This is the balancing item of the enterprise capital account for 1947, 1955, and 1956.

Borrowing from the foreign sector (item 3.C). This entry includes long-term loans; "payments and clearing agreements," which represent short-term capital transactions; liabilities to the International Monetary Fund and the International Bank for Reconstruction and Development; and some minor items unspecified in our source.

Gold sales to the foreign sector (item 4). This is the net amount of transactions made in 1948 under the title of monetary gold.

Capital purchases from the enterprise sector (item 5.A). See the comment to the corresponding entry in Table 2 A (p. 35).

Gold purchases from the foreign sector (item 5.B). See the comment to the gold sales entry above.

Value of imputed wages (item 5.C). See the comment to imputed wages from the government sector in Table 1 B, item 2.B.(4) (p. 28). The present entry represents an integral part of government investment.

Capital transfers to the enterprise sector (item 6.A). See the comment to capital transfers from the government sector in Table 2 C (p. 39).

Capital transfers to the foreign sector (item 6.B). This entry includes, in 1947 and 1948, the amortization of municipal debt and of long-term government debt and subscription to the International Monetary Fund and to the International Bank for Reconstruction and Development. The figure for 1956 represents a grant to Hungary.

Lending to the household sector (net) (item 7.A). This is the counter entry to the balancing item in the household sector capital account for 1947.

Lending to the enterprise sector (net) (item 7.B). This is the counter entry to the balancing item in the enterprise sector capital account for 1948.

Lending to the foreign sector (item 7.C). This entry includes, for 1947 and 1948, short-term capital transactions and minor liabilities not specified in the source. For 1955 and 1956, the figures are the counter entries to the balancing items of the foreign sector capital account; they represent the nation's surplus on current account increased by the net transfers received from abroad.

FOREIGN SECTOR ACCOUNTS (Tables 4 A–4 C)

The foreign sector accounts show the external transactions of the domestic sectors. Transactions on the production account correspond in principle to those of the balance of trade, and transactions on the capital account to those of the balance of payments. Since we had no information on factor payments to or from abroad, the appropriation account merely transmits the surplus or deficit of the production account to the capital account.

Individual entries in the foreign sector accounts correspond to counter entries in the domestic sector accounts, which have been discussed above. In Appendix D, the reader will find detailed description and sources of the figures shown in Tables 4 A–4 C.

Our figures for 1947 and 1948 are based on the detailed Czechoslovak balance of payments as published by the International Monetary Fund; they appear to be reliable. By contrast, our 1955 and 1956 figures are among the weakest of our estimates. Official data are limited to the import and export of commodities, valued in foreign exchange crowns, that is, in import and export prices expressed in foreign currency and multiplied by the unrealistic official exchange ratios between the domestic and foreign currencies. Invisible imports and exports go unrecorded, as do capital transactions. Invisible items were roughly estimated on the basis of the 1947 and 1948 ratios between the corresponding items and commodity transactions.

The official method of valuation in terms of foreign exchange crowns has the consequence that foreign trade magnitudes are incommensurate with individual components of the GNP expressed in domestic prices. The distortion in question is of the same nature as any other where subsidized sales are involved. For purposes of comparison, it would be desirable to have all components of GNP expressed in domestic prices, thus eliminating the distortion due to the foreign trade subsidy.

In Appendix D we converted the values of imports and exports from foreign exchange crowns to domestic crowns at the rate of 1 to 1.85, based on scattered information on the share of trade in national income as given in the Czechoslovak official definition. Using the same rate for imports and exports is something of a simplification due to lack of more detailed information.

At this point let us mention some of the soft spots of our estimates. Disregarding the special problem of foreign trade figures for 1955 and 1956, the margin of error seems to be largest in the following items, all concentrated on the enterprise sector production account: depreciation allowances (in 1947 and 1948 only), inventory changes, and subsidy receipts.

The 1947 and 1948 capital consumption allowances can at best be considered crude approximations, based as they are on the difference between official estimates of gross and net investments. Any error here obviously will affect both the estimate of the net product and that of the gross national product. Moreover, since the change in inventories was estimated as a residual on the receivable side of the enterprise production account, it will reflect the crudeness of the estimate of capital consumption allowances.

The uncertainty about subsidy receipts in 1955 and inventory changes in 1956 is linked to the necessity of using residuals as estimates; these items estimated as residuals carry the burden of the statistical discrepancy with its distorting effect. In addition, the 1956 subsidy receipts actually depend, on the one hand, on the estimate for the preceding year, obtained as a residual, and, on the other hand, on the estimated rate of increase of subsidies between 1955 and 1956. The possible error in the 1955 estimate of subsidies is thus carried into the 1956 estimate and affects the 1956 estimate of inventory changes. It is, therefore, not excluded that, in reality, subsidy receipts were larger and inventory changes smaller. One would be tempted to suspect an error of this kind in view of the 3.5 fold increase in inventory changes in 1956 over 1955. However, there is nothing a priori improbable about relatively large changes in a volatile item such as inventories. As noted in Appendix B (p. 142), the increase in inventory changes is partly due to the movement of unfinished construction: a net decrease in 1955, followed by a net increase in 1956. Moreover, economic repercussions of the events in Poland and Hungary in the fall of 1956 may have easily contributed to the abnormal increase in inventories (increase in work-in-progress due to bottlenecks in the supplies of material, piling-up of finished products for exports due to transportation difficulties, both offsetting the working-off of existing stocks, which were probably small to start with, and the reduction of stocks in retail trade due to scare-buying). Although not very satisfactory, the procedures we used seemed to be the least arbitrary among the possible alternatives.

The error in subsidy receipts may also affect the 1955 and 1956 estimates of transfers of working capital from the government to the enterprise sector. These capital transfers were estimated as residuals in a broader category of budget expenditures in which the estimate of subsidies obtained in Table 2 A was an important element.

Finally, our 1955 and 1956 estimates of government sector current purchases from the enterprise sector seem to call for a comment. One might expect these purchases to grow in step with the budget outlays, but in our estimates they decline, from 20.3

to 16.4 billion crowns. This decline, however, may be the result of a redistribution of military outlays in time, as compared with the published planned annual budget figures; actual military expenditures exceeded the planned figure by 2.2 billion crowns in 1955 and fell short of it by about 1.5 billion crowns in 1956 (see Appendix Table 36, p. 201).

With minor exceptions, all of our figures are either taken directly from official data or derived therefrom by inference, interpolations, or reconstruction to match our classifications. We have avoided ready-made official national income aggregates; indeed, the aim of the present work is to provide measures independent of such aggregates. Still, one must, at some level, rely on the published official statistics since the alternative of supplanting them is impracticable. Thus we have depended on official figures of employment, wages, physical outputs, various categories of sales, and other data in value terms. Where possible, we have checked the data for consistency with related data and for correspondence to our statistical categories, and we have tried to indicate the quality of our estimates in instances where questions of reliability occurred.

One might with good cause expect imperfections, inaccuracies, and distortion in the official statistics, in view of the motivations facing the reporting units. For reasons of maximizing personal gain or reducing loss, one could expect some factory managers, taxpayers, and other economic units to distort the statistical information they are required to submit to the government. Moreover, the professional shortcomings in the statistical services could well be expected to contribute to erroneous information. But there is little that one can do to correct such imperfections beyond seeking alternative approaches, also based on official data, to replace the suspect items.

With these limitations in mind, we believe that, by the standards of national income work done in comparable areas, our aggregates and their main structural relationships are reasonably satisfactory.

III. GROSS NATIONAL PRODUCT AT FACTOR COST

OUR sectoral and consolidated accounts in Chapter II correspond to actual or imputed money flows, that is, they reflect the current market prices at which the transactions were recorded. Such accounts are immediately useful for analysis of money flows, of the composition of consumer expenditures, of government incomes and outlays, and of similar phenomena expressed in current market values. These current values may also serve as a starting point for international or intertemporal comparisons of national product.[1]

We have already indicated at the outset some uses of national income data in current market prices. Certainly such data must serve as a starting point for revaluations in terms of other prices. Thus, it should be possible, and indeed it would be interesting, to show the Czechoslovak gross national product, both in aggregate terms and in detailed structure in rubles, or dollars, or in the currencies of other countries of East Central Europe. International comparisons along these lines obviously show the size and composition of national product in terms of scarcity relationships and institutional factors underlying the prices in the chosen currency. Such revaluations, though very tempting, are too laborious to be undertaken in the present study.

It is equally interesting and, what is more important, also feasible within the limits of the present study, to begin with the Czechoslovak gross national product in the given market prices and, where necessary, to adjust these prices and the values that

[1] See Gilbert and Kravis, *An International Comparison of National Products and the Purchasing Power of Currencies.*

depend on them to correspond to Czechoslovak resource costs. The merit of such a revaluation is that it makes explicit the pattern of resource allocation in the economy; it shows at once in what proportions the nation's productive power was used (1) by the various sectors of production and (2) to satisfy the final uses—personal consumption, government consumption, and gross investment.

We shall show that the more recent Czechoslovak current market prices do not meet this requirement, and they must be transformed to correspond to more basic phenomena. The reasons for this will become apparent when we study the current market prices in relation to our factor cost standard. For the present, two observations should suffice: (1) because of the uneven incidence of the turnover tax, one crown's worth of consumer goods represents a much smaller claim on productive resources than one crown's worth of investment goods or armaments; (2) because of the fiscal convenience of concentrating the turnover tax on the industrial sector, its relative share of the gross national product will be inflated accordingly.

Advantages of Factor Cost Valuation

Czechoslovak market prices afforded an indication of the ratios in which consumers may substitute one consumer good for another and enterprises one investment good for another. However, one crown's worth of one consumption (investment) good may contain more resources than one crown's worth of another consumption (investment) good; similarly, the resources behind one crown's worth of different final uses may differ widely as we have noted above. If we express the values of all goods in terms of the resources that go into the production of these goods, then, (1) we get a more accurate estimate of the allocation of productive resources among different end uses or among different branches of production; and (2) we get a better estimate of the alternatives that are open to the economy and of the relative order of quantities of one type of commodity that can be obtained by giving up other types of commodities. The latter point is not as compelling as the former one because, while there is nothing equivocal when we measure the resource cost of various uses, some difficulties appear when we consider the possibilities of substitution among end uses through reallocation of factors of production. These difficulties relate to the likelihood of diminishing returns from an extramarginal reallocation and to the difficulties of transferring factors of production in the short run. Still, valuation of commodities in terms of their factor cost enables us to measure at least with some accuracy the effects of marginal reallocation of resources on output. Market prices do not permit even this.

DEFINITION OF THE FACTOR COST STANDARD

For the purpose of revaluation of the gross national product we define a factor cost standard in terms of the following characteristics:[2]

1. All prices of goods and services fully resolve into the factor charges directly or indirectly incurred in the production of the commodities. In other words, the national product is considered to be equal to the sum of the values of the services of factors of production—labor, capital, and land—used up in production.

2. Wages paid to labor reflect the average differences in marginal productivities and in disutilities of labor in the various occupations.

3. The charge for capital consists of (i) a capital consumption allowance and (ii) a net return at a uniform rate to the present value of the capital in the various branches of production. Both fixed and working capital are included in establishing the present value of capital by branches.

4. The charge for land, or rent, represents the differential return to superior land.

---

[2] See Bergson, *Soviet National Income and Product in 1937,* for a discussion of ideal standards of national income valuation and for a revaluation of Soviet national income in 1937 at "adjusted factor cost." Our factor cost standard corresponds to Bergson's, but in its application we differ in some substantial respects.

5. Prices of goods and services are uniform within any given market area.

In the discussion that follows we shall examine Czechoslovak prices to see to what degree they conform to our standard and to determine what corrections are necessary to eliminate the major distortions in the structure of gross national product introduced by the given market prices.

MARKET PRICE VALUATIONS IN RELATION TO FACTOR COST

We shall now discuss the Czechoslovak prices in relation to the requirements of our factor cost standard in order to identify points of divergence and, later, to make the necessary adjustments to the values in current market prices so as to approximate factor cost. Our results, comparing the structure of gross national product before and after adjustment to factor cost, will be summarized in Tables 6 and 7, below.

AGGREGATE FACTOR COST

We feel justified in basing our work on the assumption that in Czechoslovak market prices there appears to be room for compensation of all factors, although the compensation is not correctly distributed among the prices of particular commodities. For example, we may have a situation where the returns to capital in the production of commodity A are collected in the selling price of commodity B. In a socialized economy with highly centralized planning and control, the central authority can exercise some arbitrariness in pricing as regards recouping factor charges; indeed, it is in the implementation of control over economic activity through financial measures that the arbitrariness manifests itself.

When we assume that the value of the gross national product in crowns is the same in market prices as in factor cost, we proceed not from theoretical arguments but simply from a sense of what seems reasonable in the particular instances. This amounts to saying that, taking the actual returns to labor as more or less correct, the residual in the market price value of gross national product is fully exhausted by reasonable capital consumption allowances and by a reasonable rate of return on the investment. Whether more than the residual, or less, should be taken for nonlabor factors or whether labor returns are too low or too high are questions that we cannot answer from a strictly theoretical viewpoint.

Before we consider some details of our procedure, two general questions must be considered. First, do the labor returns given by the actual wages, salaries, and social security contributions in fact conform to the factor cost standard? And, second, what justification have we for accepting aggregate nonlabor returns as equal to the value of gross national product at market prices less the labor returns?

Both questions were resolved not in theory but as practical choices among other possible choices. We wanted to show the structure of gross national product in terms having some meaning in the Czechoslovak context. The actual compensation of employees meets this test; although some arbitrariness, it may be argued, was shown in accepting the given market values for labor, it would be more arbitrary to depart from this important basic element in Czechoslovak economic accounting. Clearly this does not answer the question as to whether labor was paid more or less than its share determined by the calculus of marginal productivities; but the way in which wage rates were differentiated by occupations suggests that to some extent this calculus was faced, albeit imperfectly and in some instances grossly so.

As for our second choice, in 1955–56 the nonlabor returns represent a rate of about 12 percent, based on the present value of fixed and working capital, and apparently a lower rate in 1947–48, although the lack of capital valuations in 1947 and 1948 prices prevents a more precise statement.[3] These rates seem reasonable when account is taken of the low market prices at which capital goods are valued and of the absence of an explicit

[3] See Appendix Table 39, col. 3, and Appendix Table 43. These tables imply a return of 12 to 13 percent, whereas our alternative calculation on the assumption that all net income in agriculture at the realized prices represents returns to labor implies a return of 11 to 12 percent.

return to land. Capital goods were for the most part exempt from the turnover tax.

Three elements affecting price formation require special consideration: (1) indirect taxes, especially the turnover tax, the principal source of state budget revenue; (2) subsidies; and (3) accounting profits. Our concern is how these elements cause the structure of gross national product at market prices by final use and by sector of origin to diverge from the corresponding factor cost structure.

Indirect Taxes. In our adjustment, the market price total of gross national product is fully resolved into factor charges, and these charges then determine the components of gross national product from both the origin and end-use sides. The distinction between direct and indirect taxes as regards national income in the Soviet bloc countries and to a much lesser degree in other parts of the world is a conventional matter that is being undermined by changes, sometimes abrupt, from dependence on one kind to the other kind of tax for government revenue, and this revenue in increasing instances is becoming a species of "profit" in its allocation in large measure to support enterprise investment or to meet current factor charges. It would perhaps be startling, but not unimaginable for a government to switch entirely from complete dependence for revenue on income and profit taxes to complete reliance on sales taxes, for example. Would this mean that the gross national product at factor cost had changed? It seems preferable to have a gross national product total at factor cost defined in such a way as to be invariant under such tax shifts. This may cause some arbitrariness in delimiting factor rewards, but it introduces a useful symmetry in that a meaningful total of sales of final product at market prices is matched against the same total construed as factor charges.

As regards structure by final use, we concluded that in 1947–48 indirect taxes (including profits of state monopolies) raised the market-price share of consumption in gross national product slightly above what it would be at factor cost but that subsidies had an opposite effect, substantially offsetting the divergence introduced by indirect taxes. Accounting profits in these years were relatively low as a share of the gross national product, and there is little evidence that they were distributed disproportionately among final uses.

By 1955–56, indirect taxes had become the prime means of achieving "socialist accumulation," [4] and at the same time the major cause of divergence of market prices from factor cost. These taxes impinged mostly on consumer goods and services; in principle, investment goods and services were exempt.[5] In practice, the tax was collected mostly at the producer's level; thus, consumer goods [6] and services bought by the government or entering inventories in trade are valued at prices including the turnover tax.[7]

Subsidies. Adequately detailed information on the distribution of subsidies is lacking, but the scattered information that exists, taken together with the estimated total amount of subsidies, indicates that they did not cause significant divergence from the factor cost structure by final use. Thus, of the total estimated subsidies, 6.4 billion crowns in 1955 and 7.7 billion in 1956

[4] This term is used to designate the resources used primarily to finance investment and government expenditures.

[5] Boreš and others, *Problémy nové soustavy plánování a financování československého průmyslu,* p. 149; see also Veltruský and others, *Československé finance,* p. 340.

[6] Official sources use the term "consumer goods" for commodities sold to households, enterprises producing services, and governmental institutions on current account.

[7] The following quotations from Veltruský and others, *Československé finance,* pp. 345–47, give a more precise specification of the coverage of the turnover tax:

"[Transactions in prices net of turnover tax, comprise mainly:] (1) Sales of products for investment purposes to buyers in the socialist sector; (2) Sales of products for capital repairs of buildings which are in socialist ownership; (3) Sales of products to [producers branch] supply and marketing organizations and purchasing enterprises, insofar as they are being purchased for resale; (4) Sales of products to foreign trade enterprises, insofar as they are purchased for resale abroad; (5) Sales of products to other enterprises in the socialist sector, insofar as they are used for further processing. . . .

"Organizations not entitled to the retail rebate are: organizations of the socialist sector buying commodities for retail prices for their own use (nonmarket use), budget organizations, and agricultural cooperatives."

(see Table 2 A), more than half can be identified as relating directly to consumption-type goods and services affecting mostly personal consumption as a final use but to some extent entering government, defense (military subsistence and clothing) and gross investment (changes in inventories).[8]

Another large component of subsidies went to coal mining and metallurgy.[9] These are sectors whose products eventually enter all final uses, although gross investment probably benefited more than proportionately. With more detailed information on the distribution of subsidies, and even more so with the additional help of a detailed input-output table, more reliable measures of the divergence from factor cost structure by aggregate final use could be established, but, in view of the magnitudes involved, no serious change in structure could be expected.

Accounting Profits. Accounting profits in 1955–56 clearly failed to correspond to the contribution of capital to production; but it is difficult, lacking more detailed information, and—what would be most helpful—an input-output table, to quantify divergence from factor cost structure of gross national product by final use on this account. Thus, for 1955, an incomplete percentage distribution of total profits was as follows: electric power—4.3, chemicals—8.7, engineering products—19.6, timber and wood products—5.9, light industry—16.3, food processing—10.9, construction—7.2, and transportation—6.8.[10] In relation to capital invested, profits realized in engineering products, food processing, and light industry seem to have been proportionately too big since the same source shows blanks—presumably indicating losses—in ore mining and metallurgy and in fuels. But, it is difficult to judge, even by branches, which final use was affected most by the profits collected. For example, at first sight engineering products would seem to relate mostly to gross investment, and profits in this branch accordingly might be considered to cause gross investment at market prices to constitute

[8] See notes to Table 2 A, item 3 (p. 146).
[9] *Ibid.*
[10] *Finance a úvěr,* 1958, No. 4, p. 206.

a higher share of gross national product than at factor cost. However, the possibility must be considered that most of the profit in this branch was earned on consumer durables and thus impinges on personal consumption; the same might be true of chemicals and electric power. Construction, on the other hand, should relate exclusively to gross investment, whereas transportation (shown in the source as a branch of material production) contributes in undefined shares to all final uses. A generalization in these circumstances is difficult to support, but, very probably, on balance profits cause the share of personal consumption to be greater at market prices than at factor cost.

On the whole, it seems reasonable to believe that in 1955–56 subsidies, as well as accounting profits, affected prices of consumer goods slightly more than proportionately. Owing to their opposite effects on market prices, however, we would expect that the divergencies from factor cost introduced by these factors substantially offset each other at the level of aggregate consumption.

FACTOR COST OF INDIVIDUAL ITEMS

If the question be posed simply in terms of individual commodities, then, without doubt, in both periods the effect of indirect taxes, subsidies, and the formal accounting profits in numerous instances resulted in relative prices being out of proportion to factor costs. To attempt to correct each individual commodity price to factor cost would be beyond the scope of this study, and, moreover, where the concern is with structure of gross national product by major categories of final uses and sectors of origin of product, such detailed revaluation is unnecessary. What is required here is that the features in the price system which cause divergences from factor cost be identified, quantified, and, where possible, eliminated by suitable adjustments to aggregate values in market prices.

WAGES

On the whole, the requirement for wages to correspond to average marginal productivities and disutilities of labor in various occupations seems to have been met reasonably well in the years under consideration. In both 1947–48 and 1955–56, there were legal and administrative restrictions on the mobility of employees, yet wage incentives and wage differentials continued to serve as a means of labor allocation. The requirement with regard to disutilities was impaired in 1947–48 by the presence of rationing of consumer goods, but even in those years the prospect of derationing, which occurred in part in 1949 and in full in mid-1953, gave significance to wage differentials.

CAPITAL CHARGES

Depreciation Allowances. Business accounting in most instances provided explicit charges for capital consumed in the course of production. These charges, however, in the earlier period were based on various book values of capital and hence failed to reflect comparable charges among various branches of production with regard to the current replacement value of capital. For the later period, a capital census showing the replacement value of capital at the end of 1954 in July, 1954, prices was available, and, presumably, depreciation allowances were subsequently based on this capital revaluation. Even so, the question as to adequacy of the allowances still remains open, since capital goods as a group appear relatively underpriced at the official prices in relation to factor cost. This group was almost entirely exempt from the turnover tax, which, it will appear later, can be considered to include returns to capital. In both periods, and particularly in the more recent years, investment in the socialized sector was financed by interest-free grants, and interest as such figured in business accounting predominantly on short-term loans to meet seasonal needs for extra working capital.

Possible divergences from factor cost on account of the practice followed on depreciation allowances would be most noticeable in comparisons of structure of gross national product by sector of origin, but it would be difficult to quantify divergences as regards final uses in view of the dispersion of intermediate and final products of given branches to various final uses.

Profits. The second return to capital, namely profits, clearly did not meet our factor cost requirement of a uniform rate of return to the present value of capital in the various branches of production. Some entire branches operated at a loss and required subsidies, for example, the production of fuels and ore mining and metallurgy in 1955. For others the apparent returns did not seem proportionate to the distribution of capital by branches.[11]

The boundary between the turnover tax and accounting profits is essentially formal. The state as the quasi-universal entrepreneur can choose the form in which it gets a return on capital by reimbursing the producer for the noncapital costs and by allocating the margin between such costs and the selling price to three portions: (1) the turnover tax; (2) "profits" left at the disposition of the enterprise; and (3) "profits" paid into the state budget as a profit tax. In practice, a very substantial part of the sum of the turnover tax and profits tax is handed back to the enterprise sector to finance investment. These technicalities are related more to the requirements of financial control than to the theory of distribution.

Charge for Land. Through price control and the regimen of compulsory deliveries by farmers to state procurement organizations, the government in the postwar period was in a position to control farmers' net income. A comparison of average farmers' income with average wages earned in other sectors of employment shows some improvement by 1955–56, but the continued migration of labor away from the farms, despite the effort of the government to reverse the movement, suggests that the government may have extracted practically all the nonlabor returns from farming.[12] This does not mean that a return to land and capital in agriculture was not included in prices charged to eventual consumers; indeed, the turnover tax and profits of processing industries realized in such prices provided ample room for nonlabor returns to agriculture. In comparison with other uses,

[11] See *Finance a úvěr*, 1958, No. 4, p. 206, and State Statistical Office, *Statistická ročenka*, 1957, p. 292.

[12] It was the intention of the government to raise the permanent labor force in agriculture by 320,000 persons during 1955–1957; see *Zemědělské noviny*, October 5, 1956.

then, consumption at market prices on this score would show a larger share in the gross national product than in a breakdown at factor cost. On the other hand, in a breakdown by origin, agriculture at prices received by farmers would show a smaller share than at factor cost.

UNIFORMITY OF PRICES

The factor cost requirement that prices of goods and services be uniform within any given market area was not met on at least three counts in the actual situation: (1) the presence of rationing of consumer goods at controlled prices in 1947–48 alongside a black market; (2) multiple prices for agricultural products in 1955–56; and (3) the turnover tax, which raised prices to consumers above the level at which the goods in general were available to other users. The divergence from factor cost introduced by the turnover tax has already been discussed; we turn briefly then to the other points.

Rationing limits real wages, and, where the principle of rationing is equality, it reduces the incentive behind wage differentials. In Czechoslovakia, however, rationing was differentiated in 1947–48 according to the importance of work performed; the prospect of derationing must have been considered to some extent by wage earners; and the black market in conjunction with the expectations mentioned in the preceding point served to some extent to give fuller meaning to money wages. In any event, it would be difficult to quantify divergences from factor cost introduced by rationing; in the present case such divergences were not considered serious.

Multiple prices for agricultural products must be considered in connection with the turnover tax by means of which the prices charged to final users were raised. Insofar as agricultural products served more than one final use (consumption, gross investment as affected by farm stocks and exports, and so forth) the incidence of the tax on some uses and not on others caused the structure of gross national product at market prices by final uses to diverge from the factor cost structure. As regards structure by sector of origin, the scheme of multiple prices was the means used by the state to regulate factor incomes in agriculture, and on this count we must reckon with divergence from factor cost.

Our next step will be to make adjustments to the components of gross national product at market prices to correct for the major divergencies from factor cost identified in the discussion above.

GROSS NATIONAL PRODUCT AT FACTOR COST BY SECTOR OF ORIGIN

METHOD OF ADJUSTMENT

Our conclusion from the above discussion of Czechoslovak prices is that labor as a factor of production was more or less rewarded in keeping with the factor cost standard of valuation, but that the nonlabor factors were in general undercompensated and nonuniformly compensated. Our adjustment, shown in Table 6 and described in detail in Appendix G, consists of taking the market price value of gross national product as the correct value of gross national product at factor cost and reallocating

TABLE 6

GROSS NATIONAL PRODUCT BY ORIGIN AT FACTOR COST, 1947–48 AND 1955–56

	1947	1948	1955	1956	1947	1948	1955	1956
	(Billion current crowns)				(Percentage of total)			
1. Industry	94.5	109.3	57.8	61.6	38.3	38.2	38.2	38.0
2. Agriculture	36.5	52.4	23.8	25.0	14.8	18.3	15.7	15.4
3. Forestry	4.7	5.2	2.2	2.4	1.9	1.8	1.4	1.4
4. Construction	9.5	10.1	11.9	13.8	3.8	3.5	7.9	8.5
5. Transportation, communications	28.1	30.9	15.4	16.3	11.4	10.8	10.2	10.1
6. Trade, banking, insurance	21.8	23.1	11.6	12.5	8.8	8.1	7.6	7.7
7. Housing	13.8	14.9	12.9	14.1	5.6	5.2	8.5	8.7
8. Government	26.9	28.4	11.5	12.2	10.9	9.9	7.6	7.5
9. Other	11.2	11.8	4.1	4.4	4.5	4.1	2.7	2.7
10. Gross national product	246.8	286.1	151.2	162.2	100.0	100.0	100.0	100.0

NOTE: Figures do not necessarily add up to totals because of rounding. For sources and computation see Appendix G.

the nonlabor returns in this total to (1) capital consumption allowances and (2) net returns to nonlabor factors in the various branches of production at a uniform rate, in proportion to their present values of fixed and working capital.

A basic assumption underlying Table 6 is that the return to labor as a factor of production in agriculture in 1947–48 is equal to the total net income from farming at the realized prices and that in 1955–56 it is equal to the value of total net income calculated at compulsory delivery prices. An alternative assumption of equal validity in the absence of reasons to the contrary would be to take, as in 1947–48, the total net income at the realized prices as equal to the returns to labor in 1955–56. On this basis, but in other respects following the methodology used for Table 6, the resulting composition of GNP at factor cost is as follows (1955 and 1956 percentages of total, respectively): industry—37.4, 37.0; agriculture—18.0, 17.8; forestry—1.4, 1.4; construction—7.7, 8.3; transportation, communications— 9.8, 9.7; trade, banking, insurance—7.4, 7.4; housing—8.0, 8.1; government—7.6, 7.5; other—2.7, 2.7; total GNP—100.0, 100.0. The difference from Table 6 is the rise in the share of agriculture by a little over 2 percent of GNP and the compensatory decline in other sectors. We shall refer to this alternative adjustment at various points below.

We may ask at this point: Would the factor cost adjustment be significantly different from that shown in Table 6 if we had taken aggregate nonlabor returns, in 1955, for instance, at a much lower figure than gross national product at market prices less labor returns? One answer to this question was given by assuming nonlabor returns in 1955 to be in the same proportion to labor returns as in 1948, and again distributing the nonlabor returns among sectors of origin in proportion to their current values of fixed and working capital. All the necessary data were taken from Appendix Tables 39 and 43, and our calculation, implying a 3.9 percent return on the current fixed and working capital, showed the following percentage composition of the redefined total gross national product: industry—40.1, agriculture —15.3, forestry—1.5, construction—8.4, transportation and communications—9.3, trade, banking and insurance—7.4, housing—5.5, government—9.8, other sectors—2.8. There is very little change from the structure exhibited in Table 6.

The decline in housing and the increase in government in the above example as compared to Table 6, in each case by about 2 percentage points of total GNP, may be noted as a caution against reading judgments of relative growth of sectors based on changes in structure presented in current market or factor prices. Constant price structures and indexes of growth in constant prices are required for such judgments, whereas current factor prices are more informative in questions of resource allocation in a single given year.

Despite this stricture, it is interesting to note that over a considerable range of rates of return to capital, the structure of gross national product at "factor cost" would not change very significantly. Sectors that are heavy in the use of one factor and light on others (for example, government with respect to labor and housing with respect to capital) would be most affected by such a change in rates, but relationships among the larger sectors—industry, agriculture, transportation and communications, and construction—would not be seriously disturbed in the Czechoslovak instance.

RETURNS TO LAND

We have said nothing so far in our factor cost adjustment about returns to land, having included them in the total of nonlabor returns, which we distributed on the basis of the present value of fixed plus working capital in the various sectors of production. Thus, land is included only insofar as its value is included in our capital figures. In agriculture these figures include irrigation and drainage facilities, orchards, and similar improvements in the value of fixed capital. We have also reflected to some degree in our estimates of working capital the differential contribution of superior land by including the value of growing crops and farm products stored on the farm. But we must leave it to the reader to decide whether further adjustment is required and how it might be accomplished.

If one would prefer to see a lower rate of return to capital in agriculture than in other branches, then there would be room within our present estimate of the return to agriculture for a greater return to land.

LABOR RETURNS IN AGRICULTURE

Our factor cost adjustment in agriculture required that a judgment be made as to the character of the returns realized by farmers. After a comparison showed that the net return to farmers in 1947–48 was equal to only about half the wages earned by hired farm labor, we decided to treat net farm income as purely labor income. Whether this ratio is appropriate or not, we leave to the reader to consider. The availability of housing in the countryside as well as factors not expressed in money may have made it worthwhile for farmers to continue farming. A similar comparison in 1955–56 showed some gain for the farmers relative to hired farm labor, and for these years we assume the labor component in net farm income to be equal to the net income that would result from valuation of all farm products at compulsory delivery prices and the balance to be regarded as income to factors other than labor. The above assumptions relate to the factor cost figures shown in Table 6.

An alternative judgment was also made for 1955–56 to parallel the assumption made for 1947–48, namely, the entire net income in agriculture was taken as returns to labor. This assumption implies average wage-type returns in agriculture in 1948 at about 39 percent of the average wage level in the nonagricultural sectors and in 1955–56 at about 55 percent. By comparison, the assumption underlying Table 6 implies for 1955–56 an average wage in agriculture about 43 percent of that in the nonagricultural sectors. Despite the apparent relative gain in agriculture by 1955–56, labor was still migrating from the farms to the cities, and this was occurring in the face of an announced government policy to reverse the movement. In view of the decline in agricultural employment and the increase in agricultural capital, one would expect a relative increase in average returns to labor.

ALLOCATION OF RETURNS TO CAPITAL

It will be recalled that we distributed nonlabor factor returns to the various sectors of production at a uniform rate in proportion to their current, depreciated values of fixed capital plus their annual average levels of working capital. For our estimates of fixed capital we relied on the official data for the full replacement value (that is, the cost of equivalent new units) in 1955 prices, from which we calculated the actual value present in each year (that is, the full replacement value less the accumulated depreciation), also in 1955 prices.[13] These prices represent the current costs of production plus a more or less uniform profit margin, although this probably failed to cover the contribution of capital adequately; no turnover tax was included. We do not need to question the correctness of the valuation at this point, however, since we are primarily interested in the proportions of the total capital held by the various sectors. If capital goods were uniformly underpriced (or overpriced), the proportions would not be affected.[14]

By equalizing the rates of return to fixed capital in various sectors of production, we in effect imply that the relative prices of capital correspond to the sums of the discounted future returns (net profit or interest plus depreciation). In other words, we establish a uniform rate of net product to the given values of capital. In this connection we need to examine briefly the relative prices of capital of different durabilities.

The return to capital or the net product as defined above

[13] The official capital census was carried on in prices of July, 1954, but there was no significant change by 1955. According to the Czechoslovak State Statistical Office, *Statistická ročenka*, 1958, p. 17, fixed capital is shown at reproduction values, i.e., in value before the subtraction of accumulated depreciation. *Ibid., Generální inventarisace základních fondů v Československu, Otázky Statisticky*, 1957, No. 3, p. 24, makes it clear that depreciation norms are applied to the reproduction prices to arrive at current residual values.

[14] For the sake of comparison we also calculated the distribution of GNP at factor cost in 1955 following the same procedure as Table 6 but allocating profits among sectors on the basis of the full, undepreciated values of capital. The resulting percentage distribution of GNP is close to that shown in Table 6, namely: industry—38.4, agriculture—15.9, forestry—1.4, construction—7.3, transportation and communication—9.9, trade, etc.—6.9, housing—9.6, government—7.6, and other—2.9.

(interest plus depreciation) can be regarded as a rental charge on the fixed capital. A constant absolute return would imply a constant marginal physical product per year over the life of the capital good (the one-horse shay case). And, as we shall show below, a declining rental would be consistent with the use of the present, depreciated values of capital. It would be unrealistic to expect that wear and tear would leave production capacity per year unaltered. The net product or rental charge to be associated with capital equipment should decline somewhat, though perhaps not as rapidly as implied by straight-line depreciation. The Czechoslovak official replacement values of fixed capital make no provision for wear and tear.

In the ideal situation we should like to ascertain the market value of each item of fixed capital (in the sense of the present, discounted value of future returns) at the beginning and end of each year, thus establishing the economic depreciation as the difference. The accepted Czechoslovak practice is straight-line depreciation, a simplified expedient that may or may not correspond to economic depreciation as defined above. Another possibility to consider is constant annual net physical product over the lifetime of the unit of fixed capital and the economic depreciation that this would imply.

These two alternative ways of calculating depreciation result in different present values (after depreciation) of capital, and hence a possibly significant difference may appear in the relative sizes of sectors of origin of gross national product after allocation of returns to capital at a uniform rate as described above.

Let us assume, for example, that we have two machines whose annual net marginal physical product is the same, and that one will last two years and the other only one year. If the price of the machine with the longer life is $2,000 and the prevailing rate of interest (or return) is 10 percent, the equilibrium price of the other machine is $1,047.62 (calculated from $2,000 = X + X/R$, where $R = 1 + 0.1$). Now straight-line depreciation and a 10 percent return in the case of the machine with a two-year life implies a net return of $1,200, or $1,000 for depreciation and $200 for profit. In the same way, for the machine lasting one year, we have $1,047.62 for depreciation and $104.76 for profit, or a net product of $1,152.38. But this contradicts our assumption that both machines have the same annual net product.

If, however, we assumed that net product changes with time as implied by straight-line depreciation, we could use the above approach for distributing profits according to the actual value of the fixed capital. The annual net product here would be given by the straight-line depreciation plus interest or profit at a uniform rate on the present, depreciated value of the fixed capital, that is by $(C_0/n)[1 + i(n - t + 1)]$, where C_0 is the value of the capital when new, i is the uniform rate of return, t is the given year, and n is the life of the asset in years. The decline in the annual net product depends on i and n, being equal to iC_0/n, namely the return on the value of capital consumed in one year. We may also express this decline as equal to $i/(1 + ni)$ times the net product in the first year. Thus, if we had a 10 percent rate of return and a twenty-year life, the annual net product implied by straight-line depreciation would be decreasing each year by 0.5 percent of the initial value of the capital, or by $3\frac{1}{3}$ percent of the first year's net product (profit plus depreciation).

Without doubt, there is no uniform rule for changes in net product for the entire capital stock of a country. Lacking better information, we decided to use the current value of capital as determined by straight-line depreciation plus the annual average value of working capital for allocating profits among sectors of production. Although this choice implies an assumption of declining annual net product per unit of fixed capital over time, we are confident that the result insofar as structure of gross national product is concerned would not change considerably if we had assumed instead a constant annual net product per unit of fixed capital.

Our inclusion of working capital in the basis for allocating profits among sectors took account of the average annual values of raw materials in stocks, work in progress, and inventories of finished products. It may be noted that some of the inventories on hand reflect inefficiency; however, we are concerned with the cost of resources, leaving aside questions of relative efficiency among sectors of production. For this reason, we must stress once more that our results cannot be used uncritically for conclusions of relative growth drawn from changes in structure at current factor cost. Conceivably the output of a sector could increase significantly because of greater efficiency in the use of given resources. Our calculations do not show such changes.

Gross National Product by End Use at Factor Cost

In discussing Czechoslovak market prices in relation to our factor cost standard, we pointed out the difficulties of identifying in a precise way the individual contributions of land, labor, and capital to each final-use category. Conceptually, given a sufficiently detailed input-output table, wherein the industry sectors would be small enough to assume fairly uniform proportions of the services of factors of production entering the various products of each industry sector, and knowing the labor and capital inputs in each sector as well as the incidence of accounting profits, indirect tax, and subsidies, one could arrive at final-use totals within which the factor contributions could be specified. Such information, however, is not available.

Even without an input-output table, given sufficiently detailed information on indirect taxes, accounting profits, and subsidies by branches of production, some alignments might be made between branches of production and final uses in order to quantify roughly the divergence from factor cost introduced by the nonuniform incidence of the price-distorting elements. Our information was not adequate to attempt a detailed calculation along these lines. Instead, as indicated above, we concluded on the basis of the available data that in 1947–48 the indirect taxes caused the share of consumption to rise in market prices vis-à-vis other uses to a small degree, but that this rise was probably offset by the influence of subsidies, with accounting profits more or less uniformly distributed and, in any event, sufficiently small so as not to cause serious distortions from factor cost. Hence we accepted the market price structure as reasonably close to factor cost.

Similar considerations for the years 1955–56 led us to conclude that only in the case of the indirect tax was there serious divergence of market prices from factor cost, the other divergences being either small or mutually offsetting at the level of aggregate final uses.[15] Our adjustment for the indirect tax is explained in Appendix H, and our results showing the estimated structure of gross national product by use appear in Table 7.[16]

TABLE 7

GROSS NATIONAL PRODUCT BY USE, 1947–48 AND 1955–56

(*Percentages of total*)

	At Current Market Prices				At Factor Cost	
	1947	1948	1955	1956	1955	1956
Personal consumption	72.5	65.1	55.0	53.1	44.4	43.8
Government	13.3	12.6	12.4	12.3	10.6	10.7
Defense	6.0	5.0	8.4	5.0	11.5	6.5
Gross investment	8.2	17.3	24.2	29.5	33.5	39.0
Gross national product	100.0	100.0	100.0	100.0	100.0	100.0

In our adjustment for indirect tax in 1955–56, we first identified subcategories of final uses subject to the tax; then, assuming a uniform rate of taxation, we subtracted the tax to get all categories net of the tax. Finally, we classified certain categories of uses as ineligible to be increased by reallocation of the factor charges caught up in the indirect tax, and to the remaining categories we distributed the tax total at a uniform rate in proportion to their values net of tax. The principal items considered ineligible to be increased by the reallocation of factor charges caught up in indirect taxes were those that either consisted entirely of labor contributions (domestic services, pay to government employees, and unpaid labor in farm and community investments) or already included returns to nonlabor factors (farm market purchases and gifts from abroad).

This procedure, though lacking detailed theoretical justi-

[15] See above, pp. 54–56.

[16] For a more detailed breakdown, especially in the government sector, see below, Table 13 (p. 87).

fication, probably is closer to the theoretically correct results than might seem at first sight. The adjustment amounts to raising uniformly the values of components of final uses at current prices less the indirect tax, that is, values in which labor cost forms the major part. As already explained, the rates of accounting profits and subsidies, varying by branches of production, will probably be equalized to a large degree in the process of regrouping the output of individual branches according to the final aggregate uses.

If this assumption is correct, the reallocation of the indirect tax on the basis of the values excluding the tax would then be roughly proportionate to the labor cost in each use category. But we regarded the indirect tax as embodying nonlabor returns; accordingly it should be distributed in proportion to the contributions of fixed and working capital, which we take to represent the nonlabor factors. To reallocate the tax in proportion to labor cost would be correct only if we could assume a uniform capital intensity in all the major final-use categories. This assumption does not seem so arbitrary when we consider the same averaging effect as in the case of accounting profits and subsidies. Thus, the adjustment for indirect tax may turn out to be quite adequate in correcting for divergence from factor cost by major final uses.

The reader will notice that gross rent enters mechanically into the calculation of the factor cost adjustment in Appendix Table 52 at its market price valuation and is subsequently raised upward as part of the uniform adjustment for nonlabor factor charges caught up in the redistributed indirect taxes. Accordingly, the resulting figure for gross rent as it enters the factor cost total for personal consumption is not to be considered comparable to the gross value added by housing shown in GNP at factor cost by sector of origin. If an approximation to gross rent at factor cost within the total for personal consumption shown in Table 7 is desired, one would need to take the gross value added by housing at factor cost as given in the adjustment by sector of origin and increase this by the estimated current purchases by housing from other sectors. When such a gross rent figure is then subtracted from the factor cost value of total personal consumption, the result can be regarded as the factor cost value of personal consumption excluding gross rent.

At this juncture we present an alternative calculation of GNP by end use at factor cost in 1955–56 in which we carry over directly to consumption as gross rent the gross value added by housing at factor cost as shown in the "alternative" estimate to that of Table 6 (p. 61) plus the estimated factor cost value of current purchases by housing from other sectors. In all other respects our calculation parallels that underlying Table 7, but the total of indirect taxes to be distributed among the eligible final-use components in proportion to their values net of tax is of course reduced by the amount of tax already incorporated into the factor cost value of gross rent. The results shown as percentages of GNP at factor cost are tabulated below; some details of the estimating procedure are given in Appendix H.

	1955	1956
Personal consumption	48.2	47.7
Gross rent	8.7	8.8
Other	39.5	38.9
Government	10.2	10.3
Defense	10.7	6.1
Gross investment	30.8	35.9
GNP	100.0	100.0

Our procedure in this treatment of gross rent parallels that followed in shifting certain direct services measured solely by their labor cost at their sector of origin valuation to the end-use side of GNP, except that in gross rent it is capital cost that predominates. If the remaining end uses at their values net of indirect taxes are more or less equally capital intensive, the procedure can be justified. There is no detailed statistical information on the Czechoslovak economy that would answer this question; however, there are some general considerations that suggest the approach is reasonable.

There is some commingling of the products of most sectors of origin in serving final uses that serves to level out capital intensity. Thus, some of the output of highly capital-intensive heavy industry branches finds its way into personal consumption through inputs into agriculture and consumer goods industries. Similarly, in Czechoslovakia, a part of the final production of heavy industry may be regarded as entering personal consumption when exported in exchange for imports of food and raw materials. Personal consumption also contains some highly capital-intensive items, such as passenger transportation and utilities, whereas investment contains value added in construction, which is very labor intensive. Other components in gross investment are highly capital intensive. On balance our assumption may prove reasonable. In any event the structures of GNP at factor cost that follow from our two approaches are reasonably close.

CONSISTENCY OF SECTOR OF ORIGIN AND END-USE ADJUSTMENTS

Because of the complexity of the input-output relationships involved and our lack of knowledge of intersectoral transactions, it is impossible to insure detailed consistency between the factor cost estimates by sectors of origin and those by end uses, except for some elements of production (such as direct labor services in government and gross value added in housing) that go directly to final demand. An extremely rough check is possible, however, for consistency between the gross value added by agriculture and the food component of personal consumption. We carried through such a check for 1956, first, between the estimates in Tables 6 and 7, and second, between the alternative estimates to these two tables.

In each check we estimated, first, the value at factor cost of the food component of personal consumption from the end-use side of GNP. On the basis of our accounts in current market prices and some data on the composition of retail sales, we estimated the percentage of food consumption in total personal consumption, excluding gross rent. Assuming that the incidence of the turnover tax was proportionately about the same on foods as on the other items, we applied this percentage to the value of personal consumption at factor cost, excluding the value of gross rent at factor cost consisting of gross value added by housing on the origin side plus estimated purchases (at factor cost) from other sectors. The result is a crude estimate of food consumption at factor cost.

Second, we estimated the value of food consumption at factor cost by building it up from the gross value added by agriculture, the inputs into agriculture from other sectors, value added by food processing, the inputs into food processing, and the trade margins. Use was made of some interindustry relationships shown in the Polish 1957 input-output table, and some judgments had to be made on such matters as the percentage of farm production going into foods, the fraction of output passing through the food processing industry, and trade.

The results of our test proved consistent for both sets of our GNP estimates. In the first instance, Table 6 vis-à-vis Table 7, the value of food consumption at factor cost was on the order of 37 billion crowns from both the sector of origin and end-use approaches. In the second instance, the alternative GNP estimates (on the sector of origin side, taking the entire net income from agriculture as returns to labor and on the end-use side carrying over the factor cost value of housing explicitly into the gross rent figure in consumption) yielded from both sides a value for food consumption at factor cost of about 42 billion crowns. Taking into account the extremely rough calculations, our sector of origin and end-use estimates are considered broadly consistent on the point of food consumption and value added by agriculture.

COMPARISONS WITH CZECHOSLOVAK OFFICIAL DATA

The most readily accessible Czechoslovak estimates of national income for 1947–48 are found in a United Nations publication.[17] We show a summary comparison of these figures with our own in Table 8. It is impossible to trace all the differences between the two sets of figures to their causes because no detailed explanation of Czechoslovak official definitions, estimating procedures, and sources is available. The most obvious diver-

[17] United Nations, *National Income Statistics of Various Countries, 1938–1948*, pp. 58–60.

TABLE 8
COMPARISON OF CZECHOSLOVAK OFFICIAL FIGURES AND
OUR ESTIMATES, 1947–48
(*In billion crowns*)

	1947		1948	
	Ours	*Czechoslovak*	*Ours*	*Czechoslovak*
1. National income (at factor cost)	196.8	194.4	231.6	213.1
2. Indirect taxes minus subsidies	36.0	29.0	40.0	40.7
3. Net national product (at market prices)	232.8	223.4	271.6	253.8
4. Net domestic investment	10.5	14.0	37.1	30.0
5. Depreciation	14.0	n.a.	14.5	n.a.
6. Gross national product	246.8	n.a.	286.1	n.a.

n.a. = not available.

gences, however, are due to the following peculiarities of the Czechoslovak national income framework.

In the official Czechoslovak estimates, social security contributions by employers are treated as indirect taxes rather than supplements to wages and salaries; estimates of payments to the government that would qualify as indirect taxes by their nature if not by name are omitted; tobacco monopoly profits are treated as legitimate profits rather than indirect taxes; withdrawals from blocked savings accounts are considered as part of current income of households, whereas in our accounts they are interpreted as dissaving and thus are not explicitly recorded on the household appropriation account; estimates of agricultural investments in kind are omitted.

Substantial differences between the Czechoslovak figures and our estimates seem to exist in the case of inventory changes and capital depreciation. Otherwise, wherever definitions could be presumed identical, the two sets of estimates were in close agreement. There is not much point in pursuing this comparison in further detail or in questioning the reliability of one set of estimates in the light of the other. From mimeographed interoffice memoranda that we had the opportunity to consult, it is apparent that at the time Czechoslovak economists made their estimates they did not adhere strictly to any standard methodology; further, they often had to rely on rough guesses just as we did, and in a number of instances they had less data at their disposal than we did ten years later.

For the years 1955 and 1956, the comparison with official data is complicated by the fact that Czechoslovak estimates are not available in absolute figures and have to be reconstructed.

The official Czechoslovak definition, like its Soviet prototype, identifies as national income the value added in production in the sphere of "material production," and this excludes services not directly related to material production (for example, government services). Some arbitrary decisions must inevitably have been made concerning the boundary between "productive" and "nonproductive" economic activity. Basically the official method of calculation is to begin with the gross value of the output at market prices and to subtract therefrom "material cost," comprising capital consumption allowances and purchases of materials and "productive services," in order to arrive at national income.

It is possible to derive an absolute figure for Czechoslovak national income in 1955 from the percentage of national income (Soviet definition) originating in construction, that is, the so-called "net product" (7.6 percent),[18] and our estimate of value added in construction (9,764 million crowns, which is the sum of labor cost, including social security contributions, 8,618 million crowns, as seen in Appendix Table 32, and profits estimated as 7.2 percent of the profit total of 15,923 million crowns given in Table 2 B, items 3.B.(2) and 4.B).[19] Our concept of value added and the Czechoslovak concept of net product differ by the value of some "nonproductive" services purchased by the sector. The use of the estimate of construction recommends itself, since there is no evidence of subsidies to construction, and turnover tax is relatively unimportant in this sector. Thus our estimate avoids inaccuracies that would arise in the case of other branches. On this basis we estimated the Czechoslovak official figure of national income in 1955 at about 128 billion crowns.

As mentioned above, the official estimate should be larger

[18] See *Rudé právo*, December 8, 1956.
[19] The percentage is from *Finance a úvěr*, 1958, No. 4, p. 206.

than our estimate by the value of "nonproductive" services purchased by the material enterprise sector. For this reason we
rounded the calculated figure upward to 135 billion crowns as an
approximation of the official estimate of national income. We
checked this estimate by calculating the net product of the construction sector using information in Polish sources on its structure.[20] The result was very similar.

We also approached the official figure independently by adjusting our aggregates for "nonproductive" services. We reduced
our estimate of GNP (Table 5 A) by the value added in communal services, housing, passenger transportation, "nonproductive" communication, health, welfare, culture, education, social
organizations, public administration, science and research, internal security, and national defense. (See Appendix Table 32
for the wages, salaries, and social security contributions in the
branches mentioned.) We allocated one half of the totals under
transportation and communication as belonging to the "nonproductive" sphere. We also deducted depreciation (see Table
5 A). There are some nonproductive services in the private
sector, but we omitted these from our rough calculation as negligible. Deducting the estimated total value of the "nonproductive"
services and depreciation (21 billion crowns) from our GNP
figure, we obtained 130 billion crowns. This sum again was
rounded up to 135 billion crowns to account for the value of
nonproductive services purchased by enterprises in the material
production sector and thus included in official estimate of national income.

It may be instructive to compare the Czechoslovak distribution of national income by origin and by use in 1955 (Table 9)
with our own breakdown at factor cost (Tables 6, 7, and 13)
and to point out the main reasons for the striking divergencies.
First of all, our breakdown refers to gross national product in
the Western definition whereas the Czechoslovak breakdown refers to the narrower Soviet definition of national income. Some
additional divergencies result from differences in particular estimates, different definitions of economic branches, and from the

[20] Poland, Central Statistical Office, *Dochód narodowy polski, 1956,* p. 31.

Table 9
NATIONAL INCOME (SOVIET DEFINITION) OF
CZECHOSLOVAKIA IN 1955
(*Czechoslovak data; in percentages of the total*)

Distribution by Origin		Distribution by Use	
Industry	65.5	Consumption	80.6
Agriculture	15.1	Accumulation	19.4
Construction	7.6		
Other	11.8		
	100.0		100.0

SOURCE: *Rudé právo*, December 8, 1956.

fact that our breakdown is in terms of factor cost whereas the official one is in terms of market prices and thus reflects the distortions introduced by the nonuniform incidence of indirect taxes, subsidies, and accounting profits.

The Czechoslovak procedure in calculating the shares of different industrial branches consists in deriving net production from the wholesale value of gross production and adding the turnover tax according to an arbitrary rule. Industrial gross production is calculated officially as the sum of the output of individual enterprises in wholesale prices. Agricultural gross production represents the sum of the values of individual farm products valued at realized prices. The gross output of construction includes the value of all objects constructed; transportation includes only the gross income derived from carrying goods; and gross production in trade consists of the sum of the trade margins. Similar procedures are used for deriving gross production in other "productive" sectors. The value of capital consumption allowances and intermediate products used up in the process of production is subtracted to arrive at net production. The turnover tax is then added only to the output of industry and of agriculture in the proportions "in which it is collected as a part of the price of the final industrial or agricultural products." [21]

The upshot of the differences is the much larger share of national income originating in industry exhibited by the official figures. The economic significance of such a breakdown based on current market prices is of course very limited, if not nil—a

[21] *Politická ekonomie*, 1955, No. 6, p. 449.

fact of which Czechoslovak economists seem to be well aware. In an article devoted to the subject, we read:

The calculation of shares of national income of individual sectors . . . is not to be considered as shares of national income actually produced by individual sectors. The calculation of shares according to the realized prices, that is, in the way it is being done, necessarily includes a certain element of redistribution of national income—transfers of value between sectors—by means of prices.[22]

The Czechoslovak breakdown by use is not comparable with our figures for reasons similar to those for the breakdown by origin. As far as differences in definitions and coverage are concerned, it should be kept in mind that the official breakdown purports to show the shares in net "material production" of net investment, or "accumulation" (new fixed capital investment plus capital repairs plus inventory changes minus depreciation), and of "consumption" in the sense of all other uses of material product, including the "material component" of defense and other government outlays. It is obvious that the large share of consumption has an entirely different meaning from that which one is used to understand by this term in Western practice. The same is true of the relatively low share of "accumulation"; besides the effect of valuation in terms of given official market prices and probable discrepancies in estimates of specific values (for example, inventory changes), the divergence between the shares in the official breakdown and ours is due to the exclusion of depreciation in the former and its inclusion in the latter. If we recompute official "accumulation" in absolute figures (using our estimate of official national income as equal to 135 billion crowns in 1955), it will amount to 26.2 billion crowns. Our estimate of gross domestic investment in the same year amounts to 35.9 billion crowns in current prices (see Table 5 C). The difference should represent the value of depreciation, but it is broader than the bookkeeping concept of "capital consumption allowances" estimated in our accounts at 6.0 billion crowns (see Table 5 C). It is broader by depreciation in the "nonmaterial sector," and this, while reducing net accumulation, is added to

22 *Politická ekonomie*, 1955, No. 5, p. 451.

the value of consumption, the share of which is correspondingly raised.

There has been almost no mention in Czechoslovak sources of the distortions in relative use shares of national income due to the existing structure of prices.[23] Thus, our attempt to calculate the distribution of the national product by use in terms of economically meaningful prices reflecting factor cost is probably the first applied to the Czechoslovak economy.

[23] Only in the case of the distribution of national income by origin is it admitted that the share originating in agriculture is undervalued because "average realized prices express the value to 70–80 percent." *Politická ekonomie,* 1955, No. 6, p. 452.

IV. ECONOMIC IMPLICATIONS

ON THE BASIS of results presented in the previous chapters we shall now point out some of the peculiarities of the structure of the Czechoslovak economy and its changes during the years under study. Comparisons with other periods or countries will remain incidental. The points selected for discussion include sources of finance and some questions of resource allocation.

SOURCES OF FINANCE

In Table 10 we show the funds used for government and enterprise sector finance in a breakdown identifying the various institutional and formal means by which funds were made available. The table reveals a distinct change in emphasis on the different ways in which funds were provided in the period 1947–48 as compared to 1955–56. Although indirect taxes were by no means unimportant in 1947–48, the shift can still be described as one toward a general pattern familiar to students of Soviet-type economics: the small share of household savings and dependence upon indirect methods to enforce abstinence from current consumption, with the turnover tax towering over the rest. The absence of any state loan, compulsory or voluntary, may be noted in passing.[1] Whereas this was the dominant characteristic of the change, some interesting shifts took place in the absolute level and relative weight of specific items. Fore-

---

[1] The launching of a state loan was under consideration in 1952, prior to the monetary reform of 1953, but, unlike Soviet Russia, Poland, or Hungary, Czechoslovakia did not use state loans as a means of finance in the postwar period.

TABLE 10
SOURCES OF CZECHOSLOVAK FINANCE, 1947–48 AND 1955–56

Item	(1) 1947	(2) 1948	(3) 1955	(4) 1956	(5) 1947	(6) 1948	(7) 1955	(8) 1956
	(Million crowns)				(Percent of total) *			
1. Retained earnings of enterprises	− 1,094	12,113	3,098	2,779	− 1.1	9.0	3.6	2.9
2. Capital consumption allowances	14,000	14,500	6,012	10,835	14.1	10.8	6.9	11.1
3. Enterprise payments to government	60,604	70,295	64,939	67,137	60.9	52.3	74.6	68.9
a. Social security contributions	8,385	12,481	5,573	5,938	8.4	9.3	6.4	6.1
b. Indirect taxes	42,630	46,106	45,428	46,724	42.8	34.3	52.2	48.0
c. Direct taxes and other payments	9,589	11,708	13,938	14,475	9.6	8.7	16.0	14.9
4. Savings of households	4,823	12,347	2,239	5,235	4.8	9.2	2.6	5.4
5. Household payments to government	21,244	25,151	10,805	11,427	21.3	18.7	12.4	11.7
a. Social security contributions	5,985	9,817	351	353	6.0	7.3	0.4	0.4
b. Direct taxes, including imputed tax	12,437	11,928	8,638	9,391	12.5	8.9	9.9	9.6
c. Dues to quasi-governmental organizations	1,100	1,500	670	740	1.1	1.1	0.8	0.8
d. Other payments	1,722	1,906	1,146	943	1.7	1.4	1.3	1.0
Total	99,577	134,406	87,093	97,413	100.0	100.0	100.0	100.0

SOURCES: *Row 1:* See Table 2 B, item 4. *Row 2:* See Table 2 A, item 6. *Row 3a:* See Table 2 B, item 3.B.(1). *Row 3b:* See Table 2 A, item 5. *Row 3c:* See Table 2 B, item 3.B.(2) and (3). *Row 4:* See Table 1 B, item 4. *Row 5a–d:* See Table 1 B, item 3.C.(3), (2) and (5), (1), and (4), respectively.

* The sum of individual items may not equal the indicated totals because of rounding.

most among these were household savings and capital consumption allowances.

Household savings show a steep absolute rise from 1947 to 1948 as well as from 1955 to 1956. It would be wrong to base far-reaching conclusions on our estimates, because, as we must constantly keep in mind, they contain the statistical discrepancy of the household sector appropriation account. Caution seems to be called for, particularly in the case of the rise from 1947 to 1948. This increase goes counter to the direction of change of household time deposits, one of the main components of household savings.[2] But, assuming that our estimate reflects the movement correctly, an increase in cash balances compensating the decline in time deposits, we may ask whether such an increase was compatible with other contemporaneous facts. It has been argued that the political and economic situation created by the Communist coup in 1948 became a source of uncertainty concerning, among other things, the future worth of liquid assets. It would be logical to expect a "flight to commodities." However, the question is whether in 1948 there were enough commodities to take flight to. Rationing, instead of being relaxed, had to be tightened because of the food shortages resulting from the extremely poor harvest in 1947. The large increase in imports of essential foodstuffs was accompanied by a nearly corresponding drop in imports of nonessential industrial consumer goods in order to relieve the pressure on the country's balance of payments, even though domestic production of industrial goods still lagged considerably behind the prewar output. Moreover, soon after it had assumed control, the Communist government took the first steps toward a massive reallocation of resources in favor of heavy industry that was to be fully carried out during the first Five-Year Plan (1949–1953). Under these circumstances, the opportunities for the consumers as a whole to resort to "a flight to commodities" obviously were limited. A fairly substantial part of the 1948 savings may thus be taken to represent involuntary

[2] Time deposits with banks servicing the population (*ústavy lidového peněžnictí*) and postal saving service increased by 10.3 billion in 1947 and only by 5.5 billion in 1948 (see *Statistický zpravodaj*, 1949, No. 9, p. 327).

savings. As for the decline of deposits accompanying the increase in cash balances, the uncertainties of the times could well be used as a general explanation.[3] There probably was a tendency to keep liquid assets in cash form so as to protect them from easy state control. Further, people whose future was in jeopardy for political reasons would have had a preference for immediate liquidity, and their number was certainly large enough to have had an effect upon the structure of household savings. The transactions requirements for money on the black market also would have increased cash in the household sector. Such exchanges between households are not recorded in our accounts.

The more than twofold increase in household savings from 1955 to 1956 is subject to less doubt. Time deposits moved parallel to estimated total savings (a rise of about 58 percent), and this reinforces the credibility of the saving estimates and their movement. The doubling of total household savings could be rated as truly spectacular, given the absence of violent economic fluctuations, which presumably is a permanent feature of planned economies. In our view, the rise is to be interpreted as a corollary of a substantial recovery of the household real income from the reduced level of the early 1950s. The increase in real income was used, as soon as its absolute level permitted, to increase the saving-income ratio in order to rebuild the stock of household liquid assets that the monetary reform of 1953 had reduced to extremely low levels.

To show what we mean by the tendency to rebuild household liquid assets we have compiled in Table 11 data illustrating the prewar, postwar, and post-monetary-reform ratios of time deposits to household income. There is a marked decline in this ratio over the years. Our hypothesis, which takes the 1955–56 increase to form part of a trend, amounts to postulating a recovery from the low ratios of the period following the 1953 monetary reform. The ultimate goal of such a trend would

---

[3] *Rudé právo,* June 8, 1948, contains a denial of any intention of monetary reform. Even when goods are scarce, the possibility of exchanging money for existing goods among the population always exists. The more trusting or the less sophisticated segment of the population might be left holding the cash when a reform is effected.

TABLE 11

RATIOS OF TIME DEPOSIT BALANCES TO THE ANNUAL
HOUSEHOLD INCOME, 1937, 1947–48, AND 1955–56

Year	(1) * Household Income	(2) † Time Deposit Balances	(3) Ratio of Column (2) to Column (1)
	(Billion current crowns)		
1937	58.2	57.1	0.98
1947	205.1	21.2	0.10
1948	223.8	28.2	0.13
1955	96.3	5.7	0.06
1956	102.9	8.3	0.08

* For 1937, see Stádník, *Národní důchod a jeho rozdělení*, p. 181, row: "Soukromý (osobní) důchod úhrnem," net of undistributed corporate profits; for all other years, see Table 1 B, total income of households (items 1 and 2).

† For 1937, 1947, and 1948, see *Statistický zpravodaj*, 1950, No. 2, p. 73; for 1955 and 1956, see *Finance a úvěr*, 1957, No. 5, p. 234.

probably not be the high prewar ratio. The decline in the ratio probably reflects the people's attitude toward savings as influenced by the developments during and after the war, and probably by the redistribution of income that took place after 1945. But it seems reasonable to expect the "normal" level of this ratio desired by the households to lie somewhat closer to the 1947–48 levels.

As far as capital consumption allowances are concerned, little can be inferred from the 1947 and 1948 estimates, the reason being that official estimates on which our figures are based probably represent attempts to evaluate the physical deterioration of fixed capital rather than to estimate capital consumption allowances in the bookkeeping sense.[4] To the extent that depreciation is larger than bookkeeping would show, our profit estimates are lower. For this reason rows 1, 2, and 3 C of Table 10 should be read together.

Bookkeeping depreciation allowances up to 1956 seem to

[4] Compare the remark by Miloš Stádník: "It is undoubted that the investment activity, especially in building, was small in the Czech lands, so that the capital (*sic*) deteriorated. Some specialists in the sphere of nationalized industry estimate unrealized (*sic*) amortization at 14 thousand million Kcs, but specialists in the Ministry of Finance quote a lower sum." (Stádník, *Czechoslovak National Income and the Methods of Its Assessment,* note to Table VIII/2.)

have been entirely divorced from the reality of physical deterioration and technical obsolescence of fixed capital and the
corresponding decline in current value of assets. It appears that
depreciation was calculated on the basis of original cost, that is,
prewar or wartime cost. As a result of wartime and early postwar
scarcities, the general price level rose sharply, while the bookkeeping value of fixed capital assets as well as depreciation
allowances seem to have remained unadjusted. Profit margins of
nationalized enterprises were thereby more or less safeguarded,
but the possibility of distinguishing gross from net capital formation in any real sense was greatly impeded.

Between 1955 and 1956 capital consumption allowances
rose by 80 percent in absolute terms, and their share in the
total of sources of finance rose by 60 percent (from 6.9 percent
in 1955 to 11.1 percent in 1956). This jump reflects a fundamental change in the state's policy with respect to questions of
capital formation.

Investment policies of the first Five-Year Plan (1949–53)
were marked by a striking disregard of the maintenance of existing fixed capital. Implicit in this attitude was the belief that massive new sources of finance would take care both of the need
to keep capital intact and of the desired expansion. As a general
proposition and under certain conditions, this may be true. However, the failure to account for current capital consumption in
a meaningful way has serious drawbacks for central planners.
They ended by being unable to judge objectively the dimensions
of fixed capital, as well as replacement needs, whether by economic branches or by enterprises or regions. Characteristically,
demands of factory managers for new investments used to be
rejected in the period of the first Five-Year Plan as manifesta-
tions of the so-called "plant patriotism." One inconvenience of
the described practice of writing-off capital was the difficulty of
making comparative cost analyses between old and new plants;
new plants, with high depreciation allowances based on current
cost, sometimes had higher costs than old ones, with nominal
depreciation.

In 1955, the state undertook a reappraisal of all existing
fixed capital stock in current replacement cost, as well as a de-

tailed estimate of the prospective useful life of individual assets. This pioneering operation provided a basis for upgrading depreciation allowances from formal bookkeeping entries to a rational monetary estimate of the actual capital consumption.[5] As a result, depreciation allowances were increased.[6] As an apparent corollary to the increase in depreciation allowances, the total profits increased less and the share of the "profit tax" among the sources of finance suffered a relative decline (from 16.0 percent in 1955 to 14.9 in 1956).

Finally, in Table 12 we show the importance of indirect taxes in gross national product. We note also that indirect taxes accounted for about 51 percent of the value of consumer purchases (see Appendix Table 51).

TABLE 12
THE INDIRECT TAX AS AN ELEMENT OF CZECHOSLOVAK PRICES,
1947–48 AND 1955–56

Item	1947	1948	1955	1956
1. Total indirect tax as percent of the gross national product *	17.3	16.1	30.4	29.2
2. Total indirect tax receipts net of subsidies as percent of gross national product †	14.6	14.0	25.0	23.0

* Computed from figures in Table 5 A (gross national product) and in Table 2 A, item 5 (indirect taxes).

† Computed from figures in Table 5 A (gross national product) and in Table 2 A, item 5 (indirect taxes) minus item 3 (subsidies).

HOUSEHOLD TAX BURDEN

Some of the analytic problems posed by the merger of the state as political organ with the state as entrepreneur have already been broached in Chapter III. Let us state the basic problem once more.

In Soviet-type economies, the state, while performing functions assumed normally by the state as it developed in Western societies, simultaneously appears as the ultimate owner of the bulk of the means of production and the almost exclusive entre-

[5] Although the official economic doctrine admitted, around 1955, that obsolescence does operate under socialism, the revised rates of depreciation allowances do not include allowances for obsolescence.

[6] *Plánované hospodářství*, 1956, No. 6, p. 417.

preneur except in agriculture. Given this type of monopoly, a strict differentiation between taxes and enterprise profits, or between indirect and direct taxes, loses much of its significance. Such charges against the product, whatever their form, end up by being at the disposal of the state, and the question of household tax burden is fully answered by the only relevant fact that all of the sources of finance are ultimately derived from households. Their abstention from consumption makes resources available for other uses. It is, of course, possible to postulate that a "return to capital" is contained in enterprise profits, and from this it would follow that the profits tax is a direct tax incident upon the enterprise as final payer. Although the question could be explored further, any broader discussion would be of little use at the level of analysis maintained in the present study.

Instead of speaking narrowly of burdens and benefits of taxation, it would seem more appropriate to speak of final use shares in gross national product at factor cost. In Table 13, we observe a fairly stable share of resources allocated to government, including defense (from 17 to 22 percent over the years 1947–48 and 1955–56), a falling share for consumption (from 72 percent in 1947 to 44 percent in 1956), and a rising share for gross investment (from 8 to 39 percent). The question of burden is a matter of choice and valuation. If the population had freely elected to distribute factors of production in the indicated proportions to final uses, and if these resources were efficiently used, then no burden would be involved. These conditions, however, were not fulfilled: the allocation of resources was imposed on the population, and there were numerous instances of poor investment choices and other cases of inefficiency that imposed a real burden on the population.[7]

[7] The official press is an inexhaustible source of supporting evidence of inefficiency. We quote just a few samples picked at random:

Deploring as unnecessary the large share of building and construction in investment, one source states: "In our country the share of machinery in total investment amounts to about 35 percent, while in some developed capitalist countries it reaches up to 65 percent." *Podniková organisace*, XII (1958), No. 1, p. 20.

"Fulfillment of the investment plan, as well as payments of bonuses, is being verified by means of the funds spent on construction. . . . Materials are

RESOURCE ALLOCATION

The allocation of gross national product at factor cost to final uses in Table 13 is one of the major goals of our study. For 1947–48 the structure derived from current market prices, for reasons given in Chapter III and Appendix H, was accepted as reasonably close to factor cost, but for 1955–56 the divergence of the market price structure from that at factor cost shown in Table 13 is indeed striking. When expressed in factor

TABLE 13

RESOURCE ALLOCATION, 1947–48 AND 1955–56

(*In percentages of GNP*)

	At Market Prices and at Factor Cost		At Factor Cost		At Market Prices	
	1947	1948	1955	1956	1955	1956
1. Personal consumption	72.5	65.1	44.4	43.8	55.0	53.1
2. Government	13.3	12.6	10.6	10.7	12.4	12.3
a. Administration	6.4	5.8	1.6	1.4	1.6	1.4
b. Education	3.4	3.3	2.9	2.9	3.4	3.4
c. Culture	0.1	0.1	0.7	0.8	0.8	0.9
d. Health	0.7	0.9	2.7	2.6	3.3	3.1
e. Science and research	0.6	0.6	1.4	1.7	1.7	1.9
f. Social welfare	1.5	1.5	1.0	1.0	1.2	1.1
g. Quasi-governmental organizations	0.5	0.4	0.4	0.4	0.4	0.5
3. Defense and security	6.0	5.0	11.5	6.5	8.4	5.0
4. Gross investment	8.2	17.3	33.5	39.0	24.2	29.5
a. Domestic	9.7	17.9	32.8	37.5	23.8	28.5
b. Foreign	−1.5	−0.6	0.7	1.5	0.4	1.0
	100.0	100.0	100.0	100.0	100.0	100.0

SOURCES: Appendix Tables 52 and 53 and Table 5 C.

---

being built into constructions, even superfluously, just in order to spend money." *Rudé právo,* November 28, 1957.

"The worst phenomenon in our enterprises is the inventory of raw materials and products unnecessary for planned production. . . . While some enterprises do not fulfill the plan for lack of metallurgical products, total inventories of metallurgical products have reached almost the level of six-months' production of metallurgical industry." *Rudé právo,* May 6, 1954.

"The low level of ore production has another unfavorable effect, namely, that the expansion of our metallurgical industry is hampered by the lack of ore. The construction of HUKO, the big metallurgical combine in eastern Slovakia, had to be slowed down because in the coming years the production of ore will lag . . . and we would not have any ore for our new combine if it were completed at the date fixed originally." *Pravda* (Bratislava), April 27, 1953.

cost, consumption declines about one fourth and gross investment increases about one third from the shares at market prices.
The share of government changes relatively less.

We do not show a detailed breakdown of consumption in
Table 13 because our adjustment of market prices to factor cost
assumed equal capital intensity for major parts of the final use
aggregates. This assumption, however, becomes much less ten-
able if we start to deal with finer subdivisions of these aggregates. Values of the principal components of consumption at
current market prices can be readily identified from Table 1.A,
item 3.A and 3.B and the notes thereto. Subcategories of gross
investment and defense and security at market prices are given
in Appendix Table 52.

Government services are shown in Table 13 broken down
into several categories, thus making it possible to calculate such
broader alternative measures of consumption as may be required
for comparison purposes. Health and education outlays, for example, may be counted as consumption. The treatment of cultural services as part of consumption may also come under consideration, but here we should be very hesitant to do so without
reservations, in view of the extensive propaganda content of
cultural services that consumers would not seek to provide for
themselves by free choice. The same objection would apply in
part to education because of its heavy dose of indoctrination in
Communist ideology. By any standard, however, if we value the
various uses in terms of their factor costs, the share of consumption in the national product will be far lower than indicated in
official Czechoslovak sources, where different definitions of uses
and total aggregates, together with the warped price system,
convey the impression of a relatively high share of consumption.
In 1955, the "consumption fund" ("personal" and "collective")
represented 80.5 percent of the national income (Soviet definition).[8] In 1956, the share of personal consumption was 64 percent and of collective consumption, 17 percent; the rest was
accumulation plus reserves.[9]

[8] See *Rudé právo*, December 8, 1956.
[9] See *Životní úroveň v ČSR*, p. 6.

The share of gross investment at adjusted factor cost, 33.5 percent in 1955 and 39.0 percent in 1956, is high considered by itself, as well as in comparison with other countries. Thus, for example, in the USSR this share was about 23 percent in 1937 and 26 percent in 1948.[10] However, in 1944, at the peak of the war effort, the combined share of Soviet gross investment and defense outlays as recorded in the state budget is slightly higher than the combined percentage share of defense, security, and gross investment in Czechoslovakia in 1955. Even if the shares were made somewhat more comparable by the inclusion of investments in facilities for public administration and expenditures on the internal security apparatus in the Soviet instance, the relative drain on resources in the two countries would still be close. On the other hand, the Czechoslovak combined percentage share in these uses of gross national product in 1955 and 1956 (around 45 percent) is close to one fifth higher than the comparable Soviet figure for 1948.

We have already noted the rather erratic pattern shown by defense and security outlays in 1955 and 1956, and we have suggested explanatory hypotheses in Chapter II. By Soviet peacetime standards (1937 and 1948), the Czechoslovak shares of gross national product allocated to defense and security in 1955 and 1956 do not appear surprising. However, we are dealing with a category of outlays particularly subject to official secrecy, and we cannot be sure that all military expenditures fall within the published state budget category of defense and security.

The remarks above on resource allocation relate to our adjustment of GNP to factor cost as shown in Appendix Table 52 and the derivative Tables 7 and 13. If we rely instead on the alternative adjustment described above (p. 70), we should take

[10] See Bergson and Heymann, *Soviet National Income and Product, 1940–48*, p. 71. These percentages are based on values in adjusted prices in a procedure not fully analogous to ours. Unfortunately comparable figures for other years are not available. In view of some recent information, it seems that the share of gross investment was higher between 1929 and 1936 than in 1937. See, for example, USSR Central Statistical Administration, *Narodnoe khoziaistvo v 1959 godu* (The National Economy in 1960), (Moscow, Statistical Publishing House, 1960), p. 554, and *American Economic Review*, May 1961, p. 518.

account of a somewhat higher share of personal consumption (48 percent) in GNP in 1955–56 and more or less proportionately lower shares of the remaining final uses. At the present time we lack the necessary statistical information on the Czechoslovak economy to specify the factor cost of final uses of GNP with precision. Our two estimates are reasonably close at the level of the major final-use aggregates.

At this point it might be worthwhile to repeat our caution against indiscriminate international and intertemporal comparisons of structure of gross national products. Such caution is particularly in order for comparisons of market price structures where institutional factors enter price formation. Less hazard is involved in factor cost comparisons, but even here relative factor charges may differ significantly from country to country. One would expect similarities to emerge among the Soviet bloc countries, yet close scrutiny may be warranted.

APPENDIX A: NOTES TO HOUSEHOLD
SECTOR ACCOUNTS (TABLES 1 A, 1 B, 1 C)

NOTES TO TABLE 1 A

1. Sales to household sector appropriation account

A. Domestic services

Our estimates are shown below (in million crowns) and are explained in the notes that follow.

	1947	1948	1955	1956
1. Money wages	707	770	157	163
2. Wages in kind	434	467	156	162
3. Social security contributions by employers	48	52	47	49
Total	1,189	1,289	360	374

1. Money wages

1947. We multiplied the average annual employment (51,313 wage workers and 254 salaried employees) by the average annual earnings (13,614 crowns for wages and 33,989 crowns for salaries). For employment data, see Slovakia, State Planning and Statistical Office, *Statistická príručka Slovenska, 1948,* pp. 56–59; *Statistický zpravodaj,* 1947, No. 5, pp. 194–95; State Statistical Office, *Statistical Bulletin of Czechosolvakia,* 1947, Nos. 5–6, p. 78; *ibid.,* 1948, No. 8, pp. 140–41. The sources yielded an almost complete set of quarterly data (as of first of February, May, August, November). The missing data were interpolated either by simple arithmetic interpolation or by using the trend from available quarterly data for other periods. The annual figures were then increased by 1.2 percent to correct for the understatement of employment in National Health Insurance data, which we used, as compared to the figures of the State Statistical Office, covering employment in industry and handicrafts. This adjustment factor was used in instances cited below where only the health insurance data were available.

Sources for the 1947 wages and salaries were quarterly data in *Statistický zpravodaj*, 1947, No. 12, p. 454, and *ibid.*, 1948, No. 9, pp. 322–23. Missing quarterly data were interpolated arithmetically. Data on daily wages were converted to annual data using 313 workdays per year, the same as in Czechoslovak sources of that period. The figures thus computed were increased by 3.755 percent to compensate for the understatement in the health insurance data we used in comparison with the wage and salary data given by the State Statistical Office (State Statistical Office, *Průmyslové zprávy*, 1948, Nos. 7–8, pp. 42, 47; and State Statistical Office, *Zprávy*, 1949, Nos. 15–17, pp. 117, 126).

1948. Our estimate is the product of employment (50,116 wage workers and 227 salaried employees) and the average annual earnings (15,196 crowns for wages and 37,938 crowns for salaries). For employment data, see *Statistický zpravodaj*, 1948, No. 9, pp. 320–21 (February 1, 1948, data were taken to represent the annual average). The 1947 earnings figures were increased by 11.617 percent, corresponding to the increase in average industrial earnings calculated from data in State Statistical Office, *Průmyslové zprávy*, 1948, Nos. 7–8, pp. 42, 47; and State Statistical Office, *Zprávy*, 1949, Nos. 15–17, pp. 117, 126.

1955. The 157 million crowns shown above is one half of 313 million crowns, the other half representing the estimated wages in kind (see below); the 313 million crowns represent the 1956 estimate (see below) less 3.7 percent, which is the difference between 1956 and 1955 average wages in the socialized sector (see *Statistické zprávy*, 1957, No. 2, p. 15). Employment was assumed to be the same as in 1956.

1956. The 163 million crowns is one half of the product of employment (40,000 persons), the annual working time (2,808 hours, assuming a 9-hour day and a 6-day week), and the hourly wage (2.89 crowns). The other half was assumed to represent wages in kind (see below).

Employment was estimated roughly at 80 percent of the 1947 figure of 51,567 persons (see above). The decline was assumed to be the net result of the decrease in employment in former "bourgeois" households, the compensating increase in the new upper-class households, and the forces making for a larger inflow of new labor to other types of employment (change in preferences of labor, official pressures).

The hourly wage (covering both cash pay and compensation in kind) was estimated as the simple arithmetic average of 1956 maximum wages in three categories of domestic servants (2.18, 2.40, and 2.64 crowns of basic pay plus 20 percent permissible supplement; see wage decree in Ministry of Interior, *Úřední list,* 1956, No. 49).

2. Wages in kind

1947. This is the sum of the value of board (376 million crowns) and the lodging (58 million crowns) supplied to domestic servants. The value of board is the product of employment (51,567 persons, see above) and the estimated annual per capita value of board (7,300 crowns). In the case of lodging, the per capita value (1,500 crowns) is imputed to only 75 percent of employees.

The cost of board per day per adult person was assumed to have amounted to about 20 crowns in 1947; this was the cost of board per person per day in agriculture. In that year, agricultural workers without board received 20 crowns more per day than those with board. The value of lodging represents approximately the cost of lodging per adult worker on the farm, and this amounts to about 50 percent of the official—that is, legally authorized—urban rental (in 1947, one room with a kitchen was quoted at 3,400 crowns per year, see State Statistical Office, *Cenové zprávy,* 1947, p. 58).

1948. This was estimated under the same assumption as for 1947, but using 1948 employment and taking the per capita value of room and board 10 percent higher than in 1947.

1955 and 1956. Estimated at one half of the wage bill calculated on the basis of wage rates covering both cash wages and wages in kind. A detailed calculation of the per capita expenditure for food and housing supported this estimate.

3. Social security contributions by employers

1947 and 1948. Contributions by employers on behalf of domestic servants, amounting to 6.8 percent of money wages in both years, include compulsory health and accident insurance only. (See Vratislav Busek and Nicolas Spulber (eds.), *Czechoslovakia,* p. 214; the 1948 rate was applied for both years.)

1955 and 1956. Estimated at 15 percent of the wage bill including wages in kind, the rate applicable in the private sector (see the decree of September 28, 1953, in National Assembly, *Sbírka zákonů,* 1953, No. 84).

B. *Services of nonprofit organizations*
   This is the sum of the following components:

	1947	1948	1955	1956
1. Current purchases	200	239	14	14
2. Wages and salaries	612	718	42	43
3. Social security contributions	37	65	4	4
Total	849	1,022	60	61

1. Current purchases

1947 and 1948. Estimated at approximately one third of the respective wage and salary bills (see 2, wages and salaries, below). The proportions were based on expenditures of the government central administration (see below, pp. 132, 178, 182).

1955 and 1956. Estimated roughly at one third of wages and salaries, following the assumptions used for 1947 and 1948.

2. Wages and salaries

1947 and 1948. These are products of employment (10,439 and 11,885 persons in 1947 and 1948, respectively) and average annual salaries (58,623 and 60,443 crowns in 1947 and 1948, respectively). Employment covers employment in religious associations, social welfare organizations, and physical culture and amateur sports organizations. (Political parties, together with trade unions, are subsumed under the government sector for reasons explained in Chapter II.) The 1948 figures were computed by interpolating between the data for January 31, 1948, and January 31, 1949, published in State Statistical Office, *Zprávy,* 1948, Nos. 99–102, pp. 764–65, and 1949, Nos. 55–58, pp. 446–47. The 1947 figures were obtained by extrapolating the 1948 figures to July 1, 1947.

The annual wage rates applied here are those calculated for the entire group of nonprofit organizations (including those serving other sectors than households), on the basis of the following sources: State Statistical Office, *Zprávy,* 1948, Nos. 99–102, pp. 755, 772; *ibid.,* 1949, Nos. 55–58, pp. 431, 441, 450. The results based on employment and basic earnings were adjusted upward to include an estimate of supplementary allowances, based on the ratio between earnings in the state administration (including state enterprises) with and without supplementary allowances.

1955 and 1956. These figures are the product of employment (5,000 persons) and annual average wages prevalent in the entire group of "social organizations" (8,424 and 8,508 crowns in 1955 and 1956, respectively; see State Statistical Office, *Statistická ročenka,* 1959, p. 96). The employment figure is a rough guess, made on the basis of 1947–48 figures, and reflects a probable decline.

3. Social security contributions

1947 and 1948. Estimated at 6 and 9 percent of the wages and salaries in 1947 and 1948, respectively. The source for the 1948 rate is Busek and Spulber, *Czechoslovakia,* p. 214 (assuming no family allowances and no unemployment insurance contributions). In view of the 1947–48 increase of more than 50 percent in total social insurance contributions (see note 3.C.(3) to Table 1 B and note 7.C to Table 2 A), we assumed that rates increased 50 percent from 1947 to 1948 and that higher employment and wages accounted for the rest of the aggregate increase.

1955 and 1956. Estimated at 10 percent of the wage bill, according to the rates valid in the socialized sector (see below, p. 189, note to Appendix Table 32, column *8*).

2. Current purchases by nonprofit organizations

See note to entry 1.B., above (item 1 of the tabulation).

3. Value added by sector

See notes to entries 1.A and 1.B, above, for details on employee compensation.

NOTES TO TABLE 1 B

1. Value added by sector
See Table 1 A, item 3.
2. Income from other sectors
A. Enterprise sector
(1) Cash income
a. Wages and salaries
See Appendix E (Appendix Tables 29, 31, 32).
b. Entrepreneurial income
1947. The 18,053 million crowns is the difference between private entrepreneurial cash income before taxes (20,567 million crowns) and the amount of the general profit tax (2,514 million crowns, see State Statistical Office, *Zprávy,* 1949, Nos. 31–33, pp. 235, 241). Entrepreneurial income before taxes was estimated on

the basis of published data on income reported for taxation purposes (19,588 million crowns, see State Statistical Office, *Zprávy,* 1949, Nos. 31–33, pp. 240–49), increased by an estimated 5 percent for under-reporting.

1948. The 15,000 million crowns is a rough estimate. Entrepreneurial income before taxes was first assumed to be about the same as in 1947 (20,500 million crowns, see above); from this we subtracted (1) the amount of the general profit tax paid in 1948 (4,106 million crowns; see note 3.B.(2) to Table 2 B) and (2) an adjustment for the profits of the highest profit recipients, reclassified as a consequence of the 1948 nationalization (1,500 million crowns). The amount of this last adjustment was estimated in view of: (1) the highest income group of independent entrepreneurs, the "industrialists," diminished by 1,872 from 1947 to 1948 (State Statistical Office, *Průmyslové zprávy,* 1948, Nos. 7–8, p. 42; *ibid.,* 1949, Nos. 15–17, p. 117), (2) the income of the two highest income groups of independent entrepreneurs, numbering 1,825 persons, amounted to an estimated 1,023 million crowns (State Statistical Office, *Zprávy,* 1948, Nos. 11–15, p. 72), (3) profits were on the increase after 1946, as can be inferred from the budget proceeds of the general profits tax in 1947 (2,506 million crowns, based on 1946 profits, see *ibid.,* 1949, Nos. 31–33, pp. 235 and 241) and in 1948 (4,106 million crowns, based on 1947 profits, see note 3.B.(2) to Table 2 B); the increase is over 50 percent, indicating a similar increase of profits from 1947 to 1948. The starting assumption of unchanged entrepreneurial income in 1948 is justified only by our ignorance of the net effect of changes in demand, supply, pricing, and costs that occurred in 1948.

1955 and 1956. Owing to institutional changes after 1948, the majority of private enterprises ceased to exist. Thus, income included here pertains to net money receipts of craftsmen and members of free professions. Given the nature of such business, it was impossible to distinguish between labor and other income. For this reason this entry includes total net income of self-employed.

(i) *Handicrafts.* The number of private handicrafts and of similar trade enterprises was used to represent the 1956 number of self-employed in this category (47,000; State Statistical Office, *Statistická ročenka,* 1957, p. 180). Their number was estimated at 50,000 in 1955, on the assumption that it moved parallel to the number of self-employed outside agriculture (*ibid.,* 1957, p. 68). For both years, we estimated average net income at 20,000 crowns per person, a rough figure derived in relation to wages and sales in "communal enterprises." The average annual wages were 12,221 crowns for 1955 and 12,137 crowns for 1956, while average annual sales per employee amounted to 31,580 and 27,906 crowns (derived from figures in State Statistical Office, *Statistická ročenka, 1957*, p. 175).

Private handicrafts probably were able to furnish analogous services at considerably lower cost and still realize a net income above the wages paid in communal enterprises. Private handicrafts have most certainly a lower overhead. Further, there are reports indicative of the ability of private handicrafts to pay high wages to hired employees. (See, for example, New York *Times,* February 18, 1958.) Average net income of private handicraftsmen might be expected to lie somewhere between the wage and the sales figures of "communal enterprises." An estimate of about 20,000 crowns annually seems plausible if compared with the wages of skilled workers in industry and building trades, which were roughly between 18,000 and 22,800 crowns annually. We lacked any basis for making a good guess on the direction and magnitude of the change, if any, in average earnings from 1955 to 1956.

(ii) *Doctors.* The great majority of the members of professions in 1955 and 1956 were government employees. There is little doubt that some of them were able to supplement their regular salaries by income from private practice. Our rough estimates of such incomes are given here for the sake of completeness rather than as reliably accurate magnitudes.

There were 18,322 doctors in 1955 and 19,347 in 1956 (State Statistical Office, *Statistická ročenka, 1957*, p. 255). If we use for doctors the average earnings of persons working in "science and research" (1,499 and 1,550 crowns per month in 1955 and 1956, respectively), the total earnings of doctors will amount to 330 million crowns in 1955 and 360 million crowns in 1956. Assuming that their extra earnings amounted on the average to one fourth of their regular salary, this additional income would be 82 and 90 million crowns in 1955 and 1956, respectively.

(iii) *Other liberal professions.* It is difficult to approximate in any reliable way the incomes of nurses, lawyers, private instructors, architects working as self-employed. The figures we use in place of more inductive estimates have, to a large degree, the character of symbolic stand-ins. We assume that these earnings amounted to 100 million crowns in 1955 and to 107 million crowns in 1956 (an increase parallel to that of the total wage bill).

In summary, the cash income derived from self-employed activity was added and rounded (to avoid the appearance of precision) to 1,200 million crowns in 1955 and 1,100 million crowns in 1956.

c. Income of farmers

1947 and 1948. This represents farmers' cash income after the agricultural tax (see Dolanský, *Výklad k rozpočtu,* 1949, p. 235).

1955 and 1956. The total net cash income of farmers was obtained as the product of the net cash income per permanently working person in collectives and private farms (excluding agricultural tax), and the respective numbers of collective and private farmers at the end of each year. The calculation is given in Appendix Table 1.

APPENDIX TABLE 1

CALCULATION OF FARMERS' CASH INCOME, 1955–56

Item	1955	1956
1. Net cash income per permanently working person (crowns)		
(a) Collectives	6,416	6,730
(b) Private farms	3,960	4,409
2. Permanently working persons (thousands)		
(a) Collective farmers	320	361
(b) Private farmers	1,315	1,180
3. Total net cash income (million crowns)	7,260	7,632
4. Total net cash income (rounded, million crowns)	7,300	7,600

NOTE TO APPENDIX TABLE 1

Sources: Item 1: Nová mysl, 1958, No. 7, p. 614. *Item 2:* State Statistical Office, *Statistická ročenka,* 1959, p. 93. *Item 3:* Item 1 times item 2.

The results in Appendix Table 1 were checked by an independent detailed calculation of farmers' net cash income in 1956: total gross sales (including free market sales and income from ancillary production) less money production costs (including depreciation charges in collective farms only, and excluding the agricultural tax, which was considered as a direct tax rather than a business expense for both collectives and private farms). The net cash income according to our detailed calculation (after adjusting farmers' free market sales upward by 394 million crowns because of their understatement in our calculation) yields the same figure as the official estimates used here. We do not show the check here for lack of space.

d. Income from forestry

1947 and 1948. See United Nations, *National Income Statistics of Various Countries, 1938–48,* p. 59.

1955. Estimated at 5 percent of the total value added in forestry, which was derived from the remaining 95 percent of value added created in the socialist sector of forestry and estimated as equal to the wage bill (1,216 million crowns, calculated from employment and average-wage data in State Statistical Office, *Statistická ročenka,* 1957, p. 69, disregarding apprentices). The proportion between the private and the socialist sector (5 to 95), applied here to value added, was that between gross output produced in the private and socialist sectors in 1957 (Ministry of Interior, *Úřední list,* Part 9, February 11, 1958, p. 65).

1956. Same procedure as for 1955. The 1956 wage bill in the socialist sector was 1,319 million crowns.

e. Director's fund

1955 and 1956. These entries represent a rough estimate of disbursements from the so-called "director's fund" of socialized enterprises that was financed overwhelmingly from retained profits and to some extent from funds supplied by the government. Neither the aggregate sum of "director's funds," nor their allocation, were made public. Our estimate is based on the following considerations. The top limit to the size of the director's fund is 5 percent of the annual wage fund. This would represent about 2,600 million and 2,800 million crowns in 1955 and 1956, respectively. At least 30 percent of the fund is supposed to be distributed to individual employees in various forms, mainly as rewards in socialist competition. Allowing for the probability that director's funds did not reach their upper limit and that disbursements were not made to the full extent prescribed—undistributed residuals of director's funds amounted to 370 million crowns in 1955 and to 602 million crowns in 1956—we set our estimate at 500 million crowns in 1955 and 600 million in 1956, considerably below the estimated maximum amounts. (For information on director's fund see Baláž, *Chozrasčot priemyselných podnikov,* pp. 111–12; for information on undistributed director's funds see *Rudé právo,* February 10, 1956, and April 18, 1957.)

f. Other cash income

1955 and 1956. Here we group miscellaneous categories of cash income received from the enterprise sector, not included in the figures on wages and salaries. The latter correspond to the official category "personal wage fund"; the types of income covered by our estimates fall in the categories of "non-personal fund" and "other compensations," and these include (see Blahušiak, *Organisace práce a mezd; mzdové fondy,* pp. 78–79) the following:

1. Cash compensations to persons not on regular payrolls (literary fees, compensations for lectures, consultations of experts, and so forth)

2. Wages paid for one-time services performed by individuals not on the regular payroll of the enterprise

3. One-time cash bonuses to employees

4. Bonuses for inventions and technical improvements

5. Scholarships paid by enterprises

Other payments made by enterprises, such as travel allowances, compensations for tools and protective garments bought by the employees, as well as reimbursements for expenses incurred by employees in the performance of their duties, are not considered as household income but as transactions within the enterprise sector, even though they may represent disguised supplements to wages and salaries.

(*i*) *Nonpersonal fund.* According to Polish data for 1955 the "nonpersonal fund" amounted to about 3 percent of the personal wage fund in the socialized sector (Poland, Central Statistical Office, *Rocznik statystyczny,* 1957, p. 270). Applying this rate to item 2.A.(1)a in Table 1 B, we get 1,621 million crowns in 1955 and 1,727 million crowns in 1956.

(*ii*) *Other compensation.* Only one element of this group could be estimated with any precision—rewards for inventions and improvements—and this amounted to 74 million crowns in 1955–56 (*Práce,* July 20, 1957). We may allocate this sum between the two years according to the number of the so-called improvement suggestions (*zlepšovací návrhy*), that is, in the proportion 137,000:166,000 (*ibid.*), and this results in 33 million crowns in 1955 and 41 million crowns in 1956. Other elements of this group of income payments (individual rewards, prizes, and so forth), probably were considerable, though smaller than the nonpersonal fund payments. We estimated these "other compensations" roughly at one third of the nonpersonal fund payments, and considered the rewards for improvements and inventions included therein. These income payments would then amount to 540 million and 578 million crowns in 1955 and 1956, respectively.

The sum of the nonpersonal fund and other compensations was rounded to 2,200 million and 2,300 million crowns in 1955 and 1956, respectively.

(2) Income in kind
a. Wages and salaries in kind
1947 and 1948. These are the sums of the following rough estimates (in million crowns):

	1947	1948
1. Industry	1,300	1,500
2. Agriculture	1,500	1,600
3. Industrial crafts and trades	600	600
4. Trade and services	800	900
Total	4,200	4,600

These components were estimated as follows:

1. Industry. Estimates at about 3 percent of the total wage bill (see Appendix E, last note to Appendix Table 29).

2. Agriculture. We arbitrarily assumed that of the total number of employees in agriculture (265,423, see Appendix E, notes to Tables 29 and 31), 70 percent received board and 25 percent received lodging. The annual value of board and lodging (7,300 and 1,500 crowns in 1947, 8,030 and 1,650 in 1948) was estimated as explained in the notes to Table 1 A, (item 1.A.(2), wages in kind of domestics).

3. Industrial crafts and trades. Of the total number of employees (387,813 in 1947 and 325,150 in 1948, see Appendix E, notes to Tables 29 and 31), we assumed that 20 percent received board and 10 percent had lodging. The value of board and lodging was taken the same as for agriculture; see above.

4. Trade and services. We proceeded as in notes to items 2 and 3 above. The branches selected were those known to have furnished board and lodging to some of their employees: trade, hotels and restaurants, health services, hygiene and cosmetics, and professional services. We assumed that one third of the employees received board and one tenth lodging. Employment in all these branches combined was 325,167 in 1947 and 321,075 in 1948 (see notes to Appendix

Tables 29 and 31). The value of board and of lodging per person was taken the same as in agriculture (see above).

1955 and 1956. Compensation in kind in industry, which amounted to 0.4 percent of the total industrial wage fund both in 1955 and 1956 (State Statistical Office, *Statistická ročenka,* 1957, p. 97), that is, to 117 and 123 million crowns, respectively, was roughly rounded upward to 145 and 150 million crowns to allow for compensation in kind granted in other branches of the economy.

b. Income in kind of farmers
1947 and 1948. This was calculated from adjusted data on the 1946 average annual food consumption from own production (at prices paid to farmers) per hectare of agricultural land, based on a sample of 458 farms in the Czech lands (see Institute for Agricultural Accounting and Management, *Zprávy,* 1949, No. 1, p. 51). We used these data for the whole country (that is, including Slovakia) even though the average value of food consumption was higher in the western part of the country (Bohemia and Moravia) than in Slovakia. Because of the greater extent of commercial farming in the Czech lands, farmers were able to supplement their consumption in kind by larger market purchases. We assumed that the composition and real volume of consumption in kind remained constant in the period between 1946 and 1948; available statistics in the volume of agricultural production and sales indicate that the 1947 drought affected agricultural sales rather than consumption on the farms.

The adjustment of the original data consisted of two operations. The first was a recomputation in terms of food consumption per hectare of arable land, instead of agricultural land. Using the original data would have probably overstated the average since in the sample the proportion of arable land in agricultural land was 82 percent, that is, 11 points above the country average. Second, to take account of price changes between 1946 and 1947–48, the 1946 figure was adjusted by the wholesale price index for food for 1947 and 1948, published in State Statistical Office, *Cenové zprávy,* 1948, No. 23, p. 163. This index, we believe, reflects fairly well the changes in food prices paid to farmers.

The adjusted averages were then multiplied by the number of hectares of arable land for the whole country in the two years (see Slovakia, State Planning and Statistical Office, *Statistická príručka Slovenska,* 1948, p. 77). The results were checked by an alternative calculation using the estimated per capita food consumption on the sample farms and the total number of independent farmers and their family members. The two sets of results differed by less than one percent.

1955 and 1956. Official estimates of this item, according to *Politická ekonomie,* 1958, No. 2, p. 105, amount to 10 billion crowns in 1956 (5,274 crowns per permanently working person in collectives and 6,859 crowns in private farms multiplied by 361,000 and 1,180,000 permanently working persons in collectives and private farms, respectively, see State Statistical Office, *Statistická ročenka,* 1959, p. 93). However (according to *ibid.,* p. 223), the farmers' consumption in kind amounted to 18.4 percent of the gross agricultural production in 1957 valued in average realized 1957 prices received by farmers. In value terms, this amounted to 6.0 billion crowns in 1957, which is 40 percent lower than the former estimate for 1956. The reason for this large difference may be in the use of the retail prices for the valuation of income in kind of farmers given in *Politická ekonomie.*

For the calculation of national product, farm income in kind in 1955 and 1956 was estimated in terms of average realized prices received by farmers on the assumption that in both years it was equal to the 1957 value. The 1957 figure was merely adjusted for changes in prices received by farmers to obtain values in current prices for 1955 and 1956. This procedure seems to be supported by the relationship of the official estimates of consumption in kind between 1957 and 1958. In these two years the volume of consumption in kind remained constant although the number of permanently employed in collective and private farms decreased by about 5 percent

APPENDIX TABLE 2

CALCULATION OF FARMERS' INCOME IN KIND, 1955–58

(*Billion crowns*)

Item	1955	1956	1957	1958
1. Gross agricultural production in 1955 prices	31.5	32.5	31.1	32.9
2. Share of income in kind in gross agricultural production (percent)	...	...	18.4	17.4
3. Value of income in kind in 1955 prices	...	...	5.72	5.72
4. Index of prices received by farmers	100.0	104.3	105.7	106.2
5. Income in kind in current prices, rounded to nearest 100 million	5.7	6.0	6.0	6.1

(see State Statistical Office, *Statistická ročenka,* 1959, p. 93) and the volume of gross agricultural production increased by about 6 percent (see *Plánované hospodářství,* 1959, Nos. 7–8, p. 492). These findings show that during a short period of years farm consumption in kind is practically constant. Our estimates are shown in Appendix Table 2.

NOTES TO APPENDIX TABLE 2

SOURCES: *Item 1: Plánované hospodářství,* 1959, Nos. 7–8, p. 492. *Item 2:* State Statistical Office, *Statistická ročenka,* 1959, p. 223. *Item 3:* For 1957, 18.4 percent of item 1; for 1958, 17.4 percent of item 1. *Item 4:* State Statistical Office, *Statistická ročenka,* 1959, p. 389. *Item 5:* Item 3 for 1957 adjusted for change in prices given in item 4.

Our independent detailed calculation of income in kind of collective farmers, private farmers, and part-time farmers (not shown here for lack of space) yielded almost the same figures (5,623 million crowns in 1955 and 5,978 million crowns in 1956).

c. Income in kind in trades and professions
    1947 and 1948. From Dolanský *Výklad k rozpočtu,* 1949, p. 235.
    1955 and 1956. Income in kind of self-employed outside agriculture was considered negligible in 1955–56.

(3) Cash and imputed net rental income
    1947 and 1948
a. Cash, and
b. Imputed
Our estimates are summarized in Appendix Table 3 and explained in the notes.

APPENDIX TABLE 3
CASH AND IMPUTED RENTAL INCOME, 1947–48
(Million crowns)

	Cash		Imputed	
	1947	1948	1947	1948
1. Gross receipts	4,200	4,300	2,100	2,150
2. Less: Maintenance cost	387	433	193	217
3. Less: Taxes	805	805	402	402
Net income	3,008	3,062	1,505	1,531

1. Gross receipts. The cash receipts were given in Dolanský, *Výklad k rozpočtu,* 1949, p. 235, net of the value of rents from leased agricultural property (700 million crowns for both years, see United Nations, *National Income Statistics of Various Countries, 1938–1948,* p. 59).

Imputed rental receipts were set at one half of the cash receipts, which is roughly the prewar ratio as estimated on the basis of detailed documentation by Stádník, *Národní důchod a jeho rozdělení,* pp. 152–160, 180–181. (Note: The postwar official estimate of 1 billion crowns in 1947 and 1948 given in Dolanský, *Výklad k rozpočtu,* 1949, p. 235, implies an average imputed rent equal to about one fourth of the average cash rent—a ratio that strikes us as too low, even if we take into account the poor quality of some rural and urban owner-occupied housing).

2. Maintenance cost. The total maintenance cost, estimated at 580 million crowns in 1947 and 650 million crowns in 1948, was allocated between rented and owner-occupied dwellings in proportion 2 to 1, which is roughly the ratio of corresponding gross rents, cash and imputed. The maintenance cost total is a rough estimate based on a figure approximating maintenance cost in the prewar years (120 million current crowns, see Stádník, *Národní důchod a jeho rozdělení,* p. 159) and on an index of average wages in the building industry, as representative of all cost items in housing maintenance. This index was derived from an estimate of average monthly wages in construction in the years 1930–34 (700 crowns, based on data in State Statistical Office, *Annuaire statistique,* 1938, p. 229) and in 1947–48 (3,400 crowns in 1947, 3,800 crowns in 1948, see employment and wage bill data in State Statistical Office, *Průmyslové zprávy,* 1948, Nos. 7–8, pp. 42–44, 47–49; and its *Zprávy,* 1949, Nos. 15–17, pp. 117–118, 126–127).

3. Taxes. For 1947 (see Dolanský, *Výklad k rozpočtu,* 1948, p. 162) 1,207 million crowns; for 1948, we used the same figure, in view of the fact that conditions in housing supply and rents changed but little in the postwar period, as reflected in the insignificant change of house taxes from 1946 to 1947 (see *ibid.*). The totals were allocated between rented and owner-occupied dwellings in the same proportion as maintenance costs.

1955 and 1956

a. Cash

Net cash rental income was estimated to be close to zero, on the basis of a comparison of the estimated gross cash rents received by private landlords with their estimated costs. The estimated annual gross private rents, amounting to 490 million crowns in 1955–56, seem to have been barely sufficient to cover (1) maintenance charges amounting to an estimated minimum of 147 million crowns, and (2) the house tax, the total amount of which lay probably somewhere between 220 and 245 million crowns.

Gross cash rents received by private landlords were calculated as the difference between the estimated total of cash rents paid by all households and cash rents paid to the socialized sector of housing. Total gross rent apparently amounted to 1,045 million crowns in 1954 (*Rudé právo,* March 23, 1955; since the text did not specify the period, we assumed the statement to refer to the year immediately preceding the statement). In 1955 and 1956 total gross rent very probably rose, not because of any general rise in the rent rates but because of a net increase in available space. Appendix Table 4 and supporting notes summarize our estimates.

APPENDIX TABLE 4

CALCULATION OF GROSS CASH RENT, 1954–56

	1954	1955	1956
1. Newly rented dwellings (number)	27,793	35,592	33,169
2. Vacated rented dwellings (number)	6,667	6,924	6,508
3. Gross increment to rent (in million crowns)	27.7	35.6	33.2
4. Gross decrement of rent (in million crowns)	0.8	0.9	0.8
5. Net increment to rent (in million crowns)	26.9	61.6	67.1
6. Annual gross rent (in million crowns)	1,045	1,107	1,174

NOTES TO APPENDIX TABLE 4

1. See State Statistical Office, *Statistická ročenka,* 1957, p. 72, for newly available housing units.

2. *Ibid.,* p. 73; vacated rented dwellings were assumed to represent two thirds of all vacated dwellings, one third being allowed for owner-occupied dwellings; the figure for 1954 was estimated at the approximate level of subsequent years.

3. Rent and new housing was calculated at 2,000 crowns annually per dwelling, in keeping with a statement by a deputy of the National Assembly, who declared that rent in a modern two-room apart-

ment in Prague was 2,200 crowns (see *Rudé právo,* December 21, 1956). We assumed that the new dwellings were put into use and the vacated dwellings were withdrawn from use at regular intervals throughout the year, and hence we calculated the annual total increment or decrement of rent using one half of the relevant number of dwellings in each year.

4. The rate applied in vacated housing was estimated at 250 crowns annually on the assumption that in vacated, that is, mostly condemned apartments, rents were substantially below the average level of 500 to 600 crowns (see below).

5. The net increment in 1955 and 1956 is composed of two elements. First, there is the amount of the net increment of the preceding years, that is, 26.9 million crowns in 1955 and 34.7 million crowns in 1956. The dwellings newly occupied in 1954 earned only half their annual rent because they passed into use successively, and this half already appears in the 1954 total. Therefore, the other half of their annual rent has to be counted in the increment in 1955, and this is added to the 1954 total (line 6) to get the 1955 total. The same holds for the increment in 1956 with respect to the rent from the net space added in 1955. Second, there is half of the annual rent from apartments newly occupied during the current year diminished by half the annual rent from the apartments vacated during the current year.

6. See *Rudé právo,* March 23, 1955, for the 1954 figure.

Gross cash rentals going to socialized housing property were estimated on the basis of the percentage breakdown of services furnished to the population by state and cooperative organizations (*Životní úroveň v ČSR,* p. 27). The total value of these services was reconstructed by using the absolute amount of one of the components, namely, sales by barbershops (240 million crowns, see State Statistical Office, *Statistická ročenka,* 1957, p. 175), in relation to its share (2.87 percent) of the total in 1954. Sales of barbershop services was the only item available in absolute figures with considerable precision. On this basis, estimated rent paid in the socialized sector, being equal to 6.64 percent of the total in 1954, amounted to 555 million crowns. In order to obtain total rent in this sector for 1955 and 1956, we added to this basic figure the entire increment of total estimated rent in all sectors (that is, 62 and 67 million crowns in the two respective years, see Appendix Table 4).

A cross-check on the magnitude of gross rent in state and cooperative housing is supplied by information according to which rent in state housing alone amounted to 670 million crowns, presumably in 1957 (according to Minister of Finance J. Ďuriš, in *Rudé právo,* February 14, 1958).

Gross private rent was obtained as a residual in total gross rent (in million crowns), as follows:

	1954	1955	1956
Total gross rent	1,045	1,107	1,174
Less: Gross rent in state and cooperative housing	555	617	684
Equals: Gross rent in private housing	490	490	490

The estimate of the minimum amount of maintenance costs in private rental housing, that is, 147 million crowns, is based on the stipulation of the House Tax Act according to which at least 30 percent of the rent paid to private landlords and subject to collection on a special bank account is compulsorily set aside for the purpose of repair work (National Assembly, *Sbírka zákonů,* 1952, No. 80, section 12).

Our estimate of the total amount of house tax incident upon rents received by private landlords is based on the stipulation of section 6 of the same law according to which the tax rate equals 45 or 50 percent of the tax base, the higher rate applying when the tax base is higher than 6,000 crowns. (See also Choděra, *Domovní daň,* p. 9.)

Even assuming that landlords were left with a net residual after the deduction of obligatory maintenance charges and the incident house tax, it is safe to assume that it is so small as to be spent entirely on current operating cost of housing, leaving no provision for capital consumption and net return.

b. Imputed

Gross imputed rent was estimated at one half of gross cash rent on the same basis as in 1947–48. Net imputed rent was set equal to zero parallel to the treatment of cash rent.

c. Farm rents

1947 and 1948. See United Nations, *National Income Statistics of Various Countries, 1938–1948,* p. 59.

1955 and 1956. Farm rents paid in 1955–56 were insignificant.

(4) *Interest*

1947 and 1948. From Boris Pesek, Czechoslovak Monetary Policy, 1945–53 (MS), p. 107. The figures refer to interest on savings deposits; loans to households probably were relatively insignificant.

1955 and 1956. This represents net interest payments received by households calculated as interest receipts minus interest payments. Interest was earned on savings deposits: 84 million crowns and 107 million crowns in 1955 and 1956, respectively (see State Statistical Office, *Statistická ročenka,* 1957, p. 293). Interest payments were approximated on the basis of the amount of outstanding loans and the appropriate interest rate. In 1955, there were 1,214 million crowns in 5 percent loans and 634 million crowns in 3.5 percent loans outstanding. For 1956, the figures were 1,190 million crowns in 5 percent loans and 644 million crowns in 3.5 percent loans (*ibid.,* 1957, pp. 294, 298). Total interest payments by households then amounted to 83 million crowns in 1955 and 82 million crowns in 1956.

We did not attempt any adjustments for imputed interest or imputed charges for financial services because of lack of data. Such an adjustment probably would not be significant in any event.

(5) *Imputed wages*

1947 and 1948. We assumed that all private construction was done commercially. Scarcities of building materials support this assumption.

1955 and 1956. The estimation of the value of imputed wages of private house builders is explained below in the notes to Appendix Table 12, item b. Building materials were allocated to private housing construction in these years, and the value of such construction is included in the official investment figures.

B. *Government Sector*

(1) *Cash wages and salaries*

See Appendix E, Tables 29, 31, and 32.

(2) *Income in kind (military subsistence and clothing)*

1947 and 1948. These rough estimates were based on the assumption that noncommissioned officers and enlisted men (129,000 persons, see Appendix E, note I.B, to Appendix Tables 29 and 31) received subsistence and clothing worth about 7,500 crowns per capita annually. The per capita allowance was estimated from the

1947 purchases of food, tobacco, and clothing by the population. (See Dolanský, *Výklad k rozpočtu,* 1948, pp. 162–63; for population we used the 1947 figure given in State Statistical Office, *Statistická ročenka,* 1958, p. 56.)

1955 and 1956. The rounded figures, 850 million crowns for 1955, and 700 million crowns for 1956, are the product of the estimated number of military personnel (230,000 and 191,000 in 1955 and 1956, respectively; see Appendix E) and approximate average food and clothing expenditures per member of a worker's family (3,700 crowns for both years), assuming that such outlays are roughly equal to the cost of military food and clothing. Exact figures on workers' family budgets were not available but were approximated using data pertaining to various years. The State Statistical Office, *Statistická ročenka,* 1958, p. 323, shows that, in 1957, an average worker's family spent 45.9 percent of gross income on food, and 11.4 percent on clothing. *Ibid.,* 1959, p. 380, gives an average net income of a worker's family in 1956 as 6,006 crowns per member, which was raised to account for 8.3 percent of income tax (*ibid.,* 1958, p. 323). We assumed that an average worker's family had the same income in 1955 and 1956, and that the relative distribution of expenditures, as far as food and clothing are concerned, was the same for 1955, 1956, and 1957. Such assumption is justified here, because we deal with a rough estimate of the military strength, and thus any precise adjustment of a few percentages of an average outlay would not necessarily improve the result. For the same reason, we rounded the total calculated outlays for military subsistence and clothing.

(3) Transfer payments

1947 and 1948. These sums cover the following broad categories of cash transfer payments (in billion crowns):

	1947	1948
1. Social security benefits	13.6	16.5
2. Pensions to retired employees of state enterprises	2.6	3.0
3. Pensions to retired administration employees	3.1	3.3
4. Other income transfers	5.8	5.6
Total	25.1	28.4

The 1947 total is from Dolanský, *Výklad k rozpočtu,* 1948, p. 235, and was checked as far as possible against the detailed breakdown of items given in National Assembly, *Státní závěrečný účet,* 1947, pp. 13, 14, and 24, and its *Sbírka zákonů,* 1946, p. 1428 (for students' scholarships); and Dolanský, *Výklad k rozpočtu,* 1949, p. 61. Of the 1948 figures, items 1, 3, and 4 are from *ibid.* Item 2 is from National Assembly, *Státní závěrečný účet,* 1948, p. 24 (2,996 million crowns).

1955 and 1956. Our estimates represent the sums of items 1–5, below (figures for 1955 and 1956 in that order).

1. Pensions and allowances: 6,895 and 7,386 million crowns (see State Statistical Office, *Statistická ročenka,* 1957, p. 273).

2. Social security benefits: 5,223 and 5,497 million crowns (see *ibid.,* p. 270).

3. Financing of religious organizations: 60 and 61 million crowns (see Appendix A, Notes to Table 1 A).

4. Student scholarships: 88 and 110 million crowns. According to the State Statistical Office, *Deset let,* p. 101, there were over 30,000 university students in 1955 receiving an average scholarship of 325 crowns monthly. Assuming this average scholarship went to 30,000 students 9 months a year, the total in 1955 would have been 88 million crowns. According to *Statistický obzor,* 1957, No. 3, p. 108, these amounted to "almost 110 million crowns" in 1956.

5. Other cash transfers: 1,225 and 1,522 million crowns. These payments are similar to pensions and social security benefits but are paid outside the "national social security" scheme. According to a footnote in *Statistické zprávy,* 1956, No. 2, p. 22, they include health insurance benefits paid to members of agricultural cooperatives and nonworking pension recipients, expenditures on individual social care, and expenditures on institutional care in homes for retired people, paid from the budgets of national committees. Our estimates (in million crowns) are tabulated below and explained in the notes that follow.

	1955	*1956*
a. Payments to aged and sick, by local administrative organs	103	400
b. Benefits paid to farmers	622	622
c. Retirement pensions to government employees and other similar payments	500	500
Total	1,225	1,522

a. For 1955, see *Plánované hospodářství,* 1956, No. 2, p. 158; for 1956, see *Statistický obzor,* 1957, No. 3, p. 109. The figures may include some allowances in kind (canteens and dormitories for the needy).

b. The figure for 1955, given by the Minister of Finance (see *Rudé právo,* February 10, 1956), was used for both years.

c. The latest figure available in State Statistical Office, *Statistická ročenka,* 1957, p. 273, referring to 1950 (495.8 million crowns), was used, rounded, for both 1955 and 1956. Our estimate is broadly consistent with the probable allocation of government payments to persons on other than wage account. These "personal" expenditures would amount to 2,166 million crowns in 1955 and 2,325 million in 1956, if they were equal to 23.7 percent of the government wage bill, the planned ratio for 1954 (see *Plánované hospodářství,* 1955, No. 4, p. 308). The wage bill in government proper was 9,140 million crowns in 1955 and 9,809 million in 1956 (see Appendix E, government sector, minus social organizations). From "personal expenditures" other than wages (see above), travel allowances have to be paid (1,615 million crowns in 1955 and almost 2,000 million in 1956, according to *Rudé právo,* October 9, 1957), and this leaves 551 million crowns in 1955 and 325 million in 1956 to accommodate for retirement pensions or similar outlays. Although the 1956 residual appears insufficient, it is not clearly incompatible with our estimate because of the disparate character of data on which our check is based.

(4) Imputed wages (unpaid labor on community improvement projects)

1947 and 1948. These projects were not inaugurated until after these years.

1955 and 1956. The values shown represent unpaid labor on community improvement projects, officially referred to as "Action Z" and "Action T." These figures were derived as 65.5 and 65.2 percent of the total value of these projects (664 million and 855 million crowns in 1955 and 1956, respectively, see State Statistical Office, *Statistická ročenka,* 1957, p. 71). The proportion of the value of labor was given in *Statistický obzor,* 1958, No. 6, p. 285.

3. Purchases of goods and services
A. Purchases from the household sector

1947, 1948, 1955, and 1956. (1) Domestic services; (2) Services of non-profit organizations

Transferred from household sector production account.

B. Purchases from the enterprise sector
(1) Cash purchases
a. Retail trade purchases of goods

1947 and 1948. These figures (including farm market purchases) are estimates based on Dolanský, *Výklad k rozpočtu,* 1949, p. 238. The totals given in the source (156,000 million and 162,900 million crowns in 1955 and 1956, respectively) were reduced by the official estimates of gross cash and imputed rents that the totals include (5,200 million and 5,300 million crowns, respectively; *ibid.,* p. 235) and by the value of other services (20,300 million and 28,600 million crowns in the respective years) that we show separately in entries 3.B.(1)c, purchases of services, and 3.C.(1), dues to quasi governmental organizations.

1955 and 1956. Our estimates of retail trade purchases by households (63,793 million crowns in 1955 and 65,808 million in 1956) are based on figures of total retail sales totals in current prices (*Statistické zprávy,* 1957, No. 3, p. 13). These totals include non-household purchases (for which we allowed 15.7 billion crowns in 1955 and 19.0 billion in 1956, that is, 20 and 23 percent), as explained in the discussion below.

Retail trade turnover of commodities, according to the official Czechoslovak definition, means: "Sales from market funds (*tržní fondy*) at state retail prices direct to the consumer for his personal use. These are predominantly sales to the population and to collective farms by the retail trade network and by public catering enterprises, repair shops, and establishments working on custom orders (*závody pro zakázkovou práci*)" (State Statistical Office, *Statistická ročenka,* 1957, p. 181). This definition fails to state in sufficient detail that retail purchases for production and investment purposes are effected on a large scale by private farms, collectives, and state farms, as well as private handicrafts, socialized enterprises, and government organizations. Ample evidence shows the importance of these transactions. Partial breakdowns of retail sales by commodities show such items as feed grains and feed concentrates, fertilizers, agricultural machines, and tools (see *ibid.,* 1957, pp. 190, 193). *Rudé právo,* August 15, 1957, mentions large-scale purchases of building material in the retail distribution net.

Purchases by government organs and socialized enterprises at retail have been subject to legal regulation. Decree No. 187/1953, Ministry of Interior, *Úřední list,* modified by decree No. 91/1954, forbade retail purchases of certain categories of commodities by economic, budgetary, and other organizations and designated only certain retail stores for purchases by these organizations. In 1955 a decree of the Ministry of Internal Trade and the Ministry of Finance (Ministry of Interior, *Úřední list,* No. 163/1955) limited this category of purchases to 20 crowns daily. In 1956 a subsequent decree of the same ministries (*ibid.,* No. 155/1956) changed the limit of these purchases to 600 crowns monthly in cash purchases plus 4,000 crowns in purchases paid through the bank. Purchases of these customers are not limited to any particular set of commodities. Articles sold included floor covering, curtain material, bed linen, tablecloths, blankets, nails—the source adds: "by the ton"—iceboxes, and kitchenware (see *Noviny vnitřního obchodu,* April 20, 1957), as well as furniture, office supplies, and spare parts (see *Plánované hospodářství,* 1955, No. 5, pp. 373–74).

These purchases increased rapidly in the second half of 1956 after the promulgation of decree No. 155/1956 (see *Noviny vnitřního obchodu,* April 20, 1957), and a series of controls were introduced to keep these purchases down (see F. Krajčír, Minister of Internal Trade, in *Rudé právo,* October 9, 1957, p. 4). Decree No. 161/1957 forbade local administrative organs to buy commodities of industrial origin in retail stores (*Rudé právo,* January 3, 1958, p. 4). After these restrictive measures had been introduced, purchases by "budgetary and economic organizations" in 1957 still amounted, according to the official estimate to 8 billion crowns (the report on the development of Czechoslovak national economy in 1957, in Ministry of Interior, *Úřední list,* No. 9, February 11, 1958; for additional information on "excessive retail purchases of the public sector" see *Hospodářské noviny,* 1957, No. 22, pp. 1–2).

Besides the types of transactions enumerated, it is necessary to include among nonhousehold retail sales purchases by employees of the government or enterprises from their per diem and travel allowances. We treat these purchases entirely as intrasectoral transactions of the enterprise sector, although we are aware of the possibility that part of these allowances may represent, for their recipients, an addition to household income. Further, private purchases of construction material have to be excluded from household retail sales since private housing construction is classified as enterprise sector activity.

Our estimates of the nonhousehold retail purchases are summarized in Appendix Table 5 and documented in the notes by rows.

APPENDIX TABLE 5
NONHOUSEHOLD PURCHASES OF GOODS IN
RETAIL TRADE, 1955–56
(*Million crowns*)

	1955	1956
1. Purchases for production purposes in agriculture	3,700	4,000
2. Purchases for investment purposes in agriculture and forestry	700	900
3. Per diem and travel allowances	2,300	2,600
4. Purchases for private housing construction	500	1,000
5. Purchases by independent handicrafts	500	470
6. Purchases by the government and socialized enterprises	8,000	10,000
Total	15,700	18,970

NOTE TO APPENDIX TABLE 5

1. Purchases for production purposes in agriculture. See Appendix Table 6 and notes thereto.

APPENDIX TABLE 6
AGRICULTURE: RETAIL PURCHASES FOR PRODUCTION
PURPOSES, 1955–56
(*Million crowns unless specified*)

Item	1955	1956
1. Cash production costs of collectives per hectare (in crowns)	1,226	1,301
2. Purchases of fuel, seed, building and repair materials, and other material supplies per hectare (in crowns)	306	325
3. Total agricultural land (in 1000 hectares)	7,247	7,217
4. Total purchases of fuel, seed, buildings and repair materials, and other material supplies in agriculture	2,218	2,346
5. Purchases of fertilizer, tools, and feed	1,457	1,614
6. Total purchases, item 4 plus item 5	3,675	3,960
Rounded total	3,700	4,000

NOTES TO APPENDIX TABLE 6

SOURCES: *Item 1:* For 1955, State Statistical Office, *Deset let,* 1956, p. 41, and State Statistical Office, *Statistická ročenka,* 1958, p. 226; for 1956, *ibid.,* 1959, p. 265. *Item 2:* 25 percent of item 1, or the same share of costs as for 51 collective sample farms in 1954; see Svoboda, *Prečo a ako hospodáriť* . . . JRD, 1957, pp. 234, 252. We assumed that this percentage was representative for the entire agricultural sector. *Item 3:* State Statistical Office, *Statistická ročenka,* 1959, p. 225. *Item 4:* Item 2 multiplied by item 3. *Item 5: Ibid.,* 1959, p. 347.

Essentially the same result as in Appendix Table 6 was obtained by a detailed calculation of retail purchases for private farms, collective farms, and state farms separately for 1956 (4.1 billion crowns). For 1955 the result of an earlier detailed calculation was about 10 percent higher than our above estimate because of the overestimation of certain costs when adequate data were unavailable.

2. *Purchases for investment purposes in agriculture and forestry.* We assumed that about one fifth of the estimated value of total investment in agriculture represented purchases in retail trade (see Appendix Table 7).

APPENDIX TABLE 7

INVESTMENT IN AGRICULTURE AND FORESTRY, 1955–56

(*Million crowns*)

	1955	1956
a. Investments according to the state plan	1,675	1,871
b. Collective farms	1,691	2,369
c. Private farms	124	208
Total	3,490	4,448

NOTES TO APPENDIX TABLE 7

SOURCES: a, b: State Statistical Office, *Statistická ročenka,* 1957, p. 71. c: Estimate. An official figure for total investment by private farms was not available, and only a figure for investment in buildings was given (14 million crowns in 1955 and 39 million crowns in 1956; see *ibid.,* 1959, pp. 106, 109–14. Private investment in agricultural machinery and equipment was explicitly omitted in official investment figures (*ibid.,* 1957, p. 70, note to Table 6-1). We estimated investment in machinery and equipment on the assumption that private farmers each year bought one half of the agricultural machinery sold at retail (220 and 337 million crowns in 1955 and 1956, respectively, see *ibid.,* 1957, p. 193). The smaller relative share of private farm purchases of farm machinery, evident in official statements, was taken into account by allocating to private farms one half of total purchases, even though they owned about 59 percent of total agricultural land in the period under consideration.

It should be noted that official figures on agricultural investments contain a large element of labor of collective farmers themselves. In 1957 this element accounted for 74 percent of total investments in collective farms (see *Statistické zprávy,* 1958, No. 4, p. 20), and is consistent with our estimate of retail purchases for investment purposes in agriculture.

3. Per diem and travel allowances. The amounts shown in Appendix Table 5 represent roughly two thirds of the total estimated per diem and travel allowances. We assumed that the remaining one third was spent on services, and this has been excluded beforehand from the calculation of services bought by households.

Our estimate of per diem and travel allowances is shown in Appendix Table 8.

APPENDIX TABLE 8

ESTIMATED PER DIEM AND TRAVEL ALLOWANCES, 1955–56

(*Million crowns*)

	1955	1956
a. Government	1,615	2,000
b. Industry	1,077	1,063
c. Rest of the economy	772	833
Total	3,464	3,896

NOTES TO APPENDIX TABLE 8

SOURCES: a. *Rudé právo,* October 9, 1957. b. This is 1.0 and 0.9 percent of total costs in industry, which were estimated at 107.7 billion crowns in 1955 and 118.1 billion in 1956. These totals were reconstructed on the basis of their breakdown by cost categories (see State Statistical Office, *Statistická ročenka,* 1957, p. 98) and the corresponding wage bill (see Appendix E). The 1.0 and 0.9 percent were set arbitrarily so as to correspond to one fourth of the category "other cost" in 1955 and 1956, respectively. c. For the rest of the economy we assumed the same ratio between per diem and travel allowances and the wage bill, as in industry, roughly thirty to one. Total wages including social security contributions in the rest of the economy (taken here as corresponding roughly to the socialized enterprise sector) and in industry are shown in Appendix E.

4. Purchases for individual housing construction. The commodities and services in question are primarily construction materials and equipment for homes. We estimated these retail purchases somewhat arbitrarily at about one half of the funds used for private housing construction, and this, according to our estimates, amounted to 1,007 million crowns in 1955 and 2,101 million in 1956 (see notes to Table 1 C).

5. *Purchases by independent handicrafts.* Since figures of handicraft gross sales were unavailable, we estimated their purchases of inputs at retail in relation to the income from handicrafts before taxes. In 1955 this income amounted to about 1,000 million crowns and in 1956 to about 940 million crowns (see above, note to cash income of self-employed). Guessing roughly, gross sales by handicrafts might be double this amount, of which the value of inputs purchased in retail may have been about one fourth, that is, about 500 million crowns in 1955 and 470 million in 1956.

6. *Retail purchases by enterprises, and central and local government offices and institutions.* As already noted (above, p. 114), these purchases were officially estimated at 8 billion crowns in 1957. This estimate refers to a year during which new controls were introduced and systematic pressure was applied to reduce this type of transaction. We decided to use the same figure for the year 1955 during which pressure for relaxation of regulations was mounting, and 10,000 million crowns, that is, a figure about one quarter higher, for 1956, a year in which regulations were relaxed and retail purchases started to rise.

b. *Farm market purchases*

1947 and 1948. Assumed to be included in the retail trade purchases of goods under a, above.

1955 and 1956. Free market sales for both years were calculated from information in State Statistical Office, *Statistická ročenka,* 1959, p. 39, giving the relative distribution of personal consumption by origin, and from our estimate of the official figure of national income. Purchases on the free market constituted 1.4 percent of personal consumption in both years, and according to *Životní úraveň v ČSR,* personal consumption constituted 64 percent of the national income in 1955. Applying our estimate of the Czechoslovak official figure for national income, namely, 128 to 135 billion crowns (see Chapter III), we estimated the value of sales on farmers markets to be approximately 1.1 billion crowns. Our figure for these sales in 1956 (1.2 million crowns) represents an upward adjustment of the 1955 estimate by 7 percent, in keeping with the official figure for the change in consumption (see State Statistical Office, *Statistická ročenka,* 1959, p. 35). The share of purchases on the free market remained the same in 1955, and there seemed to be no significant change in prices of these purchases (*ibid.,* pp. 39, 389).

c. Purchases of services

1947 and 1948. From Dolanský, *Výklad k rozpočtu,* 1949, p. 238. The original figures were reduced by the amount of dues paid to trade unions and political parties (see 4.a, below), which they include.

1955 and 1956. Household purchases of services were estimated on the basis of approximate household purchases of services furnished by the state and cooperative sectors, adjusted for services bought from the private sector (see Appendix Table 9 and notes thereto).

APPENDIX TABLE 9

HOUSEHOLD PURCHASES OF SERVICES, 1955–56

(*Million crowns*)

	1955	1956
a. Services furnished by the socialized sector	9,531	9,639
b. Rents paid to private landlords	476	544
c. Private health services	362	352
d. Services furnished by private handicrafts	251	255
Total (a to d)	10,620	10,790
e. Adjustment for 1956		499
f. Total household purchases of services	10,620	11,289
g. Less: Gross cash rentals (see above)	1,107	1,174
h. Household purchases of services, excluding rent	9,513	10,115

NOTES TO APPENDIX TABLE 9

a. Services furnished to households by the socialized sector were derived from a percentage breakdown of their total published in *Životní úroveň v ČSR,* p. 27. Reconstruction of the total in absolute terms in Appendix Table 10 was effected starting from sales of services by socialized barbershops (see State Statistical Office, *Statistická ročenka,* 1957, p. 175), assumed to be purchased exclusively by households. Our result differs by less than 2 percent from figures given by A. Novotný in *Rudé právo,* March 21, 1957.

b. Rents paid to private landlords were calculated as the difference between estimated total gross rent (see note 2.A.(3), above) and rent paid in state and cooperative housing (see Appendix Table 10):

| | (Million crowns) | |
	1955	1956
Total gross rent	1,107	1,174
Less: Rent in state and cooperative housing	631	630
Rent in private housing	476	544

c. According to an official estimate, in 1955 the population's expenditures on health services was about one tenth of the state expenditures on health services, that is, 524 million crowns (National Assembly, *Těsnopisecké zprávy,* 10th Session (1956), p. 44). Subtracting from this sum the value of health and social services sold by state organizations, that is, 162 million crowns (Appendix Table 10),

APPENDIX TABLE 10

HOUSEHOLD PURCHASES OF SERVICES FURNISHED BY STATE AND COOPERATIVE ORGANIZATIONS IN 1955–56

| | 1955 | | 1956 | |
	Percent	Million Crowns	Percent	Million Crowns
Transportation	40.06	3,818	39.76	3,833
Personal	38.87	3,705	38.64	3,725
Goods	1.19	113	1.12	108
Housing	25.32	2,413	24.96	2,406
Rent	6.62	631	6.54	630
Electricity, gas, water	13.04	1,243	13.20	1,272
Maintenance	3.20	305	2.90	280
Telephone	1.45	138	1.39	134
Other	1.01	96	0.93	90
Repairs and maintenance	6.59	628	6.12	590
Entertainment	11.56	1,102	11.91	1,148
Ratio and television	1.76	168	1.79	173
Movies	4.50	429	4.82	464
Theatre	0.81	77	0.79	76
Other	4.49	428	4.51	435
Hygiene	3.91	373	4.28	413
Laundries	0.29	28	0.32	31
Cleaners	0.85	81	0.91	88
Barbers	2.77	264	3.05	294
Sports, recreation, etc.	3.09	294	3.16	305
Tourism, recreation	2.08	198	2.38	229
Sports	1.01	96	0.78	75
Health and social services	1.70	162	1.92	185
Other services	7.77	741	7.89	761
Total	100.00	9,531	100.00	9,639

yields 362 million crowns. Applying the same procedure to 1956 yields 352 million crowns (one tenth of 5,375, that is, 537 million crowns, less 185 million crowns for the state sales of health services; see Appendix F).

d. Services furnished by private handicrafts were estimated at 3.5 percent of total sales of services to households, presumably including sales for private construction, part of farm purchases for production, and so forth. (*Rudé právo,* August 15, 1957, p. 2; reference is made to the current period in general, not to any particular year). The sum of items under a–c was assumed equal to 96.5 percent (10,369 million crowns and 10,535 million in 1955 and 1956, respectively). We assumed also that two thirds of the corresponding 3.5 percent represented household purchases as defined in this study, that is, net of purchases for private construction and farmers' production needs (251 and 255 million crowns).

e. An upward adjustment was made for 1956 in order to reconcile our estimates with information that the population paid 6.3 percent more for services in 1956 than in 1955 (*Rudé právo,* April 18, 1957). The 499 million crowns brings the 1956 total (item f) up to an amount 6.3 percent higher than the estimate for 1955. We decided arbitrarily to adjust the 1956 figure upward rather than to reduce the 1955 figure.

NOTES TO APPENDIX TABLE 10

The slight discrepancies between the sums of individual items and the indicated totals are due to rounding.

The magnitude of some items in Appendix Table 10 can be roughly checked by means of other available information.

(i) Total ticket sales in railroad transportation of persons amounted to 3,211 million crowns presumably in 1954 (*Rudé právo,* March 23, 1955). Ticket sales of municipal and other local transportation amounted to 879 and 819 million crowns in 1955 and 1956, respectively (State Statistical Office, *Statistická ročenka,* 1957, p. 175). These two sets of figures alone, not counting any outlays in bus and other means of transportation, bring the total beyond our estimates. This divergence suggests that total receipts of transportation enterprises were adjusted for a certain amount of nonhousehold purchases of transportation services. This procedure is clearly identifiable in the case of laundries. Total sales of laundries (socialized sector) were 64 million crowns in 1955 and 66 million in 1956 (*ibid.,* 1957, p. 175), whereas according to Appendix Table 10, household purchases of laundry services were less than half of these sums. The share of household purchases in total sales of laundries based on these data corresponds closely to their share, derived from figures published in *Hospodářské noviny,* 1957, No. 27, p. 5.

(ii) Rentals received by the state for housing services amounted to 670 million crowns presumably in 1957 (*Rudé právo,* February 14, 1958). This figure is not excessively far from household rent payments in our table (631 million crowns in 1955 and 630 million in 1956), even though the latter figures contain rents in cooperative housing in addition to rents in state and public housing. In 1950 cooperative housing amounted to only about 5 percent of total state and public housing (see State Statistical Office, *Statistická ročenka,* 1957, p. 176).

(iii) Theater receipts amounted to not quite 90 million crowns in 1956 (derived from information according to which state subsidies to theaters in 1956 amounted to not quite 180 million crowns, equivalent to about twice the amount of income from theaters' own sources; see *Hospodářské noviny,* 1958, No. 9, p. 9). This amount is compatible with household outlays for theater entertainment in our table. The difference may be due to theater income from other sources.

d. Gross cash rentals
1947 and 1948. See Appendix Table 3 above.
1955 and 1956. See the note to net cash rents above (Table 1 B, 2.A.(3)a).

(2) Imputed purchases
a. Wages in kind,
b. Income in kind of farmers, and
c. Income in kind in trades and professions
See notes to Table 1 B, items 2.A.(2) a–c, above.
d. Imputed rentals
See notes to Table 1 B, item 2.A.(3)b, above.
e. Military subsistence
See notes to Table 1 B, item 2.B.(2), above.
f. Gifts from abroad
These are estimates of the value of private gift parcels (see notes to Table 4 C, item 6.A).

C. Payments to the government sector
(1) Dues to quasi-governmental organizations
    1947. Trade union dues (767 million crowns) were roughly esti-
mated on the basis of membership put at two million (see State Statistical Office, *Statistical Digest,* p. 41, giving 2,157,732 members as
of October 31, 1947) and the dues rate set at one percent of average
earnings (see *Práce,* June 9, 1953). Average earnings, 38,336 crowns
annually, were derived from data in Appendix Table 29. As for total
dues paid to political parties, our guess is that they may have
amounted at most to one half of total trade union dues (smaller membership, smaller dues, lower dues-paying morale, no check-off system). Given some uncertainty about the precise level of dues, the
combined total for quasi-governmental organizations was set at 1,100
million crowns.
    1948. The estimating procedure was the same as for 1947. Trade
union dues were estimated at 1,297 million crowns (3 million members, see Zapotocký, *Revoluční odborové hnutí po únoru 1948,*
p. 709); 43,240 crowns annual average earnings derived from data
in Appendix Table 31. The combined total of trade union dues and
dues to political parties was roughly set at 1,500 million crowns. This
leaves about 200 million for dues to political parties, more than one
third less than in 1947, and this seems consistent with the loss of
independence of the noncommunist parties after February, 1948.
    1955 and 1956. Our estimates are rounded figures based on the
tabulation below (in million crowns):

	1955	1956
a. Dues to trade unions	447	493
b. Dues to the Communist Party	120	150
c. Other dues	100	100
Total	667	743

    a. Membership in trade unions in 1955 was around 3.6 million
(*Práce,* May 20, 1955); in 1956 around 3.8 million (*Odborář,* May
1957, No. 10). Average dues collected in 1955 were 10.35 crowns
monthly (*Práce,* April 28, 1956); the average dues applied for 1956
were those planned, namely 10.82 crowns monthly (*ibid.*).
    b. Data on membership, made public in 1954 and 1955, showed
nearly 1.4 million members and a declining trend in total membership
(see *Rudé právo,* June 12, 1954, and June 22, 1958). Average
monthly dues were estimated at 10 crowns in 1955, by analogy with

trade union dues. Total dues-paying membership was assumed equal to 1 million in both years to allow for lower morale in paying dues and for possible overestimation of average monthly dues since many members had relatively low incomes (farmers) or no incomes (housewives). The estimate for 1956, 12.50 crowns monthly, makes an allowance for an increase in dues beginning June, 1956 (see *Rudé právo,* June 17, 1956, and *Nová mysl,* 1956, No. 6, p. 214).

c. Our estimate of the dues paid to noncommunist parties of the National Front, physical culture organizations, professional associations, and so forth, is set very roughly in probable proportion to that for trade unions or the Communist Party.

(2) Direct taxes

1947 and 1948. This is the sum of personal direct taxes (11.6 and 11.0 billion crowns, in 1947 and 1948, respectively, see Dolanský, *Výklad k rozpočtu,* 1949, p. 235), and an estimate of direct taxes and fees paid by households to local government (837 million crowns in 1947 and 928 million in 1948, which is one third of the sum of receipts in items 2.a, 2.b, and 5 in Appendix Table 11 below).

1955 and 1956. See Appendix Table 36 (wage tax).

(3) Social security contributions

1947 and 1948. This is the sum of contributions (in million crowns) as follows:

	1947	1948
1. Households on behalf of domestic servants (see notes to Table 1 A, items 1.A and 1.B)	48	52
2. Nonprofit organizations serving households (same source as above)	37	65
3. Employees (see Dolanský, *Výklad k rozpočtu,* 1949, p. 235)	5,900	9,700
Total	5,985	9,817

1955 and 1956. Social security contributions by employers of domestic servants and organizations serving households are transferred from Table 1 A.

Employees' contributions to social security do not exist as a separate category in the case of wage earners. This type of payment is included, according to official interpretation, in the wage tax. Farmers and members of agricultural cooperatives, however, contribute their social security payments apart from the agricultural tax. Their contributions amounted to 226 million crowns in 1955 (see the budget message of the Minister of Finance, *Rudé právo,* February 10, 1956). We rounded this figure upward to 300 million crowns to account for social security contributions paid by artisans and other self-employed persons. In the absence of data for 1956, we used the same figure for both years.

(4) Other payments
  1947 and 1948

The 1,722 million crowns for 1947 and 1,906 million crowns for 1948 are the sums of the following items: (1) fees paid to the central government (773 million crowns in 1947 and 933 million in 1948, that is, one sixth of the totals in *Statistický zpravodaj,* 1949, No. 9, p. 321); (2) revenue fines (69 million crowns in 1947 and 140 million in 1948, that is, one half of the totals given *ibid.*); and (3) unspecified payments to local administrations (880 million crowns in 1947 and 833 million in 1948, that is, one third of the estimated total, 2,639 million and 2,499 million crowns, see Appendix Table 11). Each of the above proportions represents a rough guess, partly based on the detailed breakdown of fees in Dolanský, *Výklad v rozpočtu,* 1949, p. 206.

Appendix Table 11 and notes thereto summarize our estimates of local government revenues and expenditures in 1947–48.

NOTES TO APPENDIX TABLE 11

Expenditures

1.(a) See Appendix Tables 29 and 31.

1.(b) Estimated as the difference between the total of pensions to retired administration employees (3.1 billion crowns in 1947 and 3.3 billion in 1948, see Dolanský, *Výklad k rozpočtu,* 1949, p. 235) and those to central administration employees (2.6 and 2.8 billion crowns in 1947 and 1948, respectively, see National Assembly, *Státní závěrečný účet,* 1947, p. 13, and 1948, p. 13).

1.(c) Estimated roughly as 12.5 percent of the wage and salary bill, following the 1947 proportion of social security contributions, severance pay, and per diem allowances, to the wage and salary bill in the central administration (see *ibid.;* the total 1948 proportion was but 0.1 percent higher).

2.(a) and (b). Compiled from the following sources: State Sta-

APPENDIX TABLE 11
EXPENDITURES AND RECEIPTS OF LOCAL ADMINISTRATION,
1947–48
(*Million crowns*)

Expenditures	1947	1948
1. Current expenditures on personnel		
(a) Wages and salaries	5,041	5,351
(b) Pensions to retired employees	500	500
(c) Other	630	670
2. Other current expenditures		
(a) Debt service	1,217	1,582
(b) Material purchases	7,731	9,483
3. Capital expenditures		
Investment purchases	4,000	4,000
Total expenditures	19,119	21,586
Receipts		
1. Contributions from Central Government		
(a) Regular	5,441	5,259
(b) Special	2,672	3,696
2. Local taxes and fees		
(a) Taxes	1,411	1,416
(b) Fees	736	998
3. Investment contributions from central government	1,728	2,373
4. Transfers from miscellaneous funds	1,195	476
5. Special levies	364	369
6. Borrowing	2,933	4,500
7. Unspecified revenues (residual)	2,639	2,499
Total receipts	19,119	21,586

tistical Office, *Zprávy,* 1948, pp. 147–56, 321–30; National Assembly, *Těsnopisecké zprávy,* Third session, (1947), pp. 334–48, item 860; Slovakia, State Planning and Statistical Office, *Statistická príručka Slovenska, 1948,* pp. 249–51; Dolanský, *Výklad k rozpočtu,* 1948 and 1949, *passim.* Material purchases were adjusted for transfers between organs of local administration.

3. Dolanský, *Výklad k rozpočtu,* 1948, p. 94.

Receipts

1.(a) and (b). Estimated by adjusting planned budget figures upward in (a) by 4,073 million crowns in 1947 and 4,126 million crowns in 1948; and in (b) by 2,000 million crowns in 1947 and 2,900 million crowns in 1948 (see National Assembly, *Sbírka zakonů,* 1946, pp. 1345–651; and 1947, pp. 1361–645). The adjustment consisted in multiplying the budget figures by 1.3359 in 1947 and by 1.2746 in 1948; these are the ratios between the total of planned budget figures and the total of actual budget expenditures in items for which detailed actual figures were not available individually. Actual figures were obtained from National Assembly, *Státní závěrečný účet,* 1947, p. 14, and 1948, p. 14, supplemented by various other sources.

2.(a) and (b). Estimated by adjusting the planned budget figures upward in (a) by 970 million crowns in 1947 and 1,243 million crowns in 1948, and in (b) by 605 million crowns in 1947 and 838 million crowns in 1948 (compiled from State Statistical Office, *Zprávy,* 1948, Nos. 22–25, pp. 148, 152, and Nos. 45–48, pp. 322–29; Slovakia, State Planning and Statistical Office, *Statistická príručka Slovenska,* 1948, p. 249; 1948 data for Slovakia were estimated by applying the same rate of increase as shown in the Czech figures). The adjustment consisted in raising the planned budget figures in the same ratio as that of planned budget receipts to actual budget receipts in similar revenue categories of the central government. The ratios were: for taxes—1.455 in 1947, 1.139 in 1948; for fees— 1.217 in 1947, 1.191 in 1948.

3. Obtained as the difference between actual central government expenditures on capital account (6,627 million crowns in 1947 and 19,170 million crowns in 1948, see National Assembly, *Státní závěrečný účet,* 1947, p. 14, and 1948, p. 14) and the sum of itemized expenditures (see *ibid.*).

4. and 5. These are budget figures compiled from State Statistical Office, *Zprávy,* 1948, pp. 150–51, 326–27, and from Slovakia, State Planning and Statistical Office, *Statistická príručka Slovenska,* 1948, p. 251; the 1947 figures for Slovakia were used for both years unchanged since the figures for the Czech lands were stable in this period.

6. See State Statistical Office, *Zprávy,* 1949, Nos. 25–26, p. 187, and Dolanský, *Výklad k rozpočtu,* 1949, p. 113 (we used the upper limit of Dolanský's estimate).

1955 and 1956

This is the sum of items shown in Appendix Table 37 under "fees, duties, etc.," and "unspecified revenues from household sector."

(5) *Imputed tax* (labor for community investment)
  1947 and 1948. Non-existent.
  1955 and 1956. See item 2.B.(4) under the receivables of Table
1 B.

4. Saving
  This is the balancing item between receivables and payables; as
such, it includes the statistical discrepancy.

NOTES TO TABLE 1 C

1. Saving
  Transferred from Table 1 B.

2. Transfers from the foreign sector
  This is the sum of private remittances and other private transfers
(see Appendix D, notes to Table 4 C, item 6.A).

3. Borrowing from the government sector
  This is the balancing residual that includes the statistical discrepancy. It may reflect a decline in cash balances as well.

4.A. Lending and capital transfers to the enterprise sector
  Our estimates are tabulated in Appendix Table 12 and explained
in the notes thereto.

APPENDIX TABLE 12

HOUSEHOLD LENDING AND CAPITAL TRANSFERS TO THE
ENTERPRISE SECTOR, 1947–48 AND 1955–56

(*Million crowns*)

	1947	1948	1955	1956
a. Repayment of debts	0	0	14	105
b. Imputed wages in private housing construction	0	0	542	1,132
c. Purchases for private housing construction	0	0	761	2,076
d. Increment to saving deposits	5,957	767	1,630	2,538
e. Excess of increment to insurance reserves over claims paid	244	111	36	59
Total	6,201	878	2,983	5,910

a, b, c. 1947–48: In the absence of information we assumed that these items were negligible (see the remarks in Chapter II, p. 32).

1955–56: a. Repayment of debts represents the net repayment calculated from data in State Statistical Office, *Statistická ročenka,* 1957, Table 20-9, p. 294, showing the amount of outstanding loans to population at the beginning of each year. Gross repayment and new borrowing figures were not available.

b. This is the value of labor supplied by households for "do-it-yourself" house construction, estimated at 35 percent of the total value of the product. In Chapter II we explained the treatment of this transaction in the sectoral accounts; for the method of calculation, see item c, below.

c. The amount of cash savings used for private housing construction, 761 and 2,076 million crowns in 1955 and 1956, respectively, was estimated by subtracting the net funds lent to private builders for this purpose by the state, that is, 246 million crowns in 1955 and 25 million in 1956 (State Statistical Office, *Statistická ročenka,* 1957, p. 294), from the total estimated cash funds invested in this field, that is, 1,007 million crowns in 1955 and 2,101 million in 1956. Total cash funds spent on construction of private housing were estimated as the difference between the value of investment in private housing construction expressed in "comparable prices of 1956" (1,549 and 3,233 million crowns in 1955 and 1956, respectively, see *ibid.,* 1957, p. 71) and the estimated value of the builders' own labor, that is, excluding hired labor (542 and 1,132 million crowns in 1955 and 1956, respectively, explained below). We assumed, as in the case of investments in general, that "comparable prices in 1956" can be used as an approximation to current market prices in both years (see Appendix B, notes to Table 2 A, entry 1.E, sales to enterprise sector capital account).

The value of labor supplied by the builders themselves was estimated at 35 percent of the total value. This percentage was obtained by raising, somewhat arbitrarily, the percentage that the wage bill in the socialized construction sector represented in the corresponding total value of construction (see *Statistické zprávy,* 1957, No. 1, p. 11, for value of construction: 18,093 million crowns in 1955 and 20,150 million in 1956; and *ibid.* for the wage bill in this branch: 5,613 million and 6,014 million crowns in 1955 and 1956, respectively, obtained as product of the number of employees and the average annual wage of a construction worker). We assumed that private construction was more labor intensive than socialized labor construction.

d. The 1947 and 1948 increments to saving deposits represent net changes in "free" and "blocked" deposits combined. The latter refer to deposits that were frozen in May, 1945—the freezing also involved the discontinuation of interest payments—and completely written off as part of the monetary reform of 1953. Releases from blocked deposits required specific authorization by the Ministry of Finance that was presumably granted only in cases of demonstrable need. The 1947 figure (5,957 million crowns) represents the resultant of an increase in "free" deposits by 12,257 million crowns and a decrease in "blocked" deposits by 6,300 million crowns; the 1948 figure is the net result of an increase in "free" deposits by 6,167 million crowns and a decrease in "blocked" deposits by 5,400 million crowns. The data for the "free" deposits are from National Bank of Czechoslovakia, *Bulletin,* 1949, Nos. 11–12, p. 240; those for the "blocked" deposits are from Dolanský, *Výklad k rozpočtu,* 1949, p. 235.

For the 1955 and 1956 figures see State Statistical Office, *Statistická ročenka,* 1957, Table 20-7, p. 293.

e. The 1947–48 figures were calculated from monthly averages for life insurance purchases, published in National Bank of Czechoslovakia, *Bulletin,* 1949, Nos. 8–9, p. 173. The figures refer to the redemption value of insurance policies purchased during each year; they accordingly may underestimate the prepaid premiums somewhat.

According to State Statistical Office, *Statistiká ročenka,* 1957, p. 295, life insurance premiums paid, less payment of claims, amounted to 45.3 and 73.9 million crowns in 1955 and 1956, respectively. In the absence of data on costs of operation of the life insurance establishment, we arbitrarily allowed 20 percent of these amounts for such costs and 80 percent, or about 36 million crowns in 1955 and 59 million crowns in 1956, as the increment to reserves. These increments are regarded as a form of saving by the household sector.

4.B. Lending and capital transfers to government sector

This is the balancing item between the receivables and payables (in 1948 only). It may represent increases in cash balances as well as reflect errors of estimation in other items of the account. In 1948 the opportunities for spending money were diminished and incentives for hoarding were considerably increased in connection with the communist *coup d'état*. Private enterprise was facing gloomy prospects; food was scarcer than in 1947 as a result of the bad harvest in 1947 and the resulting buildup of livestock inventories in the following year. See also Chapter IV, p. 81.

4.C. Lending and capital transfers to the foreign sector
    Transferred from Table 4 C, items 2.A and 3.A.

APPENDIX B: NOTES TO ENTERPRISE SECTOR ACCOUNTS (TABLES 2 A, 2 B, 2 C)

NOTES TO TABLE 2 A

1. Sales to other accounts
A. Sales to household sector production account
    See note 2 to Table 1 A.
B. Sales to household sector appropriation account
(1) Cash sales of goods and services
    See notes to Table 1 B, items 3.B.(1)a–d.
(2) Imputed sales of goods and services
    See notes to Table 1 B, items 3.B.(2)a–f.
C. Sales to the government sector production account
    1947 and 1948
    This is the sum of items brought together in Appendix Table 13 and explained in the notes to rows.

APPENDIX TABLE 13
SALES OF THE ENTERPRISE SECTOR TO THE GOVERNMENT
SECTOR ON CURRENT ACCOUNT, 1947–48
(*Million crowns*)

	1947	1948
Central Government		
1. Administration purchases (excluding military purchases)	5,151	5,448
2. Military purchases	4,034	2,848
3. Purchases on UNRRA account	2,017	1,715
4. State debt service	22	12
5. Other purchases	904	1,584
Local Government		
6. Administration purchases	7,731	9,483
Rest of Government Sector		
7. Trade unions	147	175
8. Political parties	138	128
9. Social security institutions	229	260
Total	20,373	21,653

1. This is the sum of 1947 and 1948 outlays (in that order) for materials and services (4,263 million and 4,513 million crowns) and for per diem allowances (888 million and 935 million crowns) in the central administration. Purchases of materials and services are given in National Assembly, *Státní závěrečný účet,* 1947, p. 13, and 1948, p. 13. Per diem allowances were estimated as part of expenditures on personnel other than wages, salaries, and retirement pensions (1,632 million and 1,711 million crowns, obtained from data in *ibid.*). It was assumed that these expenditures consisted of social security contributions (four percent of total wages and salaries, excluding severance pay, in central administration, excluding the Defense Ministry [see note to item I.A, Appendix Tables 29, 31], that is, 522 million and 542 million crowns) and a residual that was allocated between per diem allowances and severance pay in the proportion of four to one.

2. Military purchases represent the sum of administrative material expenditures, per diem allowances, and material military expenditures other than military subsistence and standard clothing. These components are shown in Appendix Table 14 and explained in notes thereto, following the documentation of the remaining items of Appendix Table 13.

3. See National Assembly, *Státní závěrečný účet,* 1947, p. 14, and 1948, p. 14. These are the sums of the value of unspecified social and health services financed from the UNRRA counterpart funds.

4. See *ibid.,* 1947, p. 31, and 1948, p. 29, respectively. (Interest payments are separately shown; see the government sector appropriation account.)

5. This item represents one half of the sum of unspecified miscellaneous expenditures classified under the title "other administrative expenditures" in *ibid.,* 1947, p. 14, and 1948, p. 14. The total of these unspecified expenditures was obtained by adding up the residuals of "other administrative expenditures" from which we subtracted estimates of those expenditures that could be specified. The main source of actual expenditures in this category, given in a breakdown by ministries and departments, was *ibid.,* 1947, p. 14, and 1948, p. 14. The specified components of these expenditures were

obtained from various other sources or estimated, mostly on the basis of planned budget figures in National Assembly, *Sbírka zákonů,* 1946, pp. 1345–651, *passim.,* and *ibid.,* 1947, pp. 1361–645, *passim.*

    6. From Appendix Table 11, item 2.(b).

    7, 8, 9. These are the sums of per diem allowances and current purchases, estimated from the corresponding wage and salary totals (see Appendix E, Appendix Tables 29 and 31), assuming that per diem allowances and current purchases were in the same percentage relationship to wage and salary totals (taken as 100) as in the central administration, that is, 6.8 and 6.9 percent for per diem allowances and 32.7 and 33.3 percent for current purchases in 1947 and 1948, respectively (see note to item 1 of Appendix Table 13 above, and National Assembly, *Státní závěrečný účet,* 1947, p. 13, and 1948, p. 13, for the wage and salary totals).

APPENDIX TABLE 14

ESTIMATION OF MILITARY EXPENDITURES IN 1947–48

(*Million crowns*)

		1947		1948
1. Wages and salaries of administrative personnel		708		750
2. Other expenditures on personnel				
a. Social security contributions	28 ⎞		30 ⎞	
b. Per diem allowances	48 ⎬	88	52 ⎬	95
c. Severance pay	12 ⎠		13 ⎠	
3. Material expenditures of the administration		231		250
4. Military pay		1,685		1,854
5. Military subsistence and clothing		1,000		1,000
6. Allowances to dependents of draftees		575		649
7. Military material purchases (residual)		3,755		2,546
Total		8,042		7,144

NOTES TO APPENDIX TABLE 14

    1. See Appendix E, note to item I.A in Appendix Tables 29 and 31.

    2 and 3. The totals were estimated from wages and salaries (item 1) assuming that the proportions between wages and salaries, other expenditures on personnel, and material expenditures of the administration were the same in the Ministry of Defense as in the

rest of central administration as a whole. These latter proportions were calculated from data in National Assembly, *Státní závěrečný účet,* 1947, p. 13, and 1948, p. 13.

"Other expenditures on personnel" (item 2) were allocated among the three subcategories in the same way as elsewhere in the government sector: social security contributions were taken equal to 4 percent of wages and salaries; per diem allowances were assumed equal to 4/5 and severance pay to 1/5 of the residual.

4. See Appendix E, note to item I.B, Appendix Tables 29 and 31.

5. See note 2.B.(2) to Table 1 B.

6. Estimated on the assumption that the dependents of one fifth of the 150,000 draftees (see Appendix E, note to item I.B, Appendix Tables 29 and 31; see also the proportion of married men in the age group between 20 and 24 years, State Statistical Office, *Statistická ročenka,* 1959, p. 55) were receiving allowances amounting to about one half of average earnings based on data in Appendix Tables 29 and 31. These allowances were assumed to have been paid from the Ministry of Defense appropriations since they could not be traced to any other source.

7. Residual.

8. See National Assembly, *Státní závěrečný účet,* 1947, p. 11, and 1948, p. 11.

1955 and 1956

APPENDIX TABLE 15

SALES TO THE GOVERNMENT SECTOR PRODUCTION ACCOUNT, 1955–56

(Million crowns)

	1955	1956
1. Purchases of goods and services on current account from the state budget	20,873	16,706
2. Purchases by social organizations from their own resources	350	417
Total	21,223	17,123
3. Less: Military subsistence and clothing	– 850	– 700
4. Less: Purchases from foreign sector	– 50	– 50
Total	20,323	16,373

Appendix Table 15 shows the calculation of this item. To government purchases on current account (see Appendix F, note to Appendix Table 37, item E.5) were added estimated analogous purchases of "social organizations" (350 million crowns in 1955 and 417 million crowns in 1956). The sum was reduced (1) by the value of military subsistence (Table 1 B, item 2.B.(2)), which has been counted in this account as part of compensations of employees, and (2) by the value of direct purchases from the foreign sector (see item g, Appendix Table 28).

Purchases of social organizations on current account, insofar as they were financed from their own resources, were obtained as the difference between their revenues from households (670 and 740 million crowns in 1955 and 1956, respectively, see Table 1 B, item 3.C.(1) and note thereto) and their wage bill, including social security contributions (320 and 323 million crowns in 1955 and 1956, respectively; see Appendix Table 32). We believe that social organizations made additional purchases financed from government grants; unable to make an estimate, we included these grants in government purchases of goods and services on current account.

D. Sales to government sector capital account
1947 and 1948

This is the sum of outlays listed in Appendix Table 16 and explained in the notes to entries by rows.

APPENDIX TABLE 16
SALES OF THE ENTERPRISE SECTOR TO THE GOVERNMENT
SECTOR ON CAPITAL ACCOUNT, 1947–48
(*Million crowns*)

	1947	1948
1. Public housing construction by the Ministry of Social Welfare	328	375
2. Reconstruction of Lidice and Ležaky	4	53
3. Other public investment projects	3,913	6,524
4. Other investment outlays	740	651
5. Local government investment outlays	4,000	4,000
Total	8,985	11,603

NOTES TO APPENDIX TABLE 16

1. Estimated from the planned budget figures (see National Assembly, *Sbírka zákonů*, 1946, pp. 1345–651, and *ibid.*, 1947, pp.

1361–645), on the assumption that the relative difference between the planned and the realized budget figures was the same as for the totals of the Ministry of Social Welfare (for realized figures see National Assembly, *Státní závěrečný účet,* 1947, p. 14, and 1948, p. 14).

2. The outlays were for the reconstruction of two communities destroyed in 1942 by the German occupation forces (see *ibid.*).

3. *Ibid.* (under the title "Investment purchases on own account").

4. These figures represent about three fourths of the 986 million and 868 million crowns of "other investment outlays" (*ibid.*). We assumed that the total outlays in this category were divided 3 to 1 between "expenditures preliminary to the launching of investment projects" and "settlement of financial accounts on projects that had been completed but not fully paid for" (see Bedřich Spáčil, *Veřejné hospodářství československé v roce,* 1947, p. 11). We assumed that the latter represented repayment of debts to the enterprise sector.

5. Official estimates (see Dolanský, *Výklad k rozpočtu,* 1948, p. 94, and Appendix Table 11).

1955 and 1956

From the breakdown of total investment figures among sectors, given in State Statistical Office, *Statistická ročenka,* 1957, Tables 6-1 and 6-3, p. 71, we selected those that represent government investment and adjusted them to match our definition of the government sector (see Appendix Table 17).

APPENDIX TABLE 17

GOVERNMENT SECTOR INVESTMENT, 1955–56

(*Million crowns*)

	1955	1956
1. Science and research	194	336
2. Health and social welfare	297	322
3. Culture and education	594	640
4. Administration	941	898
5. Action "T"	105	88
6. Action "Z"	559	767
7. Trade unions	100	100
8. Capital repairs	480	720
Total	3,270	3,871
9. Less: Value of labor for community investments	– 435	– 557
Total	2,835	3,314

NOTES TO APPENDIX TABLE 17

The following items of Appendix Table 17 require explanation:

3. Total investments in the sector of culture and education (694 and 750 million crowns) were decreased by estimated investments in activities, which we had classified as part of the enterprise sector, amounting to 100 million crowns in 1955 and 110 million in 1956. These latter amounts represent about 10 percent of the corresponding expenditures of the enterprise sector cultural enterprises estimated at 1,000 and 1,100 million crowns (see Appendix E, Appendix Table 32, note to item II.B.1.(i)). This ratio is based on the corresponding 1955 ratio prevalent in education and culture as a whole; total purchases on capital account, amounting to 694 million crowns (see State Statistical Office, *Statistická ročenka,* 1957, p. 71), represented about 10 percent of total expenditures estimated at 6,621 million crowns (sum of 5,771 million crowns of budget expenditures in education and culture, see Appendix Table 36, plus 850 million crowns of estimated own revenue of cultural institutions, see Appendix E, note to item II.B.1.(i)).

5. and 6. Actions "T" and "Z" are designations of government investments in the field of "community improvement projects" and "construction projects serving physical culture." They are not part of the State Investment Plan.

7. Figures in State Statistical Office, *Statistická ročenka,* 1957, Table 6-1, p. 71, comprising investments of trade unions and of non-agricultural cooperatives were split between the two arbitrarily by ascribing to the trade unions 100 million crowns worth of investments in both years.

8. The value of government sector capital repairs in 1959 prices (429 million crowns in 1955 and 642 million in 1956) was taken from State Statistical Office, *Statistická ročenka,* 1959, p. 132, adding up the following categories: science and research, health and social welfare, culture and education, and administration. In the absence of relevant data in 1955 and 1956 prices, we assumed that data in 1957 prices were the best available approximation. We deflated the values in 1959 prices by an index derived by comparing the values of total Czechoslovak capital repairs in 1955 and 1956 in 1959 prices and in 1957 prices (see *ibid.,* 1959, p. 132, and 1958, p. 108).

E. Sales to enterprise sector capital account
1947 and 1948
This is the sum of gross investment outlays listed in Appendix Table 18 and explained in the notes thereto.

APPENDIX TABLE 18
GROSS INVESTMENT IN ENTERPRISE SECTOR, 1947–48
(*Million crowns*)

	1947	1948
1. Industry	6,929.2	11,008.6
2. Industrial crafts and trades	274.8	250.0
3. Transportation		
a. State railroads	6,014.0	8,005.7
b. State airlines	41.5	28.3
c. Other carriers	605.5	806.0
4. Communications	752.2	1,296.9
5. Agriculture		
a. Purchased	1,600.0	4,266.8
b. In kind	1,438.0	1,449.0
6. Housing construction	4,798.0	7,826.8
Total	22,453.2	34,938.1

NOTES TO APPENDIX TABLE 18

1. For 1947 see State Statistical Office, *Průmyslové zprávy,* 1948, Nos. 7–8, p. 49; for 1948 see State Statistical Office, *Zprávy,* 1949, p. 129.

2. The 1947 total for industrial crafts and trades was assumed to be represented by the difference between the total shown in General Secretariat of the Economic Council, *Průběh plnění hospodářského plánu,* 1947, p. 301 (presumably referring to all industrial establishments without regard to size) and to the total shown in State Statistical Office, *Průmyslové zprávy,* 1948, Nos. 7–8, p. 49 (referring only to industrial establishments employing six or more persons). The 1948 figure was estimated very roughly at about 10 percent lower than in 1947.

3.a and 3.b. See National Assembly, *Státní závěrečný účet,* 1947, p. 25, and 1948, p. 25.

3.c. For 1947 we used the difference between the total for all transportation given in General Secretariat of the Economic Council, *Průběh plnění hospodářského plánu,* 1947, p. 301, and the sum of 3.a and 3.b. The 1948 figure was estimated on the basis of the 1948 figure for 3.a and the 1947 ratio between the investment in state railroads and other carriers.

4. See National Assembly, *Státní závěrečný účet,* 1947, p. 25, and 1948, p. 25.

5.a. For 1947, see General Secretariat of the Economic Council, *Průběh plnění hospodářského plánu,* 1947, p. 301 (apparently from the data for the first three quarters on the assumption of a constant rate of investment throughout the year (see *ibid.,* 1948, third quarter, p. 16).

5.b. See Lazarcik, Production and Productivity in Czechoslovak Agriculture, p. 62, Table 10.

6. For 1947 see General Secretariat of the Economic Council, *Průběh plnění hospodářského plánu,* 1947, p. 301, and *Statistické zprávy,* 1949, No. 3, p. 108. (The total was reduced by the value of two groups of government sector investment listed in Table 16 as items 1. and 2.). The 1948 estimate was obtained in the same way as that under 5. above.

1955 and 1956

The calculation of this entry is summarized in Appendix Table 19, and explained in notes.

APPENDIX TABLE 19
SALES TO ENTERPRISE SECTOR CAPITAL ACCOUNT, 1955–56
(*Million crowns*)

	1955	1956
1. Additions to fixed capital	25,686	27,603
2. Capital repairs	5,636	6,745
3. Investment in kind by private farmers	339	379
Total investment	31,661	34,727
4. Less: Government investment (including capital repairs)	– 3,270	– 3,871
Total investment, enterprise sector	28,391	30,856

NOTES TO APPENDIX TABLE 19

1. This is the sum of investments completed under the State Investment Plan (21,160 million crowns in 1955 and 20,225 million in 1956, see State Statistical Office, *Statistická ročenka,* 1957, p. 72) and other investments outside this plan (4,526 million and 7,378 million crowns in 1955 and 1956, respectively, see *ibid.,* 1957, p.

71, Table 6-1, columns 3–9). The latter component may include some net change in unfinished construction which was disregarded. These figures were used as an approximation of values in current prices, although they appear in various publications under different and ambiguous titles, as "comparable prices of 1956" (State Statistical Office, *Statistická ročenka,* 1957), "comparable prices of 1957" (*Statistické zprávy,* 1957, No. 4, p. 11) and "budgetary prices" (*ibid.,* 1958, No. 3, p. 10).

2. From State Statistical Office, *Statistická ročenka,* 1958, p. 109.

3. Farm investment in kind amounted to 339 million crowns in 1955 and 379 million in 1956. These figures represent only investment in kind of private farms and private plots of members of collective farms. Other farm investment in kind is assumed to be included in official figures on investments of individual sectors. For detailed calculation see note 4.A to Table 2 B.

4. See note to sales to government sector capital account, above (Appendix Table 17).

F. *Sales to foreign sector production account*
    See Appendix D.
2. *Inventory changes*
    1947 and 1948
    A. *Agriculture*
    B. *Other branches*
    The totals of A and B were obtained as the balancing items in the production account and therefore include the statistical discrepancy that would appear if all items were estimated independently. The bulk of the changes in inventories, both their decline in 1947 and their increase in 1948, seems to represent changes in livestock in agriculture. Our estimates, based on various sources indicated below, show a decline in livestock inventories of about 6.7 billion crowns in 1947, as a result of a severe drought, and a rebuilding at the rate of 5.5 billion crowns in 1948. The sources used in the estimates were: for livestock as of January 1, 1947, January 1, 1948, July 1, 1948, and January 1, 1949, State Statistical Office, *Zprávy,* 1948, Nos. 132–37, pp. 991–1036; Slovakia, State Planning and Statistical Office, *Statistická príručka Slovenska,* 1948, pp. 101–2; *Statistický zpravodaj,* 1949, No. 3, p. 93; for average live weight of livestock—State Statistical Office, *Zprávy,* 1948, Nos. 29–30, pp.

207–13, Slovakia, State Planning and Statistical Office, *Statistická příručka Slovenska,* 1948, p. 112; State Statistical Office, *Zprávy,* 1948, Nos. 130–31, pp. 981, 988–89; for prices—*Statistický zpravodaj,* 1950, No. 2, p. 53, and General Secretariat of the Economic Council, *Průběh plnění hospodářského plánu,* 1947, pp. 194–95.

1955 and 1956

No official source available shows even an approximation of changes of inventories in studied years. Only one part of inventories could be calculated from figures in State Statistical Office, *Statistická ročenka,* 1957, pp. 71–72, namely, unfinished investments. These figures show a negative change in 1955 (– 1,200 million crowns) and a positive change in 1956 (2,168 million crowns). Additional information referring to inventories was published in *Finance a úvěr,* 1958, No. 5, p. 278; it states, without referring to a specific year, that the total value of inventories in the national economy was equal to more than one half of the "national income" and almost one third of the "social product." Unfortunately, this information does not lead to an estimate of inventory changes. Our estimate was made as follows.

From gross finished investments in 1955, including capital repairs, we deducted an estimate of depreciation to obtain the value of additions to fixed capital. The difference between an official figure on "accumulation" and the estimated value of additions to fixed capital is an approximation of changes in inventories (see Appendix Table 20 and notes thereto). This procedure could be used only for 1955, because we were not in a position to estimate accumulation in 1956.

APPENDIX TABLE 20

CHANGES IN INVENTORIES IN 1955

(Million crowns)

1. Gross finished investment including capital repairs	31,661
2. Less: Depreciation	9,706
3. Net addition to fixed capital	21,955
4. Inventory changes	4,235
5. Accumulation	26,190

NOTES TO APPENDIX TABLE 20

1. Gross finished investment: see Appendix Table 19 in notes to Table 2 A, item 1.E.

2. Depreciation allowances actually set aside are shown in Table 2 A, item 6, to be 6,012 million crowns. We augmented this figure by depreciation of fixed capital owned by "budgetary organizations" and by private persons in order to be consistent with the official definition of accumulation.

As of January 1, 1955 (see Appendix Table 23 for all figures), the private sector owned 88,700 million crowns of fixed capital, excluding land improvements and livestock. Total fixed capital in the socialized sector, excluding land improvements and livestock, amounted to 371,800 million crowns, of which 42.4 percent, or 157,600 million crowns, was owned by state budget organizations (*Statistický obzor,* 1956, No. 10, p. 434). Thus, private capital plus that of budget organizations subject to our estimate of depreciation amounted to 246,300 million crowns. We applied a depreciation rate of 1.5 percent based on the following considerations: The implicit depreciation rate for capital of economic organizations (214,200 million crowns, see notes to item 6 of Table 2 A, below) was about 3 percent in 1955. The capital stock of budgetary organizations and private persons consists mostly of buildings, for which the depreciation rate was about one half the average rate for economic organizations (*Statistický obzor,* 1956, No. 10, p. 437). It is necessary to point out here that we are interested in relative depreciation for the sectors. The depreciation rates applied here have no absolute meaning because we are dealing with fixed capital in current values, whereas depreciation in 1955 was calculated on the original value of capital.

3. Row 1 less row 2.

4. Row 5 less row 3.

5. Calculated from following information. We estimated income as defined officially at about 135 billion crowns in 1955 (see Chapter III, p. 75). Accumulation constituted 19.4 percent of national income (J. Ďuriš, Finance Minister, in *Rudé právo,* December 8, 1956).

Value of inventory changes in 1956 could not be calculated in the same way. It was obtained as residual.

Both figures, for 1955 and for 1956, implicitly include changes in state reserves that could not be separated, and should be considered as a rough estimate.

The striking difference between 1955 and 1956 changes in inventories should not be surprising in view of the fact that the only identifiable part of inventories, unfinished construction, showed a negative change in 1955 and a positive one in 1956. Moreover, events during the latter part of 1956—the revolt in Hungary and the political changes in Poland—undoubtedly caused disturbances in the supply of raw materials in foreign trade and in production planning in general. Thus, the direction of the change showed by our figures may be considered correct; however, the magnitude of the increase is a crude approximation.

3. Subsidy receipts
1947 and 1948

These are sums of items in Appendix Table 21 included among central government expenditures under "other administrative expenditures" in National Assembly, *Státní závěrečný účet,* 1947 and 1948.

APPENDIX TABLE 21
SUBSIDY RECEIPTS OF THE ENTERPRISE SECTOR, 1947–48
(*Million crowns*)

	1947	1948
1. Subsidy to the Association for Grain Economy and subsidy to cover losses in oil seed production	1,000	0
2. Special subsidies to farmers	2,630	1,415
3. Contribution to state enterprises for financing of current losses due to war damage	1,211	1,270
4. Deficit of the Price Compensation Fund	500	637
5. Import subsidies	266	1,969
6. Miscellaneous nonagricultural subsidies	159	33
7. Contributions to semipublic organizations serving the enterprise sector	350	334
8. Contributions to state enterprises on UNRRA account	130	43
9. Other payments	330	443
Total	6,576	6,144

NOTES TO APPENDIX TABLE 21

The sources and methods of estimation of the individual items are presented in the following notes. Budget data to which references are made are from National Assembly, *Sbírka zákonů,* 1946, pp. 1345–651 (for the 1947 budget) and *ibid.,* 1947, pp. 1361–645 (for the 1948 budget).

1. Rough estimate based on the 1947 budget figure (572 million crowns) and the official estimate of unforeseen losses in the produc-

tion of oleaginous seed due to drought (223 million crowns at 1946 prices; see *Statistický zpravodaj,* 1947, p. 392). The sum of these two figures was raised to 1 billion crowns. Scattered references to the losses in agriculture caused by the severe drought in 1947 suggest that the budgeted amount was largely exceeded independently of the special subsidies to farmers (under 2. below).

2. The 1947 figure is from Dolanský, *Výklad k rozpočtu,* 1949, p. 195; for 1948 we used the budget figure, in view of the rate of disbursements for the first ten months of 1948 (1,033 million crowns, see *ibid.*). These subsidies are extraordinary compensations for losses caused by the 1947 drought in the form of supplements to fixed prices or grants.

3. Of the indicated total, 1,163 million crowns in 1947 were paid on the account of the treasury (that is, "Central Fiscal Administration," see National Assembly, *Státní závěrečný účet,* 1947, p. 23); the remaining 48 million crowns were presumably paid on the account of other departments, and represent the difference between total losses of state enterprises due to war damages (1,211 million crowns, see *ibid.*) and the above amount covered by the treasury. The 1948 figure is from Dolanský, *Výklad k rozpočtu,* 1948, p. 96. (*Note:* In 1948 this item was treated in government bookkeeping as current cost of state enterprises, with transfers from state enterprises to the budget correspondingly reduced. The effect upon the GNP is the same in both cases.)

4. For 1947 we used the 1948 planned budget figure. For 1948 we derived our estimate from the 1948 planned budget figure on the assumption that it was exceeded in the same proportion as all the treasury outlays for which realization data could not be ascertained. The excess of this realized total over the corresponding budget total amounted to 27.46 percent (that is, 12,139 million crowns realized as against 9,524 million crowns planned, according to our detailed compilation of realized outlays). (*Note:* This subsidy represents the net balance of the Price Compensation Fund. The revenues of this fund were obligatory payments made by firms dealing in commodities for which the prices were officially fixed at a level allowing profit margins. The revenues were used to subsidize firms selling at fixed prices set at a relatively low level, often below production costs. The deficit of the fund was covered from the budget.)

5. The 1947 figure is from Dolanský, *Výklad k rozpočtu,* 1948, p. 105. The 1948 estimate was obtained in the same way as the

1948 estimate under 4. above. (*Note:* These import subsidies covered a part of the deficit due to the difference between the purchasing prices and the fixed domestic selling prices, mostly of basic consumer goods. Another part of this deficit was financed from the Price Compensation Fund, to the extent of 65 million crowns in 1947 and probably over 2 billion crowns in 1948 (compare Dolanský, *Výklad k rozpočtu,* 1949, pp. 194–95). We treated the latter transaction as a transfer within the enterprise sector.

6. Both estimates were obtained by the same procedure as the 1948 figure under 4 above. For 1947 the excess of the realized over the planned budget outlay totals, for which specific realized figures were unavailable, amounted to 33.59 percent. (*Note:* This category groups together several minor items shown in the budget under the heading "State subsidies" and "State guarantees," having the character of subsidies.)

7. Estimated as under 4 and 6 above.

8. See National Assembly, *Státní závěrečný účet,* 1947, p. 23, and 1948, p. 23.

9. See *ibid.* The figures represent each year's residual of government payments to state enterprises after the deduction of capital transfers (3,595 million and 3,228 million crowns) and of items 3 and 8 above (for 1948 only item 8; the 1948 amount of subsidies under item 3 did not appear among government payments, as explained in the parenthetical note under 3 above).

1955 and 1956

The figure for 1955 is a residual in this account.

Subsidies in 1956 were estimated to be 20 percent larger than in 1955, an increase believed to be in line with the increase in production of subsidized industries and with the simultaneous rise in production costs due to increased rates of depreciation.

It was not found possible to calculate the amount of subsidies independently; however, the available information supports the order of magnitude of our estimate. Thus, the Machine Tractor Stations were subsidized by 1,100 million crowns in an unspecified year (*Politická ekonomie,* 1958, No. 2, p. 107). Payments to trade in 1957 to cover the difference between delivery prices and purchasing prices, special discounts for fertilizers, and so forth, were planned to be 4,602 million crowns, of which subsidies probably were the major component (*Rudé právo,* May 13, 1957). Subsidies to socialized housing were expected by the Finance Minister to reach 1,314 million crowns in 1956 (*Rudé právo,* March 10, 1956). Subsidies to the coal industry, approximated on the basis of costs of production and prices of hard coal, were about 600 million crowns in 1956. In addition, subsidies were paid to the metallurgical industry, passenger transportation, and other sectors of production.

4. Purchases from foreign sector
   See notes to Table 4 A.

5. Indirect taxes
   1947 and 1948
   These are totals of tax payments presented in Appendix Table 22. The first six items are from *Statistický zpravodaj,* 1949, No. 9, p. 321; item 7 is an estimate amounting to one half of the total fees given *ibid.;* item 8, which is included among direct taxes in the original sources, is explained in note 3 to Appendix Table 3; item 9 is from National Assembly, *Státní závěrečný účet,* 1947, p. 12, and 1948, p. 12; item 10 represents one third of the sum of local taxes and fees, and special levies in Appendix Table 11 (receipts, items 2.(a), 2.(b) and 5).

APPENDIX TABLE 22
INDIRECT TAXES IN 1947–48
(*Million crowns*)

Central Government	1947	1948
1. Turnover tax	11,555	13,051
2. Luxury tax	16	1,367
3. Customs duties	778	760
4. Net surplus of tobacco monopoly	8,840	11,851
5. Proceeds from other monopolies	5,863	4,939
6. Other indirect taxes	5,975	5,363
7. Fees in the nature of indirect taxes	2,319	2,798
8. House tax	1,207	1,207
9. Net proceeds from sales of UNNRA goods	5,240	3,842
Local Government		
10. Local taxes and fees	837	928
Total	42,630	46,106

   1955 and 1956
   These are the sums of the turnover tax and tax on services and the house tax (see Appendix Tables 36 and 37).

6. *Capital consumption allowances*

1947 and 1948

For 1947 we used roughly the difference between the official estimates of gross investment (24,660 million crowns, see General Secretariat of the Economic Council, *Průběh plnění hospodářského plánu,* 1947, p. 301) and net investment (10,600 million crowns, *ibid.,* p. 303). The source (*ibid.,* p. 301) suggests that this difference refers to actually charged depreciation allowances.

For 1948 we raised the figure by 0.5 billion crowns in order roughly to account for the increment to depreciation charges due to the net increase of fixed capital. The net increase of fixed capital equals about 21 billion crowns, that is, the difference between 1948 gross investment (34,938 million crowns, see entry 1.E in Table 2 A) and the 1947 depreciation allowances (14,000 million crowns). Assuming the fixed capital purchases to be spread evenly over the year, depreciation in 1948 would be charged against one half of the value of the annual fixed capital investment. Our estimate of the increase of depreciation charges thus implies a depreciation rate of 5 percent.

1955 and 1956

Total capital consumption allowances, estimated at 6,012 million crowns in 1955 and 10,835 million in 1956, represent part of production cost as it appears in the enterprise sector bookkeeping system, not the value of actual material depreciation. This means, for example, that depreciation of state-owned housing, although part of our enterprise sector, is omitted because fixed assets under direct government management have not been subject to depreciation allowances in the actual accounting practice (see Ministry of Finance, *Plnění a kontrola státního rozpočtu v roce,* 1953, p. 99, text of the Ministry of Finance Circular No. 113/36.754/53).

1955: We derived the estimate for 1955 by applying an index for the capital consumption allowances in industry in 1955 and 1956 to the total capital consumption allowances for 1956 (see below). Capital consumption allowances in industry amounted to about 4,566 million crowns in 1955, and 8,229 million in 1956 (that is, to 16.1 percent and 27.5 percent of the wage bill, see *Statistický obzor,* 1957, No. 10, p. 461; the wage bill in industrial activity, 28,362 million crowns in 1955 and 29,924 million crowns in 1956 was derived from the number of employees in industrial activity and average wages, see State Statistical Office, *Statistická ročenka,* 1957, p. 90).

Reducing the 1956 estimate of total capital consumption allowances, 10,835 million crowns, proportionately to the change in industry results in 6,012 million crowns as the 1955 estimate of total capital consumption allowances in the entire enterprise sector. The use of the rate of increase in industry for a rough estimate for the entire economic sector is justified by the fact that capital consumption allowances of industry accounted for about 80 percent of the total.

Appendix Table 23 presents estimates of the value of fixed capital assets in the Czechoslovak economy, on the basis of which some preceding estimates were derived. This table was constructed essentially from the initial estimate of the value of fixed assets in industry (see below) and from percentage distributions of fixed capital assets in the economy given in State Statistical Office, *Statistická ročenka*, 1957, Tables 20-4, 20-5, p. 292.

First, the full replacement value of fixed capital in industry was approximated in two ways giving reasonably close results: 154,433 million and 146,577 million crowns. The first figure is the product of the 1955 number of employees in industry (1,904,000 persons) and the value of fixed capital per employee (81,110 crowns: see *Statistický obzor*, 1956, No. 10, p. 434). The second is based on information that there was 745 crowns of industrial gross production per each 1,000 crowns worth of fixed capital in 1954 (*ibid.*, 1956, No. 10, p. 435). It was assumed that this information referred to the January 1, 1955, value of fixed capital as established by the capital stock revaluation. The 146,577 million crowns was obtained by dividing the value of 1954 industrial gross production, 109,200 million crowns, by 0.745. The 1954 industrial gross production was derived from the 1955 value and the appropriate index series (1954 = 91, 1955 = 100, see State Statistical Office, *Statistická ročenka*, 1957, p. 78). The 1955 value, 120,000 million crowns, was in turn derived from the statement by Jaromír Dolanský according to which the 1956 gross industrial production was 11.4 million crowns, that is, 9.5 percent, higher than in 1955 (*Rudé právo*, March 6, 1957).

We set our estimate of the replacement value of fixed capital in industry roughly halfway between the two results, that is, at 150,000 million crowns. The total value of fixed capital for all sectors, 551.5 billion crowns, was derived by dividing the calculated value in industry, 150 billion crowns, by its share in the total, 27.2 percent. The other absolute figures shown in Appendix Table 23 follow from

APPENDIX TABLE 23

VALUE OF FIXED CAPITAL IN CZECHOSLOVAK ECONOMY, JANUARY 1, 1955 [a]

Economic Sector	(1) All Sectors		(2) Socialized Sector		(3) Socialized Sector Land and Livestock		(4) Private Sector		(5) Private Sector Land and Livestock	
	Percent	Million crowns	Percent of column 1	Million crowns	Percent of column 2	Million crowns	Percent of column 1	Million crowns	Percent of column 4 [d]	Million crowns
Productive [b]		357,900		337,000		79,100		20,900		4,500
Industry	27.2	150,000	99.7	149,600	1.5	2,200	0.3	400	1.5	0
Agriculture	8.7	48,000	58.3	28,000	22.3	6,200	41.7	20,000	22.3	4,500
Forestry	4.7	25,900	100.0	25,900	75.9	19,700	—	—	—	—
Construction	1.0	5,500	94.6	5,200	3.0	200	5.4	300	3.0	0
Transportation [c]	20.6	113,600	100.0	113,600	1.3	50,500 [c]	—	—	—	—
Communications	0.8	4,400	100.0	4,400	0.8	0	—	—	—	—
Material procurement and supply	0.6	3,300	100.0	3,300	2.5	100	—	—	—	—
Trade	1.3	7,200	97.9	7,000	2.8	200	2.1	200	2.8	0
Nonproductive [b]		193,600		118,800		4,900		74,800		2,500
Administration	1.7	9,400	100.0	9,400	3.8	400	—	—	—	—
Culture and health	6.2	34,200	100.0	34,200	2.8	1,000	—	—	—	—
Social organization	0.2	1,100	100.0	1,100	3.3	0	—	—	—	—
Housing	24.0	132,400	43.7	57,900	3.3	1,900	56.3	74,500	3.3	2,500
Communal services	3.0	16,500	98.2	16,200	9.6	1,600	1.8	300	9.6	0
Total	100.0	551,500		455,800		84,000		95,700		7,000

[a] All absolute figures are expressed at full replacement value in prices of July 1, 1954. (The actual value, that is, full value at current prices minus total past depreciation, is available for the socialized production sector where depreciation up to date was 39 percent for all capital, excluding land and livestock [Statistický obzor, 1956, No. 10, p. 437].)

[b] The division into "productive" and "nonproductive" sectors corresponds to the official usage (see State Statistical Office, Statistická ročenka, 1957, p. 69).

[c] Road construction is included in the value of capital in transportation. The value of road construction constituted 10.9 percent of fixed capital of the socialized sector, excluding agricultural collectives (Statistický obzor, 1956, No. 10, p. 434). This amounts to about 49,000 million crowns, added to the value of land in transportation in column 3.

[d] The same percentages were used as in the socialized sector, column 3.

the percentage distributions and the all sector total value. The figures were rounded in view of the rough estimate for industry.

1956: The estimate for 1956, 10,835 million crowns, represents 4.8 percent of 225,721 million crowns, which is the January 1, 1955, value of fixed capital assets of the so-called "economic organizations" (as opposed to "budgetary organizations," which omit depreciation allowances in their bookkeeping), adjusted upward for the annual increase of 5.4 percent (see below). The 4.8 percent is the average depreciation rate prevalent in "economic organizations" (*Statistický obzor,* 1956, No. 10, p. 437). The 5.4 percent increase from 1955 to 1956 represents the increase in the value of total fixed capital assets of the "productive" sector (*Statistický obzor,* 1957, No. 11, p. 509). The January 1, 1955, value of fixed capital assets of "economic organizations," 214,157 million crowns, represents 57.6 percent of total fixed capital assets of the socialized sector equal to 371,800 million crowns. (The 57.6 percent share is from *Statistický obzor,* 1956, No. 10, p. 434. The total value of fixed capital assets in the socialized sector is counted net of the value of land and livestock, not subject to depreciation allowances, that is, 455,800 million crowns less 84,000 million crowns, as calculated in Appendix Table 23.)

7. Value added by sector

The total value added was obtained from the enterprise sector appropriation account (Table 2 B) as the total payables less income from government sector (receivable item 2). The breakdown here follows the usual categories of factor returns, with a separate listing of social security contributions and incomes of self-employed (roughly corresponding to "unincorporated business" in the United States accounts). For convenience, source references and explanations of the estimating procedure will be given item by item in the notes to Table 2 B (for the most part the reader will be referred to corresponding items in Table 1 B where they are annotated in full). Here we give only the list of elements taken from Table 2 A that compose the individual categories of factor returns.

Numbers in parentheses below refer to corresponding entries in Table 2 B.

A. Compensation of employees

This contains wages and salaries (3.A.(1)a); other cash income

(3.A.(1)f); wages and salaries in kind (3.A.(2)a); imputed wages (3.A.(5)).

B. *Income of self-employed*

This contains entrepreneurial income (3.A.(1)b); income of farmers (3.A.(1)c); income from forestry (3.A.(1)d); income in kind of farmers (3.A.(2)b); income in kind in trades and professions (3.A.(2)c); part of direct taxes, that is, the agricultural tax and tax on self-employed (in 3.B.(2), see notes thereto); farm investment in kind and inventory changes in agriculture, as that part of farmers' investment which does not generate any corresponding cash income (4.A).

C. *Social security contributions* (3.B.(1))

D. *Profits*

This contains income from the director's fund as a form of distributed profits (3.A.(1)e); direct taxes excluding the agricultural tax and tax on self-employed (in 3.B.(2), see notes thereto); other transfers, as payments similar to direct taxes (3.B.(3)); other (4.B) less transfers from government sector (2).

E. *Rents and interest*

This contains net cash rentals (3.A.(3)a); net imputed rentals (3.A.(3)b); farm rents (3.A.(3)c); interest (3.A.(4)).

NOTES TO TABLE 2 B

1. Value added by sector
   See Table 2 A, item 7.
2. Current transfers from the government sector
   1947 and 1948

These are interest payments on central and local government debt. Central government's interest payments amounting to 2,841 million and 2,772 million crowns, are given in National Assembly, *Státní závěrečný účet,* 1947, p. 31, and 1948, p. 29. Interest payments made by the local government, 1,217 million and 1,582 million crowns, are from Appendix Table 11, item 2.(a).
   1955 and 1956
   None.

3. *Payments to other sectors*
A. *Payments to the household sector*
    See notes to Table 1 B, item 2.A.
B. *Payments to the government sector*
(*1*) *Social security contributions*
    1947 and 1948
    These are the sums of the following items (in million crowns), derived as indicated below.

	1947	1948
1. Social security contributions by employers	5,753	9,485
2. Pensions to retired employees of state enterprises	2,632	2,996
Total	8,385	12,481

1. Social security contributions paid by employers were not available directly. We assumed that, in principle, employer's contributions were equal to those paid by the employees. Taking the latter as the starting point, we added estimates of two items that do not have a counterpart among the employees' contributions, and from the sum we subtracted contributions of employees outside the enterprise sector. The calculation (in million crowns), and notes thereto follow.

	1947	1948
a. Contributions by employers (assumed to match employees contributions)	5,900	9,700
b. Plus: Employers' contributions on behalf of family workers	100	100
c. Plus: Excess of employers' contributions over employees' contributions in state enterprises	297	326
Subtotal	6,297	10,126
d. Less: Contributions by employees in the household sector	85	117
e. Less: Contributions by employees in the government sector	459	524
Total contributions by employers in the enterprise sector	5,753	9,485

a. Dolanský, *Výklad k rozpočtu,* 1949, p. 235.
b. Rough guess, based on an imputed wage bill of family workers (see employment figures in State Statistical Office, *Zprávy,* 1948, and average wages in agriculture and handicrafts in Appendix Tables 29

and 31) and a contribution rate equal to 6.8 percent of the wage bill, as in the case of domestic servants (see notes to Table 1 A, item 1.A).

   c. State enterprises' contributions on behalf of their employees were apparently equal to 4 precent, whereas contributions paid by the employees themselves amounted to 2 percent of their wage bill (see Bušek and Spulber, *Czeckoslovakia,* p. 214 in reference to 1948 and 1950; compare also Stádník, *Národní důchod a jeho rozdělení,* p. 178, in reference to absolute figures in the period 1929–43). The estimated excess of the employers' contributions thus amounts to 2 percent of the wage bill (net of severance pay, see Appendix Tables 29 and 31 and notes thereto).

   d. Assumed equal to item 3.C in Table 1 A, which implies the same contribution rate by employers and employees.

   e. This is the sum of contributions computed as percentages of corresponding wage bills, that is, in state and local administration (at 2 percent rate), in trade unions, political parties, and social security institutions (at 6 percent for 1947 and 9 percent for 1948). For wage bill data see Appendix E; contribution rates are estimates based on Bušek and Spulber, *Czechoslovakia,* p. 214.

   2. From National Assembly, *Státní závěrečný účet,* 1947, p. 24, and 1948, p. 24. In 1947 and 1948 state enterprises paid these retirement pensions directly out of current appropriations as part of the wage and salary bill. Here we treat them formally as contributions to the social security system (part of the government sector), whence they are paid in the form of transfers to the household sector.

1955 and 1956
See Appendix Table 32.

(2) Direct taxes
   Direct taxes paid by the enterprise sector are estimated below (in million crowns) and explained in the notes which follow.
      1947 and 1948

	1947	1948
1. Total direct tax receipts of the central government including house tax	19,324	20,184
2. Less: Direct taxes paid by the household sector	11,600	11,000
3. Less: House tax	1,207	1,207
Subtotal: Direct taxes paid by the enterprise sector to the central government	6,517	7,977

	1947	1948
4. Plus: Profits of state enterprises other than the tobacco monopoly	513	897
5. Plus: Direct taxes paid by the enterprise sector to the local government	837	928
Total	7,867	9,802

1. See *Statistický zpravodaj*, 1949, No. 9, p. 321.

2. The figures represent total direct taxes paid by households, see Dolanský, *Výklad k rozpočtu*, 1949, p. 235.

3. See note 3 to Appendix Table 3. The house tax is included among direct taxes in original sources.

4. Calculated from data in National Assembly, *Státní závěrečný účet*, 1947, p. 23, and 1948, p. 23. The figures represent gross profits of state enterprises other than the tobacco monopoly. Profits were entered on a gross basis since losses of state enterprises were covered by subsidies on the enterprise sector production account.

5. Estimated as one third of local administration revenues listed as items 2.a, 2.b, and 5 in Appendix Table 11.

Direct taxes include the following items (in million crowns) to which reference will be made below.

	1947	1948
1. Tax on self-employed ("general profits tax")	2,514	4,106
2. Agricultural tax	1,439	830
3. Tax on nationalized enterprises ("special profits tax")	2,368	2,971

Item 1, tax on self-employed, for 1947 is from State Statistical Office, *Zprávy*, 1949, Nos. 31–33, pp. 235 and 241. The rest of the figures for which actual data were not available (item 1, for 1948, and items 2 and 3 for both years) are estimates representing adjusted budget figures. The adjustment consisted of the following steps. We first calculated the totals of actual direct tax receipts that were not available in itemized detail (3,997 million crowns in 1947 and 7,973 million in 1948) and the total planned budget receipts for the same tax categories (2,194 million crowns in 1947 and 5,475 million in 1948; see National Assembly, *Sbírka zákonů*, 1946, p. 1524, and 1947, p. 1537). The actual receipts exceeded planned receipts by 82.17 percent in 1947 and by 45.62 percent in 1948 (see calculation below). We assumed that in each individual tax category actual receipts exceeded the planned receipts by the same percentage, and we adjusted the planned figures accordingly.

The calculation of the total of actual tax receipts not available individually is shown below (in million crowns).

	1947	1948
1. Total actual direct tax receipts of the central government	19,324	20,184
2. Less: Actual direct tax receipts available individually		
a. Personal direct taxes	11,600	11,000
b. General profits tax	2,514	n.a.
c. House tax	1,207	1,207
d. Special tax on dividends	1	1
e. "Tantieme tax"	5	3
3. Unaccounted-for actual direct tax receipts (1. less 2.)	3,997	7,973

(All figures were explained in the calculations above, except items 2.d and e, and these are from Tuček, *Vývoj československých financí v letech 1945–1952,* p. 33.)

1955 and 1956

Total direct taxes paid by enterprises (million crowns) consist of the following items (taken from Appendix Table 37):

	1955	1956
a. Agricultural tax	346	366
b. Handicraft tax	42	42
c. Profit tax	13,200	13,685
d. Cooperative tax	350	382
Total	13,938	14,475

(3) Other payments
  1947 and 1948

These amounts are rough estimates taken numerically equal to transfers from the household sector (item 3.C.(4) in Table 1 B).

  1955 and 1956
  None.

4. Income retained by the sector
A. Farm investment in kind and changes in inventories
   of farm products
   1947 and 1948

This is the sum of estimates of farm investment in kind (1,438 million crowns in 1947 and 1,449 million in 1948; see Appendix

Table 18), and of changes in inventories of farm products (– 6,700 million and 5,500 million crowns, see notes 2.A and 2.B to Table 2 A).

1955 and 1956
Farm investment in kind
Our estimate is shown in Appendix Table 24 and explained in notes to rows. In each case the total value of investment in kind was obtained by multiplying the area by the estimated value of investment per hectare indicated in the notes. As used here, investment in kind excludes orchards, vineyards, and hop gardens, which we show under inventory changes.

APPENDIX TABLE 24
FARM INVESTMENT IN KIND, 1955–56

	Agricultural Land (thousand hectares)		Total value of Investment in Kind (million crowns)	
	1955	*1956*	*1955*	*1956*
a. State and other public farms	1,108	1,149	60	68
b. Collective farms	1,802	1,837	97	109
c. Private plots on collective farms	110	117	9	10
d. Individual farmers	3,682	3,739	298	333
e. Part-time farmers	394	400	32	36
Total			496	556

NOTES TO APPENDIX TABLE 24

a and b. The value of investment in kind in a sample of 51 collective farms in 1955, 53.9 crowns per hectare of agricultural land (see Bača, *Za další rozvoj socialistické zemědělské družstevní velkovýroby*, p. 81), was used for state and other public farms as well as for all collective farms. For 1956 the figure was arbitrarily increased by 10 percent to 59.3 crowns.

c, d, and e. The estimates per hectare for state and other public farms and for collective farms in 1955 and 1956 were arbitrarily increased by 50 percent for our calculation for private plots of collective farmers, individual, and part-time farmers, giving 80.9 crowns in 1955 and 89.0 crowns in 1956.

The corresponding data on area were obtained from State Statistical Office, *Statistická ročenka,* 1957, pp. 112 and 117, and *Statistické zprávy,* 1957, No. 1, p. 10 (for 1955 area of private plots).

Appendix Table 25

INVENTORY CHANGES IN AGRICULTURE, 1955–56

(1)	Changes in Inventory (thousands of kilograms of live weight, units or hectares)		Average Price (per kilogram per unit or per hectare, in crowns)		Value of Inventory Changes (million crowns)	
	(2) 1955	(3) 1956	(4) 1955	(5) 1956	(6) 1955	(7) 1956
Horses (thousands of kilograms)	0	–412	3.20	3.30	0	–1
Cattle (thousands of kilograms)	24,948	10,394	6.00	6.20	150	64
Hogs (thousands of kilograms)	50,698	8,139	9.20	9.67	466	79
Sheep and lambs (thousands of kilograms)	–655	–1,694	4.20	4.40	–3	–7
Total livestock (thousands of kilograms)	74,991	16,427	8.18	8.18	613	135
Poultry (thousands of kilograms)	1,522	937	12.00	12.65	18	12
Total livestock and poultry (thousands of kilograms)	76,513	17,364	—	—	631	147
Fruit trees (thousands of units)	2,262	–244	52.70	—	119	–9
Vineyards (area in hectares)	442	3,946	10,412	10,412	5	41
Hop gardens (area in hectares)	–612	–181	20,825	20,825	–13	–4
Beehives (thousands of units)	–135	32	174	174	–23	6
Seed and feed	—	—	—	—	64	179
Total	—	—	—	—	783	360

Data for 1955 refers to the February 15, 1955 census; data for 1956 to the December 15, 1955 census.

Inventory changes in agriculture here exclude the value of inventories in state and public farms that corresponds to other categories of value added (for example, to wages paid by state and other public farms). We made our estimate as follows: First, the changes in all agricultural inventories were estimated to be 783 and 360 million crowns in 1955 and 1956, respectively, and, second, the changes in inventories in state and public farms, 166 and 72 million crowns in 1955 and 1956, respectively, were deducted. (See Appendix Tables 25 and 26 and notes thereto for details). The difference, 617 million crowns in 1955 and 288 million in 1956, was added to the investments in land estimated in the preceding section to get the entry under item 4.A in Table 2 B.

NOTES TO APPENDIX TABLE 25

Our estimates do not include goats, field stock, and working capital because the data were not available.

Inventory changes of livestock and poultry (columns 2 and 3) were obtained as the product of the change in numbers between January 1, and December 31 of each year (State Statistical Office, *Statistická ročenka*, 1957, p. 133) and the average live weight per head (State Statistical Office, *Zprávy*, 1948, Nos. 130–31, p. 981, for horses; and State Statistical Office, *Statistická ročenka*, 1957, pp. 140–41, for all other livestock and poultry).

Changes in the numbers of fruit-trees, area of vineyards and hop gardens, and numbers of beehives between the beginning and the end of each year were calculated from State Statistical Office, *Statistická ročenka*, 1957, pp. 130–31, 138.

Average prices (columns 4 and 5) were obtained as follows: Horse prices for 1955 are double the average delivery price (Ministry of Interior, *Úřední list*, 1955, No. 38, p. 163). This adjustment was made in order to keep the ratio of horse and cattle prices close to the 1947 ratio, see *ibid.*, 1947, p. 721, and General Secretariat of the Economic Council, *Průběh plnění hospodářského plánu*, 1947, pp. 194–95). Horse prices for 1956 are derived from 1955 by using the price index for cattle from 1955 to 1956 (*Politická ekonomie*, 1958, No. 2, p. 113). Cattle prices for 1955 are from *Mladá fronta*, August 4, 1955. For 1956, they are derived from 1955 by using the cattle price index (*Politická ekonomie,* 1958, No. 2, p. 113). Hog prices for 1956 are from *Zemědělské noviny,* July 4, 1957; for 1955, derived from 1956 price by using the price index for hogs (*Politická ekonomie,* 1958, No. 2, p. 113). Prices of sheep and lambs, as well as poultry, are weighted averages of delivery and above-delivery prices (Ministry of Interior, *Úřední list,* 1955, No. 38, pp. 162–63; for 1956 poultry prices, *ibid.,* 1956, No. 2). The weights used were respective shares of delivery and above-delivery sales in total sales (for sheep and lambs, see *Plánované hospodářství,* 1957, No. 3, p. 176; for poultry, data of hog sales were used, see *Politická ekonomie,* 1958, No. 2, p. 113).

Fruit tree prices were extrapolated from the 1945 price of 65.75 crowns (State Statistical Office, *Zprávy,* 1948, Nos. 3–4, pp. 106–7), up to the 1948 price by means of the wholesale price index (State Statistical Office, *Cenové zprávy,* 1948, p. 103); from 1948 to June 1953, by means of the official investment price index (*Československý přehled,* May 1954, p. 4). It was assumed that the price had not changed since 1953; it was merely converted in the ratio of 5 to 1 in consideration of the monetary reform of 1953. The hop garden price per hectare was estimated from the 1946 price (36,000 crowns, State Statistical Office, *Zprávy,* 1949) by the same method as the fruit tree price. The price of a vineyard per hectare was assumed to be one half of the hop garden price, that is, 10,412 crowns.

The price of a beehive was estimated from the 1948 price (400 crowns, see *Slovenský včelár,* July, 1948), using the same method of extrapolation as in the case of fruit tree and hop garden prices.

Value of inventory changes (columns 6 and 7) is the product of inventory changes in quantity terms (columns 2 and 3) and unit prices (columns 4 and 5). In the case of seed and feed, the estimated value of seed and feed per hectare was multiplied by the corresponding change in area (92,000 hectares for 1955 and 146,000 hectares for 1956 based on State Statistical Office, *Statistická ročenka,* 1957, p. 112). The value of seed and feed per hectare was estimated from data pertaining to collective farms (524.5 crowns in 1955, see Prouza, *Společné fondy v JZD,* p. 73), and this was increased by one third, to 699 crowns, for 1955 and by three fourths, to 1,223 crowns, for 1956. This adjustment is based on considerations of price increases of feed and litter, given in *Politická ekonomie,* 1958, No. 2, p. 113, and of the rise in the ratio of feed and litter per hectare in collective farms, mentioned in Bača, *Za další rozvoj socialistické zemědělské družstevní velkovýroby,* p. 81.

APPENDIX TABLE 26
INVENTORY CHANGES IN STATE AND OTHER PUBLIC FARMS,
1955–56
(*Million crowns*)

	1955	1956
Feed and seed	64.00	26.00
Horses	3.95	5.44
Cattle	57.45	55.11
Hogs	40.89	– 11.72
Sheep and lambs	–0.97	– 3.22
Poultry	0.44	0.47
Total	165.76	72.08

Inventory changes in state and public farms, shown in Appendix Table 26, were estimated using the same sources and price estimates as in the calculation of all agricultural inventory changes above.

B. Other
This is the balancing item in the account, and as such, it reflects any errors of estimate in the remaining items.

NOTES TO TABLE 2 C

1. Earnings retained by the sector
Transferred from Table 2 B, item 4.
2. Capital consumption allowances
Transferred from Table 2 A, item 6.
3. Borrowing and capital transfers from the household sector
See Table 1 C, item 4.A.
4. Capital transfers from the government sector
1947 and 1948
This is the sum of items listed in Appendix Table 27 and documented in the notes thereto.

NOTES TO APPENDIX TABLE 27

1. See National Assembly, *Státní závěrečný účet,* 1947, p. 14, and 1948, p. 14.
2. Obtained from the same sources and by the same methods as items 4 (1948), 5 (1948), and 6 and 7, of Appendix Table 21. These transfers represent a contribution to investment projects designed to benefit agricultural production (irrigation, conservation of natural resources, afforestation, and so forth).

APPENDIX TABLE 27
GOVERNMENT SECTOR CAPITAL TRANSFERS TO THE
ENTERPRISE SECTOR, 1947–48
(*Million crowns*)

	1947	1948
1. Capital transfers to state enterprises	3,907	3,701
2. Capital transfers to agriculture (on account of the Central Fiscal Administration)	160	25
3. Rehabilitation of agriculture	1,012	861
4. Repayment of principal by the State Debt Service	126	– 93
5. Payments on state guaranteed loans	100	180
6. Miscellaneous capital transfers to the enterprise sector (on account of the Central Fiscal Administration)	80	13
7. Rehabilitation of industry	379	320
8. Other capital transfers to the enterprise sector (on various accounts)	397	28
9. Repayment of debt on investment projects	247	217
Total	6,408	5,252

3. As under 2. above. These are transfers that were financed from the counterpart of UNRRA funds.

4. See National Assembly, *Státní závěrečný účet,* 1947, p. 31, and 1948, p. 29. The negative figures for repayment of the principal represent part of the proceeds of a loan earmarked for the redemption of matured claims against the government, but added instead to the cash balances of the Fiscal Administration; in other words, they represent a part of the net increase in state debt.

5. Assumed equal to the budget figure (see National Assembly, *Sbírka zákonů,* 1946, pp. 1345–651, and *ibid.,* 1947, pp. 1361–645). This item refers to the repayment of loans on behalf of producers (mainly nationalized industries) that had contracted loans from the banking system under a government guarantee of repayment, but were unable to meet the terms of the loan contract.

6. As under item 2 above. This item refers to contributions to miscellaneous investment projects.

7. As under item 2 above. These are transfers that were financed from the counterpart of UNRRA funds (compare item 3).

8. This is an estimate of residual capital transfers, included among "other administrative expenditures" (1,200 million crowns in 1947 and 805 million in 1948 were budgeted, see Dolanský, *Výklad k rozpočtu,* 1948, pp. 108–9). Among these expenditures we identified specifically the items listed in Appendix Table 16, item 1 and 2, and in Appendix Table 27, items 2 and 6. The budgeted total for

these items amounted to 708 million crowns in 1947 and to 760 million crowns in 1948 (for source see above, under 5), but the estimated actual total was 572 million crowns in 1947 and 466 million crowns in 1948 (see Appendix Tables 16 and 27). The actual total of the residual transfer items was derived on the assumption that the ratio of budgeted to actual outlays noted above prevailed also between the budgeted residual transfers that were not accounted for specifically (1,200 million less 708 million crowns for 1947, and 805 less 760 million crowns for 1948) and the corresponding totals of actual transfers.

9. This is an estimate of the amount of "settlement of financial accounts on projects that had been completed but not fully paid for," which, in original data, are lumped together with "expenditures preliminary to the launching of investment projects" (compare Spáčil, *Veřejné hospodářství československé v roce 1947,* p. 11). Our estimate represents one fourth of the total (986 million and 868 million crowns) given in National Assembly, *Státní závěrečný účet,* 1947, p. 14, and 1948, p. 14.

1955 and 1956

See Appendix Table 37, item D.1 (capital grants), and item D.3 less item A.6 (working capital transfers, net).

5. Borrowing from the government sector (net)

This is the balancing item for 1948; it includes the statistical discrepancy. (For the other years, see item 7, below.)

6. Gross investment by the enterprise sector

Transferred from Table 2 A, items I.E and 2.

7. Lending to the government sector (net)

1947, 1955, and 1956

This is the balancing item, including the statistical discrepancy. (For 1948, see item 5 above.)

APPENDIX C: NOTES TO GOVERNMENT SECTOR ACCOUNTS (TABLES 3 A, 3 B, 3 C)

NOTES TO TABLE 3 A

1. Imputed sales of government services to the government sector appropriation account (at cost of inputs)
   This is the sum of items 3 and 4 on the payable side of this account, less value of item 4.D.

2. Imputed sales to government sector capital account
   This is the value of imputed wages for unpaid labor on community improvement projects. For sources and method of calculation see note to entry 2.B.(4) in Table 1 B.

3. Purchases of goods and services on current account
A. From the enterprise sector
   See note to entry 1.C in Table 2 A.
B. From the foreign sector
   This is the net balance of international payments for the maintenance of diplomatic representatives abroad and similar items.
   See notes to entries 1.B and 3.B in Table 4 A.

4. Value added by sector
A. Compensation of employees
   See Appendix Tables 29, 31, and 32.
B. Military subsistence and clothing
   See note 2.B.(2) to Table 1 B.
C. Social security contributions
   1947 and 1948
   These are the sums of the following items in million crowns (see sources below):

	1947	1948
1. Pensions to retired administration employees	3,100	3,300
2. Social security contributions by the state and local administration	761	796
3. Social security contributions by the other employers in the government sector	78	126
Total	3,939	4,222

1. See Dolanský, *Výklad k rozpočtu*, 1949, p. 235. Although these payments were made on current account, we treat them here for the sake of comparability as if they were paid through the social security establishment; compare also note to entry 3.B(1), item 2, of Table 2 B.

2. Estimated as 4 percent of the corresponding wages and salaries in Appendix Tables 29 and 31; the percentage used is the same as that in state enterprises (see Bušek and Spulber, *Czechoslovakia,* p. 214).

3. Estimated as 6 percent of the corresponding wages and salaries in 1947 and 9 percent in 1948, on the same basis as social security contributions by nonprofit organizations serving households (see note to entry 1.B, item 3, in Table 1 A and Appendix Tables 29 and 31).

1955 and 1956
See Appendix Table 32.

D. *Imputed wages for unpaid labor in community improvement projects*
See note to entry 2.B(4) in Table 1 B.

NOTES TO TABLE 3 B

1. *Income from other accounts*
A. *From the household sector appropriation account*
See notes to entries under 3.C in Table 1 B.
B. *From the enterprise sector production account*
See note to entry 5 in Table 2 A.
C. *From the enterprise sector appropriation account*
See notes to entries under 3.B in Table 2 B.
D. *From the government sector production account*
See note to entry 4.C in Table 3 A.

2. *Imputed purchases of government services from the government sector production account*
Transferred from Table 3 A, entry 1.

3. *Transfers to other accounts*
A. *Transfers to the household sector appropriation account*
See note to entry 2.B(3) in Table 1 B.
B. *Subsidies to the enterprise sector production account*
See note to entry 3 in Table 2 A.
C. *Interest payments to the enterprise sector*
See note to entry 2 in Table 2 B.

4. *Saving*
Residual.

NOTES TO TABLE 3 C

1. *Saving*
Transferred from the government sector appropriation account; see note to item 4 in Table 3 B.

2. *Capital transfers from the foreign sector*
See note to item 6.B in Table 4 C.

3. *Borrowing from other sectors*
A. *From the household sector (net)*
This is the balancing item of the household sector capital account in 1948; see note to item 4.B in Table 1 C. For other years, see note to item 7.A, below.

B. *From the enterprise sector (net)*
This is the balancing item of the enterprise sector capital account in 1947, 1955, and 1956; see note to item 7 in Table 2 C. For 1948, see note to item 7.B, below.

C. *From the foreign sector*
See note to item 7 in Table 4 C.

4. *Gold sales to the foreign sector*
See note to item 8 in Table 4 C.

5. Government sector investment
A. Capital purchases from the enterprise sector
See item 1.D in Table 2 A.
B. Gold purchases from the foreign sector
See note to item 4 in Table 4 C.
C. Value of imputed wages in community improvement projects
See note to entry 2.B.(4) in Table 1 B.

6. Capital transfers to other sectors
A. To the enterprise sector
  1947 and 1948
See Appendix Table 27, p. 162.
  1955 and 1956
See Appendix Table 37, item D.1 (capital grants), and item D.3
less item A.6 (working capital transfers, net).
B. To the foreign sector
See note to item 2.B in Table 4 C.

7. Lending to other sectors
A. To the household sector (net)
This is the balancing item of the household sector capital account;
see note to item 3 in Table 1 C.
B. To the enterprise sector (net)
This is the balancing item of the enterprise sector capital account
for 1948; see note to item 5.A in Table 2 C.
C. To the foreign sector
See note to item 3.B in Table 4 C.

APPENDIX D: NOTES TO FOREIGN SECTOR ACCOUNTS (TABLES 4 A, 4 B, 4 C)

The arrangement below is first by period and second by tables.

NOTES TO TABLE 4 A: 1947–48

All figures used in the foreign sector accounts for 1947 and 1948 were obtained in International Monetary Fund, *Balance of Payments Yearbook, 1948 and 1949,* pp. 139–42.

1. Imports of goods and services
A. By the enterprise sector
   This is the sum of payments for merchandise abroad, foreign travel, transportation, insurance, interest payments (investment income paid), film royalties, licenses and patents, commissions, postal services, income from real estate, salaries, services, and so forth. We excluded 4,000 million crowns of UNRRA gift imports; their domestic counterpart value enters the accounts, but to an unknown sum.

B. By the government sector
   This entry covers only payments by the government not included in the entries under 1.A, above (contributions to international institutions, Czechoslovak representation abroad, foreign representation in Czechoslovakia).

2. Balance on production account
   Does not apply in 1947 and 1948 on the receivable side. See note to entry 4, below.

3. Exports of goods and services
A. By the enterprise sector, and

B. By the government sector
These entries include items on the export side, corresponding to those listed under item 1 above.
4. Balance on production account
This is the deficit on current transactions in goods and services.

NOTES TO TABLE 4 B: 1947–48

All entries in this account merely transfer the balance on production account to the capital account. We found no information on current factor payment to or from abroad.

NOTES TO TABLE 4 C: 1947–48

1. Deficit of nation on current account
Transferred from Table 4 B.
2. Transfers from other sectors
A. From the household sector
This is the sum of private remittances (43 million crowns in 1947 and 244 million crowns in 1948) and other private transfers) 25 million crowns in 1947 and 206 million crowns in 1948).

B. From the government sector
This entry includes amortization of municipal debt (4 million crowns in 1947 and 1 million crowns in 1948), amortization of long-term loans contracted by official institutions (235 million crowns in 1947 and 307 million crowns in 1948), and subscription to the International Monetary Fund and to the International Bank for Reconstruction and Development (165 million crowns in 1947 only).

3. Borrowing from other sectors
A. From the household sector
This is the sum of net private direct investment (6 million crowns in 1947 and 91 million crowns in 1948) and of "other," representing the net balance of purchases and maintenance of real estate (6 million crowns in 1947 and 14 million crowns in 1948). Attributing these transactions to the household sector is more or less arbitrary, but it does not introduce any significant error into the accounts because of the negligible amounts involved. Moreover, the eventual consolidation of the capital accounts eliminates these details.

B. From the government sector

This includes short-term capital transactions of official institutions under the titles of (*a*) payments and clearing agreements (288 million crowns in 1947 and 356 million crowns in 1948) and (*b*) other liabilities (177 million crowns in 1947 and 80 million crowns in 1948).

4. Gold purchases by the government sector

This entry refers to monetary gold.

5. Surplus of nation on current account

Does not apply to 1947 and 1948.

6. Transfers to other sectors

A. To the household sector

This is the sum of (*a*) private remittances (303 million crowns in 1947 and 170 million crowns in 1948) and (*b*) other private transfers (57 million crowns in 1947 and 20 million crowns in 1948).

B. To the government sector

This is the sum of (*a*) *reparations* (147 million crowns in 1947, none in 1948), (*b*) long-term capital transactions of official institutions under the title of "settlement of claims arising out of war damage" (253 million crowns in 1947, none in 1948), and (*c*) the statistical discrepancy representing the difference between the net totals of current transactions and capital transactions as recorded in the source (210 million crowns in 1947, 351 million crowns in 1948).

7. Lending to the government sector

This is the sum of (*a*) long-term loans contracted by official institutions (1,953 million crowns in 1947, 1,654 million crowns in 1948) and short-term capital transactions of official institutions under the titles (*b*) payments and clearing agreements (1,580 million crowns in 1947 and 442 million crowns in 1948), (*c*) liabilities to IMF and IBRD (302 million crowns in 1948 only), and (*d*) other (324 million crowns in 1947 and 1 million crowns in 1948).

8. Gold sales by the government sector

See item 4, above.

NOTES TO TABLE 4 A: 1955–56

All entries in Table 4 A are based on reconstructed current account transactions for the years 1955 and 1956, shown in Appendix Table 28. Item by item documentation to Table 4 A will follow the notes to the appendix table.

APPENDIX TABLE 28
CURRENT CZECHOSLOVAK FOREIGN SECTOR TRANSACTIONS,
1955–56
(*Million crowns*)

		1955			1956	
(1)	(2)	(3)	(4)	(5)	(6)	(7)
			Net			Net
Transactions	Credit	Debit	Credit	Credit	Debit	Credit
a. Goods	8,467	7,579	888	9,988	8,537	1,451
b. Foreign travel	25	80	– 55	25	80	– 55
c. Transportation	127	379	– 252	150	427	– 277
d. Insurance	10	19	– 9	12	21	– 9
e. Miscellaneous	53	242	– 189	53	242	– 189
f. Subtotal	8,682	8,299	383	10,228	9,307	921
g. Government purchases	50	100	– 50	50	100	– 50
h. Total goods and services	8,732	8,399	333	10,278	9,407	871

NOTES TO APPENDIX TABLE 28

a. State Statistical Office, *Statistická ročenka*, 1957, p. 203.

b. Estimated for both years on the basis of the 1956 number of visitors from abroad (35,000, see *Statistický obzor*, 1957, No. 3, p. 109) and to abroad (111,000, see *ibid.*), on the assumption that each of them spent roughly 100 dollars, that is, 720 crowns (for rate of exchange see State Statistical Office, *Statistická ročenka*, 1957, p. 297). The assumed average expenditure is based on information in *Statistický obzor*, 1957, No. 4, p. 160.

c. We calculated the cost of transportation at roughly 1.5 percent on exports and 5 percent on imports. These figures are based on the ratio of transportation charges to the turnover of goods in 1948 (2.03 percent for exports and 6.35 percent for imports—see International Monetary Fund, *Balance of Payments Yearbook, 1948 and 1949*, pp. 139–42), modified in the light of Hungarian figures (1.5 and 4.3 percent respectively, calculated from Hungary, Central Statistical Office, *Adatok és Adalékok a népgazdaság fejlödésének tanulmányozásához, 1949–1955*, pp. 293, 318–19, 331–32). The similar geographical positions with respect to trade partners and shifts in the geographical structure of trade toward the Soviet bloc suggested the adjustment based on the more recent data.

d. Cost of insurance was estimated to be roughly proportionate to the cost of transportation, using the 1948 ratio of the two items (see International Monetary Fund, *Balance of Payments Yearbook 1948 and 1949*, pp. 139–42).

e. "Miscellaneous," as defined in *ibid.*, includes film royalties, licenses and patents, commissions, postal services, and so forth. We used the 1948 figure for both years, adjusted for the change in currency in 1953, that is, divided by five.

f. Subtotal represents enterprise sector transactions.

g. Government transactions represent mainly the cost of diplomatic representation. We used 1948 figures for both years, roughly rounded and adjusted for the 1953 change in currency.

1. Imports of goods and services
A. By the enterprise sector

See Appendix Table 28, row f, columns *3* and *6*. The values there are in foreign exchange crowns, that is, in world prices corrected to crowns at the official rate of exchange. On the basis of scattered information on Czechoslovak foreign trade prices and on the basis of comparable situations prevailing in Hungary and Poland, it seemed clear that the official exchange rate failed to convert external values into domestic prices (Compare Alton and associates, National Income and Product of Hungary in 1955, and their National Income and Product of Poland, 1954–56). We used 1.85 as the ratio for converting foreign exchange crowns into domestic crowns on the basis of the following considerations.

Nová Mysl, June, 1958, p. 550, stated that the foreign trade turnover in 1956 amounted to 23.9 percent of the national income. We assumed this to refer to the turnover in domestic crowns, since otherwise the figure would be too large to be consistent with the data in foreign exchange crowns. We estimated the relevant national income figure according to the Czechoslovak official definition at 143 billion crowns (see above, Chapter III, p. 75; our estimate for 1955, 135 billion crowns, was increased by 6 percent for 1956 in keeping with the official index in unspecified prices in State Statistical Office, *Statistická ročenka,* 1957, p. 15). Accordingly, trade turnover would amount to 34.2 billion domestic crowns, but *ibid.,* 1959, p. 363, shows only 18.5 billion (foreign exchange) crowns. We used the ratio between these values, 1.85, to convert the values in row f, Appendix Table 28, to domestic crowns. An unknown margin of error is attached to our rough conversion factor, but on balance it seemed preferable to use such an approximation than to mix values in foreign exchange crowns with other values in domestic crowns.

B. By the government sector
See Appendix Table 28, net figures in row g, columns *4* and *7.*

2. Balance on production account
This is the balancing item; total payables less the specified receivables.

3. Exports of goods and services
A. By the enterprise sector
The figures in Appendix Table 28, row f, columns *2* and *5,* were multiplied by 1.85, the estimated average rate of exchange between domestic crowns and foreign exchange crowns (see note 1.A, above).

B. By the government sector
We show only the net figures under item 1.B.

4. Balance on production account
Not applicable on the payable side in 1955–56.

NOTES TO TABLE 4 B: 1955–56

1. Balance on production account
Not applicable on the receivable side in 1955–56.
2. Surplus of nation on current account
This was taken equal to the balance of the production account, item 2 in Table 4 A. There is no evidence of any net factor payments to the nation.
3. Balance on production account
See Table 4 A, item 2.
4. Deficit of nation on current account
Not applicable in 1955–56.

NOTES TO TABLE 4 C: 1955–56

1. Deficit of nation on current account
Not applicable in 1955–56.
2. Transfers from other sectors
A. From the household sector
No data were available.
B. From the government sector
For 1955 no information was available. For 1956 this is a grant to Hungary; see *Népszabadság,* December 31, 1956.

3. Borrowing from other sectors
A. From the household sector
No information was available.
B. From the government sector
The figures represent the balancing item of the foreign sector capital account; it serves to cover the nation's surplus with the rest of the world. Since our estimates of imports and exports are expressed in domestic crowns (see note to item 1.A of Table 4 A for 1955–56), they affect this balancing item. In particular, the latter should not be interpreted as actual obligations; these should be expressed in foreign exchange currency, since the domestic crown is not used in foreign transactions. The "borrowing" shown here follows from our accounting in domestic crowns; alternatively, the item could be construed as a mixture of borrowing and transfers required to balance the account.

4. Gold purchases by the government sector
No information was available.
5. Surplus of nation on current account
See Table 4 B, item 2.
6. Transfers to other sectors
A. To the household sector
We assumed an unchanged level of net private transfers since 1948 (see International Monetary Fund, *Balance of Payments Yearbook, 1948 and 1949,* p. 139; the net figure was divided by 5 to allow for the 1953 monetary reform). This assumption seems not unreasonable; although the amounts received by individual citizens may have decreased owing to obstacles of various kinds, the number

of persons receiving gifts probably increased because of an increase in emigration from Czechoslovakia after 1948.

B. *To the government sector*
  No information was available on this item.
7. *Lending to the government sector*
  No information was available on this item.
8. *Gold sales by the government sector*
  No information was available on this item.

APPENDIX E: EMPLOYMENT AND WAGE BILL IN THE GOVERNMENT AND ENTERPRISE SECTORS

In this Appendix we present tables showing the Czechoslovak wage bill by sectors. There are some differences between the breakdown in 1947–48 and that in 1955–56; these are due to organizational changes and to the differences in the information. Social security contributions are not shown in the tables referring to 1947 and 1948, since they could be computed independently of the wage bill. Owing to technical feasibility, the data for 1947 and 1948 are shown in separate tables, whereas 1955 and 1956 figures are found in one table.

NOTES TO APPENDIX TABLE 29

I. Government sector
A. State administration
   Employment in column (5) is based on data in State Statistical Office, *Zprávy,* 1948, Nos. 99–102, p. 745–48 (referring to January 31, 1947, and January 31, 1948, and *ibid.,* 1949, Nos. 55–58, pp. 421–23.
   Average salary in column (6) was derived from figures in columns (5) and (7).
   Total earnings in column (7) are the sum of (1) wages and salaries excluding the Defense Ministry (13,051 million crowns, National Assembly, *Státní závěrečný účet,* 1947, p. 13), (2) wages and salaries of the Defense Ministry administrative personnel (708 million crowns), and (3) severance pay (222 million crowns). Item (2) was estimated from the average salary in the state administration excluding the Defense Ministry, and from an estimate of the number of Defense Ministry administrative personnel, made on the basis of data as in column (5) above. Item (3) was estimated in the follow-

ing way. We calculated the difference between the total expenditures on personnel (shown in National Assembly, *Státní závěrečný účet, 1947,* p. 13) and the sum of the wages and salaries and pensions. It includes (*a*) employer's social security contributions, (*b*) per diem allowances, and (*c*) severance pay (see Spáčil, *Veřejné hospodářství československé v roce 1947,* p. 11).

Social insurance contributions paid by the employer (the government) were estimated at 4 percent of the gross wage and salary bill. (See information on social security contribution rates published in Busek and Spulber, *Czechoslovakia,* p. 214. This source shows 6 percent, but it is believed that employees paid 2 percent and the employer the balance as indicated in the source's footnote for 1950.) Per diem allowances were arbitrarily assumed to have accounted for 80 percent of the remainder of "other expenditures on personnel" after the deduction of employer's social security contributions; the rest was assumed to represent severance pay. (Severance pay in the Defense Ministry was regarded as insignificant.)

B. Military establishment

The 1947 figures for military pay were based on oral information from a former army officer and on assumptions that are summarized below, together with the calculations.

SIZE, STRUCTURE AND PAY OF THE ARMED FORCES

Personnel Category	Number	Average Annual Pay (crowns)	Total Pay (million crowns)
Commissioned officers	15,000	50,000	750
Warrant officers	6,000	30,000	180
Noncommissioned officers	25,000	15,000	375
Enlisted men	104,000	3,650	380
Total	150,000	(11,233)	1,685

The figure under the heading "average annual pay" for enlisted men (who received no regular pay) refers to a daily allowance of 10 crowns per man.

C. Trade unions

Salaries of trade union employees were computed from the average number of trade union officials and their average earnings. The 1947

APPENDIX TABLE 29

EMPLOYMENT AND CASH EARNINGS IN THE GOVERNMENT AND ENTERPRISE SECTORS, 1947

(1)	(2) Wage Earners	(3) Average Annual Wage (crowns)	(4) Total Wages (million crowns)	(5) Salaried Employees	(6) Average Annual Salary (crowns)	(7) Total Salaries (million crowns)	(8) Total Earnings (4) plus (7) (million crowns)
I. Government sector							
A. State administration				209,072	66,872	13,981	13,981
B. Military establishment				150,000	11,233	1,685	1,685
C. Trade unions				7,452	50,000	373	373
D. Political parties				7,000	50,000	350	350
E. Social security system				15,000	38,622	579	579
F. Local administration				100,779	50,020	5,041	5,041
Total				489,303		22,009	22,009
II. Economic enterprise sector							
A. Agriculture and forestry	252,533	20,625	5,208	12,890	34,712	447	5,655
B. Industry	1,096,358	39,049	42,812	195,528	60,490	11,827	54,639
C. Industrial crafts and trades	387,813	26,237	10,175	—	—	—	10,175
D. Trade, banking, and insurance	83,401	30,075	2,508	202,284	38,622	7,813	10,321
E. Transportation (privately operated)	31,661	30,046	951	12,257	38,622	473	1,424
F. Health service	20,745	25,418	527	18,823	35,024	659	1,186
G. Other services	31,922	19,423	620	31,588	34,974	1,105	1,725
H. Nonprofit organizations serving enterprises	3,073	58,623	180	27,525	58,623	1,614	1,794
I. State enterprises	319,828	46,977	15,025	—	—	—	15,025
J. Local government enterprises	28,325	34,069	965	—	—	—	965
Total	2,255,659		78,971	500,895		23,938	102,909
Less: Adjustment for benefits in kind in industry							1,300
Net cash total							101,609

number of officials is given as 7,452 in State Statistical Office, *Statistical Digest of the Czechoslovak Republic, 1948,* p. 41, referring to September 30, 1947, and was taken as equivalent to the number of employees; to the extent that it includes unpaid officials, their number is assumed to be equal to the number of hired personnel. The 1947 average salaries were assumed to have been 50,000 crowns, about the same as the average for local administration employees (see item F).

D. Political parties

This is a rough estimate based on the assumed membership in political parties (about 2 million), allowing for paid employees in about the same proportion as for union officials to union membership (0.35 percent, see State Statistical Office, *Statistical Digest of the Czechoslovak Republic, 1948,* p. 41) and average salaries as in local administration.

E. Social security system

Wages and salaries of employees of the social security system were computed from estimates of employment (15,000 persons) and average salaries in trade, banking, and insurance services (38,-622 crowns in 1947, see item II.D). Employment was estimated from 1933–35 data on total wage and salary bills of social security institutions, and on average wages and salaries during this period (see State Statistical Office, *Statistická ročenka,* 1937, pp. 182–86 and p. 223). Since the social security system was not subject to any major reorganization until the latter part of 1948, employment was assumed relatively stable until 1948.

F. Local administration

Employment was based on census data as of July 31, 1947, given in State Statistical Office, *Zprávy,* 1948, Nos. 54–55, pp. 394, 407.

Average salaries were calculated from data on basic earnings (excluding allowances) in local administration and enterprises combined (*ibid.,* 1948, Nos. 54–55, pp. 394, 407, and Nos. 99–102, pp. 756–57). As a first step, 1947 basic earnings in local administration and enterprises combined (for which basic data were not available) were estimated from the corresponding 1948 figure on the basis of the change from 1947 to 1948 of the combined average earnings in central state administration and state enterprises. As a second step, these combined averages were broken down into separate averages for local administration and local enterprises on the basis of the ratios between the corresponding categories in the state sector. As a third step, the resulting computations were adjusted upward by the appropriate ratios of actual average earnings (including all allowances and severance pay) and calculated basic average earnings (excluding all allowances) in the state sector. (For actual earnings, see A, above; for basic earnings, see State Statistical Office, *Zprávy*, 1948, Nos. 99–102, p. 756).

II. Economic enterprise sector
A. Agriculture and forestry

Employment figures in columns (2) and (5) were calculated as simple arithmetic averages of quarterly data; for May 1, see State Statistical Office, *Statistical Bulletin of Czechoslovakia*, 1947, Nos. 5–6, p. 78; for August 1 and November 1, see *ibid.*, 1948, No. 8, pp. 140–41; the missing February 1 figure was estimated from November, 1946, data in *Statistický zpravodaj*, 1947, No. 5, pp. 194–95, using the rate of change in agricultural employment between November 1, 1947, and February 1, 1948, given in *ibid.*, 1948, No. 9, pp. 320–21. The results were adjusted upward by 1.2 percent. This adjustment, as well as a 3.755 percent upward adjustment of average wages and salaries, is applicable to data originating with the National Health Insurance Institute as explained in Note 1.A to Table 1 A, page 91, above. Average wages in column (3) and salaries in column (6) were calculated from quarterly data given in State Statistical Office, *Statistical Bulletin of Czechoslovakia*, 1948, No. 9, pp. 159–60, and *Statistický zpravodaj*, 1947, No. 12, p. 454, and were raised 3.755 percent as indicated above.

B. Industry

Employment in Columns (2) and (5) represents annual averages calculated from monthly and quarterly data (excluding apprentices) in State Statistical Office, *Průmyslové zprávy*, 1948, Nos. 7–8, pp. 42–44. Average wages and salaries, columns (3) and (6), were derived from wage and salary totals and employment figures, without adjustment for the inclusion of apprentices in wages and salaries and their exclusion from employment.

Total wages and salaries in columns (4) and (7) are from State Statistical Office, *Průmyslové zprávy*, 1948, Nos. 7–8, pp. 47–49.

Compensation of apprentices (380 million crowns) is included. The wage total includes benefits in kind (see State Statistical Office, *Zprávy,* 1949, Nos. 15–17, p. 126); these were subtracted from the final earnings total (see below).

C. Industrial crafts and trades

Employment figures represent the sum of data for the Czech lands given in State Statistical Office, *Zprávy,* 1948, Nos. 113–17, pp. 885–87 (as of January 1, 1947) and of data for Slovakia given in Slovakia, State Planning and Statistical Office, *Statistická príručka Slovenska 1948,* pp. 161–62 (as of December 31, 1947).

Average and total wages and salaries were calculated from data for individual branches, as shown in Appendix Table 30. The employment column is from the same sources as above. The average wages in individual branches were estimated from the corresponding 1948 data and from the 1947–48 percentage change of average earnings (wages and salaries combined) in the corresponding branches of industry (sources as in B [industry], above).

APPENDIX TABLE 30
AVERAGE EARNINGS IN INDUSTRIAL CRAFTS AND TRADES IN 1947

Branch	Number of Employees	Average Earnings (crowns)	Total Earnings (million crowns)
Stone, clay and glass working	9,841	31,921	314.1
Metalworking	87,746	27,738	2,433.9
Paper and chemical plants	9,861	25,180	248.3
Textile and clothing manufacture	78,389	20,233	1,586.0
Leather processing	25,901	24,445	633.1
Woodworking	40,228	25,683	1,033.2
Food processing	52,395	22,516	1,179.7
Building and construction trades	83,452	32,916	2,746.9
All industrial crafts and trades	387,813	26,237	10,175.2

D. Trade, banking and insurance
E. Transportation (privately operated)
F. Health service
G. Other services

The method of calculation and sources are the same as above in A (agriculture and forestry), except for the November 1, 1946, employment data, and these were compiled from data on Czech lands (obtained as in agriculture and forestry) and on Slovakia (February

Appendix Table 31

EMPLOYMENT AND CASH EARNINGS IN THE GOVERNMENT AND ENTERPRISE SECTORS, 1948

(1)	(2) Wage Earners	(3) Average Annual Wage (crowns)	(4) Total Wages (million crowns)	(5) Salaried Employees	(6) Average Annual Salary (crowns)	(7) Total Salaries (million crowns)	(8) Total Earnings (4) plus (7) (million crowns)
I. Government sector							
A. State administration				215,566	67,455	14,541	14,541
B. Military establishments				150,000		1,854	1,854
C. Trade unions				8,200	53,000	435	435
D. Political parties				6,000	53,000	318	318
E. Social security system				15,000	43,102	647	647
F. Local administration				104,890	51,015	5,351	5,351
Total				499,656		23,146	23,146
II. Economic enterprise sector							
A. Agriculture and forestry	252,533	23,018	5,813	12,890	38,739	499	6,312
B. Industry	1,170,183	43,867	51,332	224,026	65,175	14,601	65,933
C. Industrial crafts and trades	325,150		8,934	—	—	—	8,934
D. Trade, banking, and insurance	78,209	33,564	2,625	207,448	43,102	8,941	11,566
E. Transportation (privately operated)	33,451	33,531	1,122	12,626	43,102	544	1,666
F. Health service	20,020	28,366	568	16,585	39,087	648	1,216
G. Other services	27,932	21,676	605	31,187	39,031	1,217	1,822
H. Nonprofit organizations serving enterprises	5,622	60,443	340	24,706	60,443	1,493	1,833
I. State enterprises	306,608	54,309	16,652	—	—	—	16,652
J. Local government enterprises	27,292	36,238	989	—	—	—	989
Total	2,247,000		88,980	529,468		27,943	116,923
Less: Adjustment for benefits in kind in industry							1,500
Net cash total							115,423

28, 1947 data were used; see Slovakia, State Planning and Statistical Office, *Statistická príručka Slovenska 1948*, pp. 56–59).

Public transportation is included in state and local government enterprises.

Wages and salaries in "hygiene and cosmetics," included in G (other services), were assumed to be the same as those of domestic servants (see note 1.A to Table 1 A).

H. Nonprofit organizations serving enterprises

We classified as such: (1) professional associations in agriculture and forestry, (2) industrial and craft associations, (3) professional associations in trade, banking, and transportation, and (4) associations for liberal professions. The employment and salary data were estimated in the same way as those of nonprofit organizations serving households (see note to item B.2, Table 1 A, above).

I. State enterprises

Employment in column (2) includes salaried personnel and was computed as the arithmetic average of data for four periods (end of January, April, July, and October, 1947) given in Dolanský, *Výklad k rozpočtu,* 1949, p. 218. Average wages (column 3) were derived from totals of employment and earnings.

Total earnings include wages and salaries (14,850 million crowns, see National Assembly, *Státní závěrečný účet,* 1947, pp. 23–24) and the severance pay, estimated as part of "other outlays on personnel" (174.7 million crowns, see *ibid.*). The estimating procedure was the same as in the case of state administration (see note above).

J. Local government enterprises

As under I.F (local administration), above.

Adjustment for benefits in kind in industry

Total benefits in kind in industry were estimated at roughly 3 percent of the industrial wage bill. Total wage supplements in cash and in kind represented about 6 percent of the wage bill (see State Statistical Office, *Zprávy,* 1949, Nos. 15–17, p. 126); we assume that the cash supplements to the wage total for all industry was 3 percent, somewhat less than in metallurgy and metal working industry (3.4 percent in 1948, see *ibid.*), which offered lower benefits in kind than the average. Benefits in kind would then represent the remaining 3 percent.

NOTES TO APPENDIX TABLE 31

1. Government Sector
A. State administration

As in Appendix Table 29. The components of 1948 total earnings in column (7) are: (1) wages and salaries, excluding the Defense Ministry (13,557 million crowns, see National Assembly, *Státní závěrečný účet,* 1948, p. 13); (2) wages and salaries of the Defense Ministry administrative personnel (750 million crowns); (3) severance pay (234 million crowns).

B. Military establishment

Employment was assumed the same as in 1947; total earnings were assumed 10 percent higher (see Table 29). Average salary was derived from employment and earnings totals.

C. Trade unions

Employment was assumed about 10 percent above the 1947 figure. The average salary of 53,000 crowns was roughly estimated following the percentage increase in average salaries in nationalized industry (about 6 percent, derived from data given in State Statistical Office, *Průmyslové zprávy,* 1948, Nos. 7–8, pp. 42–44, and its *Zprávy,* 1949, Nos. 15–17, pp. 117–18 and 126–27).

D. Political parties

Employment was estimated roughly so as to reflect the process of partial liquidation of the noncommunist parties and their administrative machines. Average salary was estimated as in the case of trade unions (see above).

E. Social security system

Employment as in 1947. As average salaries we applied those of trade, banking, and insurance services (see under II.D, below).

F. Local administration

Employment figures are based on the interpolation of data in State Statistical Office, *Zprávy,* 1948, Nos. 54–55, pp. 394, 407; and Nos. 99–102, pp. 756–57. For average salaries, see *ibid.*

II. Economic Enterprise Sector

A. Agriculture and forestry

Employment was assumed the same as in 1947. Average wages and salaries were assumed to have increased above the 1947 level at the 1947–48 rate of increase of industrial wages and salaries (11.6 percent, calculated from data in the State Statistical Office, *Průmyslové zprávy,* 1948, Nos. 7–8, pp. 42, 47, and its *Zprávy,* 1949, Nos. 15–17, pp. 117, 126).

B. Industry

Employment figures (excluding apprentices) are from State Statistical Office, *Zprávy,* 1949, Nos. 15–17, pp. 117–18. Average wages and salaries were derived from employment and earnings totals. No adjustment was made in the employment figure for the excluded apprentices. Total wages and salaries in columns *(4)* and *(7)* are from *ibid.,* p. 126. The figures include 450 million crowns of allowances to apprentices.

The 1948 coverage of data under "industry" is not entirely comparable with 1947 because of the 1948 reclassification of part of building and construction trades into industry. This was due to nationalization of enterprises in the early part of 1948.

As in 1947, the value of benefits in kind, included in the wage total, was subtracted from the final total (see below).

C. Industrial crafts and trades

Total employment is the sum of estimates for individual branches in the Czech lands and in Slovakia. The estimates for the Czech lands were obtained as averages of data for January 1, 1947 (see corresponding note to Appendix Table 29) and those for December 31, 1948 (see *Statistický zpravodaj,* 1949, No. 11, p. 413). In the case of building and construction trades, we used the December 31, 1948, data; the 1948 nationalization measures suddenly reduced the number of building trades employees classified under crafts and trades, and this made an estimate by means of averaging inappropriate. Employment figures for Slovakia are simple arithmetic averages of employment data as of January 1, 1948, or December 31, 1947 (see Slovakia, State Planning and Statistical Office, *Statistická príručka Slovenska 1948,* pp. 161–62) and of December 31, 1948 (see *Statistický zpravodaj,* 1949, No. 11, p. 413).

Average wages were derived from the employment and wages

APPENDIX TABLE 32

EMPLOYMENT AND WAGE BILL IN THE GOVERNMENT AND
ENTERPRISE SECTORS, 1955–56

	(1)		(2)		(3)
		Employment excluding Apprentices (thousand persons)		Monthly Average Wage (crowns)	
Branch of Employment		1955	1956	1955	1956
I. Government sector					
A. Administration and justice		128	125	1,233	1,242
B. Education and culture		201	205	1,057	1,125
C. Health and social welfare		155	161	1,033	1,092
D. Science and research		57	69	1,499	1,550
E. Social organizations		33	33	702	709
F. Internal security		65	65	1,197	1,243
G. Army personnel		230	191	—	—
Total I, A–G		869	849		
II. Enterprise sector					
A. Agriculture					
1. Socialized (excluding collective farms)		317	311	913	1,013
2. Collective farms		7	8	913	1,013
3. Private farms		4	3	913	1,013
Total II, A		328	322		
B. Other branches					
1. Socialized (including wages in kind)					
(a) Industry		1,904	1,950	1,280	1,315
(b) Construction		431	454	1,364	1,421
(c) Forestry		94	103	1,078	1,067
(d) Transportation, communications		329	340	1,281	1,315
(e) Trade		456	463	1,020	1,075
(f) Communal services		73	80	1,019	1,011
(g) Housing		22	25	723	800
(h) Banking, insurance		30	30	1,121	1,165
(i) Cultural enterprises		32	33	1,057	1,125
(j) Nonclassified		16	16	—	—
Total II.B.(1), including wages in kind		3,387	3,494		
(k) Wages in kind					
Total II.B.(1), excluding wages in kind					
2. Private		10	10	1,325	1,372
Total II.B, excluding wages in kind		3,397	3,504		
Total II.A and II.B, excluding wages in kind		3,725	3,826		
Total for the national economy (I and II), excluding wages in kind		4,594	4,675		

(4) Annual Wage Bill excluding Apprentices' Compensation (million crowns)		(5) Employment, Apprentices Only (thousands)	(6) Annual Wage Bill, Apprentices Only (million crowns)		(7) Total Annual Wage Bill (4) plus (6) (million crowns)		(8) Social Security Contributions (million crowns)	
1955	1956	1955, 1956	1955	1956	1955	1956	1955	1956
1,894	1,863				1,894	1,863	189	186
2,546	2,763				2,546	2,763	255	276
1,921	2,110				1,921	2,110	192	211
1,025	1,283				1,025	1,283	103	128
278	281				278	281	42	42
934	970				934	970	28	29
820	820				820	820		
9,418	10,090				9,418	10,090	809	872
3,473	3,781	13	12	13	3,485	3,794	349	379
77	97				77	97	11	15
44	36				44	36	6	5
3,594	3,914	13	12	13	3,606	3,927	366	399
29,245	30,771	33	32	33	29,277	30,804		
7,055	7,742	8	7	8	7,062	7,750		
1,216	1,319	2	2	2	1,218	1,321		
5,058	5,365	3	3	3	5,061	5,368		
5,581	5,973	10	9	11	5,590	5,984		
893	971	3	3	3	896	974		
191	240				191	240		
404	419				404	419		
409	450				409	450		
296	309				296	309		
50,348	53,559	59	56	60	50,404	53,619	5,183	5,514
145	150				145	150		
50,203	53,409	59	56	60	50,259	53,469		
159	165				159	165	24	25
50,362	53,574	59	56	60	50,418	53,634		
53,956	57,488	72	68	73	54,024	57,561	5,573	5,938
63,374	67,578	72	68	73	63,442	67,651	6,382	6,810

totals. Total wages are from *Statistický zpravodaj,* 1949, No. 11, p. 413.

D. *Trade, banking and insurance*
E. *Transportation (private)*
F. *Health services*
G. *Other services*
Employment is from *Statistický zpravodaj,* 1948, No. 9, pp. 320–21 (data refer to February 1, 1948), adjusted upward by 1.2 percent (see above, p. 91).

Average wages and salaries were assumed to have increased above the 1947 level at the 1947–48 rate of increase of industrial wages and salaries (see under II.A).

H. *Nonprofit organizations serving enterprises*
As in 1947 (see the corresponding note to Appendix Table 29).

I. *State enterprises*
Employment was calculated as the arithmetic average of data for January 31, 1948, and January 31, 1949, as published in State Statistical Office, *Zprávy,* 1948, Nos. 99–102, pp. 745–48, and 1949, Nos. 55–58, pp. 421–23.

Average wages were derived from employment and wage totals. Total earnings include wages and salaries (16,308 million crowns, see National Assembly, *Státní závěrečný účet,* 1948, pp. 23–24) and the severance pay (344 million crowns estimated in the same way as in 1947; see the corresponding note to Appendix Table 29).

J. *Local government enterprises*
Employment was estimated as above in I.F (local administration). Average salaries were calculated from data on basic earnings (excluding allowances)in local administration and enterprises combined (see State Statistical Office, *Zprávy,* 1948, Nos. 99–102, p. 755). The salary rates paid in enterprises were estimated as explained above in I.F (local government), steps two and three.
Adjustment for benefits in kind in industry
As in 1947.

NOTES TO APPENDIX TABLE 32

Explanatory notes are arranged first by columns, then by rows.

Column 1

Employment categories are defined by the main activity of the employment enterprise (see State Statistical Office, *Statistická ročenka*, 1957, p. 67). Source data were rearranged in groups matching categories of our framework of accounts.

Columns 2, 3, and 4

All data on employment and average wages, and consequently on the total annual wage bill, were obtained from *ibid.*, 1957, p. 69, unless specified otherwise in notes to individual entries.

Column 5

Data on the number of apprentices in 1955 were obtained from *Statistické zprávy*, 1957, No. 1, p. 27, and were used for the year 1956 as well.

Column 6

Data on apprentices' compensation were obtained as follows: We calculated the difference between the total wage bill of the socialized sector, including apprentices' compensation (61,595 million crowns in 1955 and 65,756 million in 1956, see *Statistické zprávy*, 1957, No. 3, p. 29) and the same wage bill excluding apprentices' compensation (61,527 and 65,683 million crowns in 1955 and 1956, respectively; see State Statistical Office, *Statistická ročenka*, 1957, p. 69). The difference was then divided by the total number of apprentices (72 thousand) to get the average apprentice compensation used in each employment category.

Column 7

Column 4 plus column 6.

Column 8

Social security contributions are those paid by the employer. (Employee's contributions to social security are considered to be included, according to some official interpretations, in the wage tax.) They were calculated in accord with the government decree of September 28, 1953, National Assembly, *Sbírka zákonů*, 1953, No. 84) specifying that social security contributions were to represent, as a rule, 10 percent of gross wages, with two exceptions: (i) a 15 percent rate applying to employees in the private sector, social organiza-

APPENDIX TABLE 33

CALCULATION OF SOCIAL SECURITY CONTRIBUTIONS IN THE SOCIALIZED ENTERPRISE SECTOR
EXCLUDING AGRICULTURE, 1955–56

(1)	(2) Number of Employees (thousands)		(3) Average Monthly Wage (crowns)		(4) Total Wages (million crowns)		(5) Social Security Contributions (million crowns)	
	1955	1956	1955	1956	1955	1956	1955	1956
15 percent rate								
a. Manufacturing cooperatives	98	101	1,280	1,315	1,505	1,594	226	239
b. Trading and catering cooperatives	113	114	1,000	1,051	1,356	1,438	203	216
c. Total a and b	211	215	—	—	2,861	3,032	429	455
10 percent rate								
d. Rest of the socialized sector outside agriculture	3,176	3,279	—	—	47,543	50,587	4,754	5,059
e. Total c and d	—	—	—	—	50,404	53,619	5,183	5,514

tions, and cooperative enterprises, including agricultural collectives; and (ii) a 3 percent rate applying to internal security employees.

In order to obtain social security contributions paid by the nonagricultural enterprise sector it was necessary to calculate separately wages of cooperative enterprises to which the 15 percent rate applied (see Appendix Table 33).

NOTES TO APPENDIX TABLE 33

SOURCES: *Row a, column 2:* State Statistical Office, *Statistická ročenka,* 1957, p. 79. *Row b, column 2: Ibid.,* p. 201. *Rows a, b, column 3: Ibid.,* p. 69. For manufacturing cooperatives the average wage in industry was used, for trading and catering cooperatives, that in trade and public catering. *Row d, column 2:* Difference between employment in the socialized enterprise sector outside agriculture (Appendix Table 32, total II.B.(1), column 2) and employment in nonagricultural cooperatives (present table, row c, column 2). *Row d, column 4:* Difference between total wages in the socialized enterprise sector outside agriculture (Appendix Table 32, total II.B.(1), column 7 and total wages in nonagricultural cooperatives (present table, row c, column 4)). *Rows a–e, column 5:* 15 percent and 10 percent of column 4, as indicated.

Specific explanations to the entries by rows in Appendix Table 32 are as follows:

I. Government sector
Government sector covers employees of government proper as well as those of the so-called social organizations, with the exception of religious institutions.

A. Administration and justice
See notes to individual columns.

B. Education and culture
Figures pertaining to the government sector were obtained as the difference between data for the comprehensive sector of "education and culture" covering government and enterprises (see column notes) and the corresponding estimates for cultural establishments in the enterprise sector (see row II.B.1.(i) and the appropriate note below). Cultural establishments of the enterprise sector were presumed

to operate independently of the budget, covering their costs largely from their own receipts (for example, ticket sales). Social security contributions in the government sector were estimated at 10 percent of the wage bill.

C. Health and social welfare

All employed persons listed under this title were assumed to be directly on government payrolls.

D. Science and research

The employment shown here is assumed to be completely in the government sector.

E. Social organizations

Employment and average wages in 1955 and 1956 from State Statistical Office, *Statistická ročenka,* 1959, p. 96, minus 5,000 persons each year for religious organizations, included in the household sector (Table 1 A).

F. Internal security

The estimated number of internal security personnel is put at 65,000, or approximately one third of the estimated strength of the regular armed forces. This proportion seems to have prevailed in Hungary, according to information from recent emigrants. Another way of using the Hungarian estimates for Czechoslovakia would be to assume the same proportion between the size of the security establishment and the number of inhabitants. If Hungary has some 50,000 internal security personnel for a population of almost 10 million, Czechoslovakia would require about 65,000 for its more than 13 million inhabitants. As average salary we used the average wage in the socialized sector of the economy, that is, 1,197 crowns in 1955 and 1,243 in 1956 (State Statistical Office, *Statistická ročenka,* 1957, p. 69).

G. Army personnel

Estimates of the Czechoslovak army strength vary between 230,-000 and 285,000 men. *Die Presse* (Vienna), June 5, 1955, estimated the then current effective force at 230,000 men. *Süd-Ost Pressedienst* (Salzburg), May 31, 1952, put it at 280,000 men for December,

1951. *Sudetendeutsche Zeitung,* March 9, 1957, put it at 285,000 men.

In the period 1955–56 the Czechoslovak government twice announced reduction in army strength—on August 24, 1955, by 34,000 men, to be effective by December, 1955 (New York *Times,* August 2, 1955), and on July 24, 1956, by a further 10,000 men (*Rudé právo,* July 26, 1956).

In the absence of better information we used the figure of 230,-000 for 1955. We reduced this by 34,000 for the cut in forces at the end of the year and by one half of the 10,000 cut announced in July, 1956, to 191,000 for our estimate for the average strength in 1956. If we take into account our estimate of 65,000 security personnel, considered to be unchanged since 1955, we get around 250,000 for the combined military and security personnel at the beginning of 1957. If some further allowance is made for paramilitary personnel other than the army and security personnel, the resulting figure would be close to the estimate of 285,000 cited above. Such a reconciliation of figures, however, is highly speculative.

We guess that there were 40,000 officers in the army in 1955 and that subsequent cuts in the armed forces did not affect the number of officers, since they probably would be left active as the basic cadres. Thus, we have an estimated 190,000 enlisted men in 1955 and 151,000 in 1956.

Before the currency reform of 1953, enlisted men were paid about 300 crowns per month, according to an oral statement by a former high government official. Allowing for the 5 to 1 conversion of old to new currency, the corresponding post-reform monthly pay would be 60 crowns per month. This figure seems to agree with a statement by the same source that border guards received about 170 to 190 crowns per month in the ranks from private to corporal and that such pay was about three times the corresponding army pay.

In the case of officers, we estimated the average pay at the average wage in the socialized sector of the economy (see State Statistical Office, *Statistická ročenka,* 1957, p. 69). In order to account for the higher pay received by the border guard members—who are part of the army, though subordinated to the Ministry of Interior—we assumed their number to be 10,000 (two thirds enlisted men, one third officers). Their pay was presumed to be three times as high as that of the regular army members. We assumed that one third of their pay, that is, the amount equal to the pay of regular army soldiers, was already included in the above estimates, and we added 120 crowns per month for the estimated 6,670 border guard privates and twice the average wage in the socialized sector for each of the estimated 3,330 border guard officers (see *ibid.*, 1957, p. 69).

Our estimates are summarized in Appendix Table 34. We rounded the figures to 820 million crowns in both 1955 and 1956.

APPENDIX TABLE 34
ESTIMATED SALARIES PAID TO ARMY PERSONNEL, 1955–56

	Number of Men	Annual Pay (crowns)	Total Pay (million crowns)
1955			
a. Enlisted army personnel	190,000	720	137
b. Army officers	40,000	14,364	575
c. Additional pay of			
(i) Border guard enlisted men	6,670	1,440	10
(ii) Border guard officers	3,330	28,728	96
Total			818
Total rounded to			820
1956			
a. Enlisted army personnel	151,000	720	109
b. Army officers	40,000	14,916	597
c. Additional pay of			
(i) Border guard enlisted men	6,670	1,440	10
(ii) Border guard officers	3,330	29,832	99
Total			815
Total rounded to			820

II. Enterprise sector

A. Agriculture

1. Socialized (excluding collective farms)
   See notes to columns.

2. Collective farms

1955: The number of hired employees in collective farms, 7,000 persons in 1955, was estimated at about one third higher than that of hired employees in the private sector of agriculture (5,000 persons, see State Statistical Office, *Statistická ročenka,* 1957, p. 139). This estimate is based on the ratio between the two categories given in a percentage breakdown of agricultural employment in 1955 (*Rudé právo,* October 6, 1956).

1956: The number of hired personnel, 8,000, is an estimated annual average falling approximately midway between 7.5 thousand persons at the beginning of 1956 and 8.6 thousand persons at the beginning of 1957. The beginning-of-the-year estimates were obtained as 2.3 percent of the corresponding total employment of collectives (327 thousand in 1956 and 372 thousand in 1957, see State Statistical Office, *Statistická ročenka,* 1957, p. 139); the 2.3 percent is the 1955 proportion derived from the total employment (300 thousand, see *ibid.*) and our estimate of hired employees (7,000 thousand, see above).

As average wages we used those paid in the socialized sector of agriculture.

3. Private farms

See State Statistical Office, *Statistická ročenka,* 1957, p. 139; for 1955 we used as annual employment the simple average of the beginning-of-the-year data; for 1956, the beginning-of-the-year number was used. As average wages we again applied those paid in the socialized sector of agriculture.

B. Other branches
1. Socialized (*including wages in kind*)

The socialized part of the enterprise sector, excluding agriculture, includes state and nationalized enterprises, as well as cooperative and municipal enterprises. Official data on wages and salaries by branches include the value of wages in kind which is given only as a total for the entire socialized sector. Therefore, it was impossible to separate the value of cash wages in kind for each individual branch.

(a) Industry

The term covers manufacturing and extractive industries.

(b) Construction

The term covers also project designing and geological surveying, in so far as it serves construction.

(c) Forestry

The term covers planting, cultivation, and preservation of forests and wild life, as well as production of timber.

(d) Transportation, communications

Figures on employment and the annual wage bill in columns (2) and (4) were computed from data given separately for the "productive" and "nonproductive" sectors (see State Statistical Office, *Statistická ročenka*, 1957, p. 69).

The average monthly wage in Appendix Table 32, column (3), was derived from the total wage bill in column (4) and employment in column (2).

(e) *Trade*

The term covers wholesale and retail trade, foreign trade, procurement of supplies (*materiální technické zásobování*), procurement of agricultural produce, and public catering enterprises (restaurants, canteens, and so forth).

(f) *Communal services*

The term covers public utilities, laundries, barbershops, swimming pools, parks, hotels, and so forth.

(g) *Housing*

The term covers occupations connected with housing services, not with housing construction.

(h) *Banking, insurance*

The term covers all banks, as well as insurance institutions outside the "national insurance" scheme, which is part of the government.

(i) *Cultural enterprises*

The basic estimate is that of wages and salaries (column 4). Employment was derived as the quotient of total wages and salaries, and the average wage in education, culture, and physical education (column (3): see State Statistical Office, *Statistická ročenka*, 1957, p. 69).

Wages and salaries shown in column (4) were derived from wages and salaries, including social security contributions (450 million crowns in 1955, 495 million crowns in 1956), which were estimated as 45 percent of 1,000 million and 1,100 million crowns, respectively, the estimated total revenues of cultural establishments presumed to operate independently of the budget and to cover their costs largely, from their own receipts (for example, ticket sales). These total revenues were estimated as the sum of estimated independent receipts, amounting to 850 million crowns in 1955 and 900 million in 1956, and government subsidies amounting to 150 million and 200 million crowns in these years. Independent receipts were estimated somewhat arbitrarily as the quasi-totality of household expenditures for entertainment in state and cooperative organizations, excluding radio and television, shown in Appendix Table 10, the residual being presumably spent on nominal fees in government-operated establishments. The amount of government subsidies was estimated roughly in the neighborhood of government subsidies to theaters in 1956 (180 million crowns; see *Hospodářské noviny,* 1958, No. 9, March 2, 1958).

The share of wages and salaries was set at 45 percent, following approximately the corresponding estimated share of wages and salaries in the 1955 total expenditures on education and culture, with government-operated and enterprise sector establishments lumped together.

These total expenditures amounted to an estimated 7,233 million crowns (sum of planned budget appropriations, 6,383 million crowns, see Appendix Table 36, and of receipts from households estimated above at 850 million crowns). Total wages and salaries plus social security contributions (10 percent) in education and culture, 3,251 million and 3,534 million crowns in 1955 and 1956, respectively, were derived from figures in State Statistical Office, *Statistická ročenka,* 1957, p. 69 (total employment 233,000 persons, monthly average wage 1,057 crowns, social security contributions equal to 10 percent of the wage bill). The estimates were divided between wages and social security contributions (which are not shown separately in column *8* of Appendix Table 32) in the usual ratio, 10 to 1.

(j) Nonclassified

This category covers miscellaneous occupations (book publishing, lawyers, scrap collecting, and so forth). Employment for 1955 was obtained from *Statistické zprávy,* 1957, No. 1, p. 27, and was assumed to have remained unchanged in 1956. The wage bill in columns *4* and *7* was obtained as a residual by taking total wages and salaries, including wages in kind (see below, Appendix Table 35, row h), and subtracting therefrom the sum of wages and salaries in 1955 and 1956, respectively: (1) in the government sector (9,418 million and 10,090 million crowns), and religious institutions (42 million and 43 million crowns), (2) in socialized and private agriculture (3,594 million and 3,914 million crowns), (3) in individual categories of the enterprise sector outside agriculture, except "nonclassified," which is to be determined (50,052 million and 53,250 million crowns in the socialized sector and 159 million and 165 million crowns in the private sector), and (4) apprentices' compensation (68 million and 73 million crowns). The small residual derived in this manner may be greatly in error; accordingly, no attempt was made to show average monthly wages.

(k) Wages in kind

This is estimated on information that wages in kind in industry amounted to 0.4 percent of the total wage fund in industry, both in 1955 and 1956 (see State Statistical Office, *Statistická ročenka,* 1957, p. 97). Applying this percentage to the wage bill in industry yields 117 million crowns in 1955 and 123 million in 1956 (see row II.B.1.(a)). These figures were rounded upward to 145 and 150 million crowns in order to allow for the value of wages in kind in the nonindustrial branches of the enterprise sector outside agriculture.

2. Private

Employment was estimated arbitrarily at 10,000 persons (in terms of full-time employees) for both 1955 and 1956, in consideration of the widespread part-time work of many persons whose main occupation is in the socialized sector. Using only official sources would yield two alternative estimates, both of which seem too low: (i) 4,834 persons in 1956, which is the difference between the total number of persons working in private handicraft and analogous trades (49,834 persons; see State Statistical Office, *Statistická ročenka,* 1957, p. 180), and the number of self-employed, not counting farmers (45,000 persons; *ibid.,* p. 68); (ii) 2,000 persons in 1956, which is the difference between 5,000 employees in the private sector (see *ibid.,* p. 68), and 3,000 hired employees working on private farms (*ibid.,* p. 139).

For the average monthly wage we used that of construction workers (1,325 crowns in 1955 and 1,372 in 1956; see *ibid.,* 1957, p. 105). This corresponds to our guess that the average wage should be somewhat above the average wage in industry but below the wages cited occasionally by the press. For example, the New York *Times,* February 19, 1958, mentioned complaints in Czechoslovakia about the "demoralizing influence" of private enterprise in paying higher than average wages to such groups of employees as private truckers, tailors, smiths, and construction workers. It cited the newspaper *Stráž míru* of Karlovy Vary as protesting wages in private enterprise as high as 9,000 crowns per month for carpenters and 6,000 for roofers and as mentioning that employees of state industry were working part-time for private employers.

Total II.B (excluding wages in kind)
Obtained by simple summation, after estimates in the category "nonclassified" had been obtained with the help of the total for the national economy established independently (see below).

Total II.A and II.B (excluding wages in kind)
Direct summation of indicated items.

Total for the national economy (I and II, excluding wages in kind)
The total wage bill (column 7) was obtained as a sum of the total wage bill in the "socialized sector of the economy" (see State Statistical Office, *Statistická ročenka,* 1957, p. 69), and of the individual estimates of categories not included in that total (see Appendix Table 32). The calculation is shown in Appendix Table 35.

APPENDIX TABLE 35
TOTAL WAGE BILL FOR GOVERNMENT AND ENTERPRISE
SECTORS, 1955–56

	Total Wages and Salaries (million crowns)	
	1955	*1956*
a. Socialized sector	61,527	65,683
b. Agricultural collectives	77	97
c. Apprentices	68	73
d. Army	820	820
e. Internal security	934	970
f. Private farms	44	36
g. Rest of private sector	159	165
h. Total	63,629	67,844
i. Less: Religious institutions	− 42	− 43
j. Less: Wages in kind	− 145	− 150
k. Total cash wages and salaries	63,442	67,651

APPENDIX F: STATE BUDGETS, 1955 AND 1956

The Czechoslovak state budgets for 1955 and 1956 had to be reconstructed from consecutive budget speeches of the Minister of Finance as well as from a report, made in the Czechoslovak legislature, on the state budget closing account for the year 1955. In Appendix Table 36 these reconstructed state budgets are presented in the official breakdown, both as planned or anticipated and as realized. For the reconstruction of the realized budget the available data had to be supplemented by estimates. In Appendix Table 37, the state budget is presented in a functional breakdown by categories corresponding to our framework of accounts. Our notes below show the sources and methods underlying our figures.

NOTES TO APPENDIX TABLE 36

A. Total revenues

1955: Planned—National Assembly, *Těsnopisecké zprávy,* Fourth Session (1955), p. 48; realized—*ibid., Seventeenth Session* (1957), p. 18. The source contains the report of the budget and economic committee on the government motion for approval of the state budget closing account for the year 1955. The report of the committee revealed only selected figures; the account itself was not published.

1956: Planned—*ibid.,* Tenth Session (1956), p. 30; realized—*ibid.,* Seventeenth Session (1957), p. 31. According to this source anticipated revenues and planned expenditures were realized to 99.6 and 98.4 percent, respectively.

1. Revenues from the socialized sector

1955: Planned—*ibid.,* Fourth Session (1955), p. 180; realized—sum of the component revenues under a, b, and c.

1956: Planned—National Assembly, *Sbírka zákonů,* No. 6, 1956,

APPENDIX TABLE 36
CZECHOSLOVAK STATE BUDGET, 1955–56
(*Million crowns*)

	1955		1956	
	Planned	*Realized*	*Planned*	*Realized*
A. Total revenues	86,209	86,425	90,304	89,943
1. Revenues from the socialized sector	73,128	73,413	77,244	76,935
a. Turnover tax and tax on services	44,935	44,992	45,830	46,288
b. Transfers of enterprise profits	13,043	13,200	14,390	13,685
c. Surplus of working capital, social security contributions, income tax of cooperatives	15,150	15,221	17,024	16,962
2. Revenues from the population	10,256	10,174	10,730	10,687
a. Wage tax	8,253	8,203	8,580	8,834
b. Agricultural tax	370	346	370	366
c. Handicraft tax	n.a.	42	42	42
d. House tax	n.a.	436	436	436
e. Miscellaneous fees	n.a. ⎱		286 ⎱	
f. Duties and various small revenues	n.a. ⎰	1,147	1,016 ⎰	1,009
3. Other revenues	2,825	2,838	2,330	2,321
B. Total expenditures	86,039	83,942	89,887	88,449
1. Development of national economy	43,864	40,757	48,093	47,586
2. Cultural and social purposes	28,276	27,073	28,779	29,349
a. Social security benefits	12,023	12,118	12,747	12,883
b. Health service	5,500	5,239	5,705	5,375
c. Education	5,065	4,576	n.a. ⎱	6,544
d. Culture	1,318	1,195	n.a. ⎰	
e. Unspecified	4,370	3,945	n.a.	4,547
3. State defense	10,430	12,643	9,606	8,105
4. State administration	3,469	3,469	3,409	3,409
C. Surplus	170	2,483	417	1,494

Appendix 1; realized—estimated in conjunction with the estimate of the realized revenues from the population (item A.2) and other revenues (item A.3). None of the three components of the realized revenues, that is, 89,943 million crowns, was available directly. Our estimates show the total distributed among the components in the same proportions as the planned total.

a. Turnover tax and tax on services
  1955: Planned—National Assembly, *Těsnopisecké zprávy,* Fourth

Session (1955), p. 78; realized—sum of the turnover tax, 43,940 million crowns, and the tax on services, 1,052 million crowns, see *ibid.*, Seventeenth Session (1957), pp. 16, 18.

1956: Planned—*ibid.*, Tenth Session (1956), p. 48; realized—*ibid.*, Seventeenth Session (1957), p. 31.

b. Transfers of enterprise profits

This official category is elsewhere referred to as profit tax.

1955: Planned—*ibid.*, Fourth Session (1955), p. 51; realized—*ibid.*, Seventeenth Session (1957), p. 19 ("Transfers of profits: plan was realized to 101.2 percent").

1956: Planned—*ibid.*, Tenth Session (1956), p. 48. Realized—*Rudé právo,* November 12, 1957: according to the source anticipated transfers of enterprise profits to government were realized to 95.1 percent and reached the sum of 13.7 billion crowns.

c. Surplus of working capital, social security contributions,
income tax of cooperatives

1955: Planned—derived as a residual. Realized—estimated in conjunction with item A.3 (other revenues): $A.1.c + A.3 = A - (A.1.a + A.1.b + A.2)$. The indicated residual in the right member of the equation was divided between the two unknowns in the left member of the equation in the ratio of the corresponding planned revenues.

1956: Planned—obtained as the residual component in the revenues from the socialized sector; realized—as in 1955.

2. Revenues from the population

1955: Planned—National Assembly, *Těsnopisecké zprávy,* Fourth Session (1955), p. 78; realized—*ibid.*, Seventeenth Session (1957), p. 16. ("Tax from the population [realized] to 99.2 percent." The source used this ambiguous term, which could mean either the total sum of direct taxes paid by the population or the total revenues from the population; we assumed it was the latter.)

1956: Planned—National Assembly, *Sbírka zákonů,* No. 6, 1956, Appendix 1; realized—see note to A.1 (revenues from the socialized sector), 1956, realized.

a. Wage Tax

1955: Planned—National Assembly, *Těsnopisecké zprávy,* Fourth Session (1955), p. 51; realized—*ibid.*, Seventeenth Session (1957), p. 19. ("The budget of the wage tax was fulfilled to 99.4 percent.")

1956: Planned—*ibid.*, Tenth Session (1956), p. 48; realized—derived from the planned 1957 wage tax revenues, which were 3.3 percent higher than the 1956 revenues (see *ibid.*, Seventeenth Session (1957), p. 53).

b. Agricultural tax

1955: Planned—*ibid.*, Tenth Session (1956), p. 39. Realized—derived from the percentage fulfillment of the anticipated tax proceeds (93.5 percent, see *ibid.*, Seventeenth Session (1957), p. 19).

1956: Planned—*ibid.*, Tenth Session (1956), p. 48; realized—derived from the agricultural tax proceeds as anticipated in 1957, that is, 324 million crowns, which was stated to be 42 million crowns less than in 1956 (see *ibid.*, Seventeenth Session [1957], p. 53).

c. Handicraft tax
d. House tax

1955: Planned—not available; realized—assumed the same as in 1956.

1956: Planned—*ibid.*, Tenth Session (1956), p. 48; realized—assumed equal to the anticipated amount.

e. Miscellaneous fees
f. Duties and various small revenues

1955: Planned—not available; realized—obtained as a residual in the total (A.2 [revenues from the population]).

1956: Planned—*ibid.*, Tenth Session (1956), p. 48; realized—as in 1955.

3. Other revenues

1955: Planned—*ibid.*, *Fourth Session* (1955), p. 180; realized—see above, note to item A.1.c.

1956: Planned—National Assembly, *Sbírka zákonů,* No. 6, 1956, Appendix 1; realized—analogous to 1955, see above.

B. Total expenditures

Same as for total revenues, see A, above.

1. Development of national economy

1955: Planned—National Assembly, *Těsnopisecké zprávy,* Fourth Session (1955), p. 63; realized—derived from the 1956 planned figure, 48,093 million crowns, which was stated to be 18 percent higher than the realized expenditures in 1955 (see *ibid.,* Tenth Session [1956], p. 30).

1956: Planned—National Assembly, *Sbírka zákonů,* No. 6, 1956, Appendix 1; realized—derived from the 1957 planned figure, 53,154 million crowns, which was stated to be 11.7 percent higher than realized outlays in 1956 (see National Assembly, *Těsnopisecké zprávy,* Seventeenth Session [1957], p. 33).

2. Cultural and social purposes

1955: Planned—*ibid.,* Fourth Session (1955), p. 49; realized—derived from the 1956 planned expenditures, 28,779 million crowns, which were stated to be 6.3 percent higher than expenditures in 1955 (see *ibid.,* Tenth Session [1956], p. 42).

1956: Planned—*ibid.,* Tenth Session (1956), p. 42; realized—derived from the 1957 planned expenditures, 31,932 million crowns, which was stated to be 8.8 percent higher than in 1956 (see *ibid.,* Seventeenth Session [1957], p. 43).

a. Social security benefits

1955: Planned—*ibid.,* Fourth Session (1955), p. 68. Realized—State Statistical Office, *Statistická ročenka,* 1957, pp. 270, 273; the figure is the sum of total health insurance benefits (5,223 million crowns) and total pension benefits (6,895 million crowns) both disbursed in the year 1955. The estimated actual outlays may not be entirely comparable with the planned outlays since the latter exclude some minor categories that the former include.

1956: Planned—National Assembly, *Těsnopisecké zprávy,* Tenth Session (1956), p. 45. Realized—State Statistical Office, *Statistická ročenka,* 1957, pp. 270, 273; the figure is the sum of total health insurance benefits (5,497 million crowns) and total pension benefits (7,386 million crowns).

b. Health service

1955: Planned—National Assembly, *Těsnopisecké zprávy,* Fourth Session (1955), p. 49; the source gives the amount as "almost five and a half billion crowns." There is an unexplained discrepancy between this information and the per capita outlays in health service planned for 1955, amounting to 385.07 crowns (see *ibid.,* Fourth Session [1955], p. 69). Multiplying this by total population, whether by that of the end of 1954, or that of mid-1955 (see State Statistical

Office, *Statistická ročenka,* 1957, p. 35), yields a product slightly above 5 billion crowns. Realized—*Těsnopisecké zprávy,* Tenth Session (1956), p. 44.

1956: Planned—derived from the statement that planned outlays in 1956 were 8.9 percent above actual 1955 outlays, above (see *ibid.,* Tenth Session (1956), p. 42); realized—derived from the planned 1957 outlays amounting to 5,638 million crowns which were stated to be 4.9 percent above 1956 outlays (see *ibid.,* Seventeenth Session [1957], p. 44).

c. Education

1955: Planned—*ibid.,* Fourth Session (1955), p. 49; as in the case of health service outlays, there is a discrepancy of about 500 million crowns between the indicated figure and the corresponding figure based on per capita outlays in education, amounting to 341.30 crowns (see *ibid.,* Fourth Session [1955], p. 69), and on the corresponding population totals given in State Statistical Office, *Statistická ročenka,* 1957, p. 35). Realized—the total of items 2.c, 2.d, and 2.e was obtained as a residual by subtracting items 2.a and 2.b from the group total, item B.2; this residual was then allocated among 2.c, 2.d, and 2.e, according to the ratios of planned expenditures.

1956: Planned—not available; realized—the sum of expenditures in education and culture (items 2.c and 2.d) was derived from the 1957 planned outlays amounting to 6,956 million crowns which were stated to be about 6.3 percent above the 1956 outlays (see National Assembly, *Těsnopisecké zprávy,* Seventeenth Session [1957], p. 43).

d. Culture

1955: Planned—product of planned per capita outlays amounting to 101.23 crowns (see *ibid.,* Fourth Session [1955], p. 69) and the population figure of end of 1954, 13,023,596 (see State Statistical Office, *Statistická ročenka,* 1957, p. 35; it was assumed that the per capita figure was calculated on the basis of current, not projected, population figures); realized—as under 2.c (education), 1955, above.

1956: Planned—not available; realized—as under 2.c, above.

e. Unspecified

1955: Planned—obtained as a residual in item B.2; realized—as under 2.c.

APPENDIX TABLE 37
STATE BUDGET, 1955–56 (ADJUSTED BREAKDOWN)
(*Million crowns*)

	1955	1956
Revenues		
A. From enterprise sector	75,916	78,941
1. Indirect taxes	45,428	46,724
2. Profit tax	13,200	13,685
3. Income tax on cooperatives	350	382
4. Agricultural tax	346	366
5. Handicraft tax	42	42
6. Transfer of working capital	1,431	1,855
7. Unspecified revenues	2,492	2,038
8. Social security contributions	5,573	5,938
9. Import price differences	7,054	7,911
B. From government sector		
Social security contributions	809	872
C. From household sector	9,700	10,130
1. Wage tax	8,203	8,834
2. Fees, duties, etc.	800	660
3. Unspecified revenues	346	283
4. Social security contributions	351	353
Total revenues	86,425	89,943
Expenditures		
D. Enterprise sector	36,836	43,214
1. Capital grants	16,264	15,031
2. Subsidies	6,406	7,687
3. Transfer of working capital	6,786	12,802
4. Export price differences	7,380	8,694
E. Government	47,106	45,235
1. Wages and salaries	9,140	1,809
a. Civilian employees	7,386	8,019
b. Internal security	934	970
c. Army personnel	820	820
2. Social security contributions		
for government employees	767	830
3. Transfers to household sector	13,491	14,576
a. Pensions and allowances	6,895	7,386
b. Social security benefits	5,223	5,497
c. Student stipends	88	110
d. Other cash transfers	1,225	1,522
e. Religious organizations	60	61
4. Purchases on capital account	2,835	3,314
5. Purchases on current account	20,873	16,706
a. Unspecified	19,973	15,956
b. Military subsistence	850	700
c. From foreign sector	50	50
Total expenditures	83,942	88,449
F. Surplus	2,483	1,494
Total	86,425	89,943

1956: Planned—not available; realized—obtained as a residual in item B.2.

3. State defense

1955: Planned—National Assembly, *Těsnopisecké zprávy,* Fourth Session (1955), p. 73; realized—within total expenditures, the residual 16,112 million crowns, covering state administration and defense, was distributed between these two categories, the planned amount being allocated to state administration, on the assumption that such outlays are regular and easy to project, and the balance to defense.

1956: Planned—National Assembly, *Sbírka zákonů,* No. 6, 1956, Appendix 1; realized—obtained by calculating the difference between total actual expenditures (88,449 million crowns) and the sum of expenditures on development of national and on cultural and social purposes; of the difference, 11,514 million crowns, the planned sum, was allocated to state administrations, on the assumption that these outlays conformed to the plan, and the balance to defense.

4. State administration

1955: Planned—National Assembly, *Těsnopisecké zprávy,* Fourth Session (1955), p. 72; realized—see note to B.3, above.

1956: Planned—as under B.3; realized—see B.3, above.

C. Surplus

1955 and 1956: Planned and realized—see above, note to item A (total revenues).

NOTES TO APPENDIX TABLE 37

Revenues
A. From the enterprise sector
1. Indirect taxes

As indirect taxes we consider the turnover tax and house tax. See Appendix Table 36, items A.1.a and A.2.d.

2. Profit tax
Iibid., item A.1.b.

3. Income tax on cooperatives

For 1956 from *Finance a úvěr,* No. 2, 1960, p. 83. For 1955 an estimate based on the 1956 figure.

4. Agricultural tax, and *5. Handicraft tax*
    See Appendix Table 36.
6. Transfers of working capital
    In both years the figure is a residual in this table. It includes surplus or working funds which some enterprises transferred to the budget, and it reflects as well any errors of estimate in other items.

7. Unspecified revenues
    This is part of item A.3, other revenues, in Appendix Table 36. The total was allocated between the enterprise sector and the household sector in the same ratio as revenues from the socialized sector and revenues from the population in Appendix Table 36 (items A.1 and A.2). A comparison with the more detailed Polish budget for 1956 (Poland, Central Statistical Office, *Rocznik Statystyczny, 1957,* p. 290) suggests that the category "other revenues" includes such items as revenues of cultural and social institutions, court fees, and so forth that originate either with the socialized sector or with the population. "Other revenues" probably also include direct payments to the government from abroad, but these were impossible to identify and therefore were disregarded.

8. Social security contributions
    See Appendix Table 32, column 8.

9. Import price differences
    See Appendix D, p. 172.
B. From government sector
Social security contributions (for government sector employees)
    See Appendix Table 32, column 8.
C. From household sector
1. Wage tax
    See Appendix Table 36, item A.2.a.
2. Fees, duties, etc.
    This is the difference between miscellaneous fees, and duties and various small revenues (items A.2.e and A.2.f in Appendix Table 36) and social security contributions of self-employed, collective farmers, and domestic servants (items 3.C.(3), Table 1 B, less item 3.C.(2), Table 1 A, the latter item not being included in the miscellaneous category of revenues from the population, but instead appearing in item A.1.c of Appendix Table 36.

3. Unspecified revenues
See notes to item A.7 above.
4. Social security contributions paid by households
See Table 1 B, item 3.C.(3).

Expenditures
As a preliminary step, we adjusted the expenditures under development of national economy and of those under the remaining three groups (cultural and social purposes, state defense, and state administration), as shown in Appendix Table 36, to make them correspond to our definition of the enterprise and government sectors. These adjusted subtotals were needed for the calculation of residuals used as estimates of transactions for which data were not available.

D. Enterprise sector
We subtracted from item B.1 in Appendix Table 36 the estimated expenditures included therein that should be classified as government sector outlays, as follows: development of technology (1,634 million crowns in 1955 and 2,085 million in 1956; see National Assembly, *Těsnopisecké zprávy,* Tenth Session (1956), p. 49); development of vegetable and animal production, agricultural research, soil improvement, etc. (1,401 million crowns in 1955, used also for 1956; see *Rudé právo,* March 23, 1955); agricultural schools (722 million crowns in 1955, used also for 1956; see *ibid.*); recruitment of labor and resettlement of the border region (164 million crowns in 1955, used also for 1956; see *ibid.*).

1. Capital grants
This is an estimate of the value of investments in the enterprise sector financed from the state budget. We took total investments within the "state investment plan" (which are financed partly by the state budget and partly by the enterprises from their own means), added thereto other investments undertaken outside the "state investment plan" but financed from the state budget (investment grants to agricultural collectives), and finally subtracted those investments of the "state investment plan" that were either financed directly by the enterprise or did not belong to the enterprise sector (investments in government proper). The calculation is shown in Appendix Table 38 and in the supporting notes which follow.

APPENDIX TABLE 38
CALCULATION OF INVESTMENTS FINANCED FROM THE
STATE BUDGET, 1955–56
(*Million crowns*)

	1955	1956
a. State investment plan	20,110	22,640
b. Capital grants to agricultural collectives	325	325
Total (a, b)	20,435	22,965
Less:		
c. Investments financed from retained profits	1,289	928
d. Investments financed from depreciation allowances	856	4,810
e. Investments in government proper	2,026	2,196
(i) Administration	941	898
(ii) Culture and education	594	640
(iii) Health service	297	322
(iv) Science and research	194	336
Total (c, d, e)	4,171	7,934
Investments financed from the state budgets	16,264	15,031

NOTES TO APPENDIX TABLE 38

a. State investment plan: See State Statistical Office, *Statistická ročenka* 1957, p. 71, Table b-1, Columns 3, 4.

b. Capital grants to agricultural collectives: see National Assembly, *Těsnopisecké zprávy,* Fourth Session (1955), p. 65; the planned figure for 1955 was used here for both 1955 and 1956.

c. Investments financed from retained profits: This represents, for 1955, 8.4 percent of total profits of nationalized enterprises amounting to 15,349 million crowns, and for 1956, 5.9 percent of 15,730 million crowns. The percentages represent the portion of total profits used for financing investments (see *Finance a úvěr,* 1958, No. 5, p. 270). Total profits of nationalized enterprises were derived from the amount of the profit tax (see item A.1.b, Appendix Table 36) and from the rate of the tax on profits (86 percent in 1955 and 87 in 1956, see *Finance a úvěr,* 1958, No. 5, p. 270). Profits used for financing investments of cooperatives were not considered because these investments are not included in the "state investment plan."

d. Investments financed from depreciation allowances: This is the difference between capital consumption allowances (6,012 million crowns in 1955 and 10,835 million crowns in 1956, see Table 2 A, item 6) and the value of capital repairs in the enterprise sector (5,156 million and 6,025 million crowns, see Appendix Tables 17 and 19); this difference is the estimated amount of depreciation allowances available for financing investments included in the "state investment plan." Depreciation allowances are not paid into the state budget as revenues (see, for example, Veltruský and others, *Československé finance,* pp. 127, 336–63).

e. Investments in government proper, (i)–(iv): See State Statistical Office, *Statistická ročenka,* 1957, p. 71. Item (ii) shown in *ibid.* was reduced by 100 million crowns in 1955 and 110 million in 1956 for estimated investment falling in the enterprise sector (see above, p. 138).

2. *Subsidies*
See Table 2 A, item 3.
3. *Transfer of working capital*
This item was derived as a residual in the group of expenditures under D; as such it reflects any errors of estimate in the other items. In particular, item 4, export price differences may possibly be incorrect, largely by the extent of the incidence of turnover tax on exports. Our assumption was that the full difference between the value of exports in domestic crowns and in foreign exchange crowns was covered by budget transfers under item 4, that is, that the possible exemption of exports from the turnover tax did not reduce the amount of the price differences to be covered by transfers.

4. *Export price differences*
See Appendix D, p. 173.
E. *Government*
The subtotal of expenditures in Appendix Table 36 under cultural and social purposes, state administration, and state defense (43,185 million and 40,863 million crowns) was increased by the value of government services originally included among expenditures under development of national economy (3,921 million crowns in 1955 and 4,372 million in 1956, see under D, above).

1. *Wages and salaries, a–c*
See Appendix E, Appendix Table 32; wages of employees of social organizations are not counted here.
2. *Social security contributions*
As under E.1, immediately above.

3. Transfers to household sector, a–e
See note to Table 1 B, item 2.B.(3).

4. Purchases on capital account
See Appendix Table 17.

5. Purchases on current account
Obtained as residual in group of expenditures under E (government).

a. Unspecified
Obtained as residual in the total under 5.

b. Military subsistence
See Table 1 B, item 2.B.(2).

c. From foreign sector
See Table 4 A, item 1.B.

F. Surplus
As in Appendix Table 36.

APPENDIX G: GROSS NATIONAL PRODUCT AT FACTOR COST BY SECTOR OF ORIGIN

In Appendix Table 39 we show our estimates of the gross national product at factor cost by sector of origin. The first three numerical columns distribute the labor returns, the adjusted returns to other factors, and the adjusted depreciation. The fourth numerical column is the sum of the other three, and serves as the basis, in absolute terms, for the percentage distribution of gross national product by origin given in Table 6. The general principles and rationale underlying our factor cost adjustments were explained in Chapter III; the actual calculation, including that of the allocation of depreciation, is presented in Appendix Tables 40, 41, 42, 49, and 50, and in supporting Tables 43 to 48.

In Chapter III we presented, in addition to Table 6, an alterna-

APPENDIX TABLE 39

GROSS NATIONAL PRODUCT BY ORIGIN AT FACTOR COST,
1947–48 AND 1955–56

(*Million crowns*)

(1)	(2)	(3)	(4)	(5)
		Returns to		
	Returns to	*Other*	*Deprecia-*	*Gross*
	Labor	*Factors*	*tion*	*Product*
1947				
Industry	73,859	10,673	9,936	94,468
Agriculture	27,366	7,111	1,995	36,472
Forestry	3,940	475	242	4,657
Construction	7,572	1,333	556	9,461
Transportation, communications	17,105	5,977	5,002	28,084
Trade, banking, insurance	18,045	3,061	669	21,775
Housing	—	8,457	5,323	13,780
Government	26,948	—	—	26,948
Other	9,401	1,108	688	11,197
Total	184,236	38,195	24,411	246,842

APPENDIX TABLE 39 (continued)

(1)	(2)	(3)	(4)	(5)
	Returns to Labor	Returns to Other Factors	Deprecia-tion	Gross Product
1948				
Industry	85,852	10,781	12,631	109,264
Agriculture	42,451	7,485	2,438	52,374
Forestry	4,463	465	296	5,224
Construction	8,054	1,319	680	10,053
Transportation, communications	18,685	5,985	6,241	30,911
Trade, banking, insurance	19,296	3,012	817	23,125
Housing	—	8,390	6,505	14,895
Government	28,368	—	—	28,368
Other	9,915	1,086	840	11,841
Total	217,084	38,523	30,448	286,055
1955				
Industry	34,600	15,469	7,757	57,826
Agriculture	14,240	8,465	1,112	23,817
Forestry	1,457	549	158	2,164
Construction	8,618	2,884	426	11,928
Transportation, communications	5,788	6,543	3,070	15,401
Trade, banking, insurance	6,992	4,145	429	11,566
Housing	218	9,401	3,286	12,905
Government	11,512	—	—	11,512
Other	2,551	1,161	406	4,118
Total	85,976	48,617	16,644	151,237
1956				
Industry	36,267	17,110	8,229	61,606
Agriculture	14,421	9,353	1,195	24,969
Forestry	1,579	607	166	2,352
Construction	9,989	3,338	448	13,775
Transportation, communications	6,135	7,045	3,130	16,310
Trade, banking, insurance	7,391	4,643	452	12,486
Housing	274	10,382	3,432	14,088
Government	12,219	—	—	12,219
Other	2,752	1,266	418	4,436
Total	91,027	53,744	17,470	162,241

tive adjustment of GNP to factor cost by sector of origin for 1955–56. The basic difference between Table 6 and the alternative calculation is that in the latter we assumed that the entire net income in agriculture (18,431 million crowns in 1955 and 19,136 million in 1956) represents returns to labor, whereas in the former a part of the net income was assigned to nonlabor factors of production. Except for this distinction, the methodology for the two approaches is

APPENDIX TABLE 40
RETURNS TO LABOR IN 1947–48
(Million crowns)

(1)	(2) Cash Wages and Salaries	(3) Wages in Kind	(4) Social Security Contributions by Employers	(5) Cash Returns to Labor of Self-employed	(6) Returns in Kind to Labor of Self-employed	(7) Total Returns to Labor
1947						
1. Industry	58,930	1,900	3,650	8,889	490	73,859
2. Agriculture	4,938	960	329	11,939	9,200	27,366
3. Forestry	2,815	540	185	400	—	3,940
4. Construction	5,884	—	329	1,359	—	7,572
5. Transportation, communications	13,306	—	2,929	870	—	17,105
6. Trade, banking and insurance	10,321	624	517	6,193	390	18,045
7. Housing	—	—	—	—	—	—
8. Government	22,009	1,000	3,939	—	—	26,948
9. Other	6,734	610	531	1,406	120	9,401
10. Total	124,937	5,634	12,409	31,056	10,200	184,236
1948						
1. Industry	68,621	2,100	6,363	8,258	510	85,852
2. Agriculture	5,623	1,008	367	13,830	21,623	42,451
3. Forestry	3,355	592	216	300	—	4,463
4. Construction	6,246	—	546	1,262	—	8,054
5. Transportation, communications	14,498	—	3,379	808	—	18,685
6. Trade, banking and insurance	11,566	711	876	5,753	390	19,296
7. Housing	—	—	—	—	—	—
8. Government	23,146	1,000	4,222	—	—	28,368
9. Other	7,002	656	851	1,306	100	9,915
10.Total	140,057	6,067	16,820	31,517	22,623	217,084

the same. We show, however, only the detailed calculations supporting Table 6.

In Appendix Tables 40 and 41 and supporting notes we show the
sources of column 2 (returns to labor) of Appendix Table 39.

NOTES TO APPENDIX TABLE 40

Column 2. Cash wages and salaries
Figures in this column are based on Appendix Tables 29 and 31.
The reference to items in the following notes refers to the notation in
these two tables.

1. Industry
Items II.B and C, excluding construction which amounted to 5,884
million crowns in 1947 and 6,246 million crowns in 1948 (see State
Statistical Office, *Průmyslové zprávy,* 1948, Nos. 7–8, pp. 47–49).

2. Agriculture, and 3. Forestry
Item II.A, which contains private agriculture and forestry, was
split between the two proportionately to employment figures for the
period from March, 1947, to February, 1948, that is, in the proportion 76 to 24 (see *Statistický zpravodaj,* 1948, No. 9, p. 320, and
State Statistical Office, *Statistical Digest of the Czechoslovak Republic,* 1948, p. 38); to agriculture were then added wages and salaries
in state farms and to forestry those in state forests (see National
Assembly, *Státní závěrečný účet,* 1947, pp. 23–24, and 1948, pp.
23–24).

4. Construction
See item 1 above.

5. Transportation and communications
This is the sum of private transportation (see item II.E) and of
state enterprises operating in this branch (see National Assembly,
Státní závěrečný účet, 1947, pp. 23–24, and 1948, pp. 23–24, and
notes to item II.I of Appendix Tables 29 and 31).

6. Trade, banking and insurance
See item II.D of Appendix Tables 29 and 31.

7. Housing

No data available. In this period before the introduction of state-operated housing the wage bill in this branch was assumed too insignificant to warrant an independent guess.

8. Government

See items I.A through I.F, Appendix Tables 29 and 31.

9. Other

Based on sources in notes to items II.F, G, H, and I, Appendix Tables 29 and 31.

Column 3. Wages in kind
1. Industry, 2. Agriculture, and 3. Forestry

Based on notes to Table 1 B, entry 2.A.(2)a. Income in kind was allocated between agriculture and forestry proportionately to their cash-wage distribution.

6. Trade, banking, and insurance, and 9. Other sectors

Wages in kind in trade and services (800 million crowns in 1947 and 900 million crowns in 1948; see notes to Table 1 B, entry 2.A.(2)a) were allocated between categories 6 and 9 in proportion to cash wages in, on the one hand, trade, banking, and insurance, and, on the other, health and other services. This proportion was 78:22 in 1947 and 79:21 in 1948 (see Appendix Tables 29 and 31, items II.D, II.F, and II.G). Wages in kind of domestic servants (see Table 1 A, entry 3.A.(2)) are covered by the present estimate under "Other."

8. Government

This is the subsistence and clothing of military personnel (see Table 1 B, entry 2.B.(2)).

Column 4. Social security contributions

For the totals see Table 1 A, entry 3.C.; Table 2 B, entry 3.B.(1); and Table 3 A, entry 4.C. The distribution of the totals among individual sectors was made on the basis of cash wages and salaries (see Appendix Tables 29 and 31) and the rates of social security contributions by employers in the different sectors (see Busek and Spulber,

Czechoslovakia, p. 214, and National Assembly, *Státní závěrečný účet,* 1947, p. 24, and 1948, p. 24).

Column 5. Cash returns to labor of self-employed

The *total* income of self-employed was obtained as follows: For 1947, figures in State Statistical Office, *Zprávy,* 1949, Nos. 31–33, pp. 240–49, were increased by 5 percent, which is our estimate of the rate of under-reporting (see above, note to item 1.A of Table 1 A, p. 91); the distribution by branches is given by the source; for 1948, see notes to Table 1 B, entry 2.A.(1)b; the 1948 total was distributed in the 1947 proportions. This total income was considered to represent only cash returns to labor in all branches where the average income of self-employed was below the level of average wages in corresponding branches. In trade, banking, and insurance, only 77 percent of the total income was considered as cash labor returns, and 23 percent (1,850 million crowns in 1947 and 1,719 million crowns in 1948) as returns to capital. This allocation corresponds to the excess of the average income of the self-employed over the average wage in these branches in 1947 (see State Statistical Office, *Zprávy,* 1949, Nos. 31–33, pp. 245–48, and Appendix Table 29, item II.D). For agriculture, see Table 1 B, entry 2.A.(1)c, and (3)c, and notes to Table 2 B, entry 3.B.(2). All income of farmers was considered as returns to labor. For forestry, see Table 1 B, entry 2.A.(1)d.

Column 6. Returns in kind to labor of self-employed
1. Industry, 6. Trade, banking and insurance, and 9. Other sectors

See Dolanský, *Výklad k rozpočtu,* 1949, p. 235. This source gives only the total for all three sectors amounting to 1,000 million crowns in each year. The total was distributed among these three sectors proportionately to the number of self-employed (see State Statistical Office, *Zprávy,* 1949, Nos. 31–33, pp. 240–49).

2. Agriculture

See Table 1 B, entry 2.A.(2)b for income in kind of farmers, and Table 2 B, entry 4.A for inventory changes and farm investment in kind.

Column 7. Total returns to labor

This is the sum of items in columns 2 to 6. In the case of agriculture all cash income and income in kind was assumed to represent returns to labor since there was no good way to differentiate among the different factor returns. Considering the differences between incomes of independent farmers and income of wage earners in agriculture, it may well be that returns to factors other than labor in agriculture were zero or negative. The average income (cash and in kind) of self-employed farmers amounted to 17,370 crowns in 1948, and the average earnings (cash and in kind) of hired labor in agriculture amounted to 34,473 crowns in the same year (calculated from Appendix Table 31, and notes to Table 1 B, item 2.A.(2)a; State Statistical Office, *Statistická ročenka*, 1958, p. 89; General Secretariat of the Economic Council, *Průběh plnění hospodářského plánu*, 1947, pp. 255–56; and State Statistical Office, *Zprávy*, 1948, Nos. 50–53, pp. 362, 366–67). On the other hand, it is possible that the total number of hours worked by independent farmers was smaller than that of the hired labor. The nonmonetary rewards of farmers, that is, independence, attachment to land, and so forth, may have compensated partly or fully for their lower returns as compared with hired labor.

APPENDIX TABLE 41

CALCULATIONS OF THE RETURNS TO LABOR IN 1955–56

(*Million crowns*)

	1955	1956
1. Industry	34,600	36,267
2. Agriculture	14,240	14,421
3. Forestry	1,457	1,579
4. Construction	8,618	9,989
5. Transportation, communications	5,788	6,135
6. Trade, banking, insurance	6,992	7,391
7. Housing	218	274
8. Government	11,512	12,219
9. Other sectors	2,551	2,752
Total	85,976	91,027

NOTES TO APPENDIX TABLE 41

1. Industry

The figures are sums of the following:

(a) Wage bill (29,277 million crowns in 1955 and 30,804 million crowns in 1956, see Appendix Table 32).

(b) Income of handicrafts, including handicraft tax (1,042 million crowns in 1955 and 982 million crowns in 1956, see notes to Table 1 B, entry 2.A.(1)b.i, and to Table 2 B, entry 3.B.(2)).

(c) "Other cash income" (1,278 million crowns in 1955 and

1,321 million crowns in 1956). This is the estimate of industry's share in the total of "other cash income" to households from enterprises and was allocated among individual branches proportionately to their wage bill as given in Appendix Table 32. The total is from Table 1 B, entry 2.A.1.(b).

(d) In addition, the total for industry contains contributions paid by cooperative enterprises (226 million crowns in 1955 and 239 million crowns in 1956, see Appendix Table 33) and contributions paid by nationalized enterprises (2,777 million crowns in 1955 and 2,921 million crowns in 1956, that is, 10 percent of the industry wage bill, as given in Appendix Table 32, excluding the wage bill of manufacturing cooperatives, as given in Appendix Table 33).

2. Agriculture

The general approach to the calculation of labor returns in agriculture is explained in Chapter III. We assumed that the labor income was equal to the actual income in agriculture recomputed in terms of compulsory delivery prices. The value of output in average realized prices, 21,601 million crowns in 1955 and 23,340 million crowns in 1956 (see Lazarcik, *Production and Productivity in Czechoslovak Agriculture,* p. 62) was multiplied by 0.806 for 1955 and 0.798 for 1956, these coefficients representing the ratios of the index of compulsory delivery prices to that of average realized prices (see State Statistical Office, *Statistická ročenka,* 1959, p. 389; both indexes have their base in 1937 market prices). The results, 17,410 million crowns for 1955 and 18,625 million crowns for 1956, were then deducted from the original output figures in average realized prices, and this gave us 4,191 and 4,715 million crowns for 1955 and 1956, respectively. These sums were then considered returns to other factors than labor.

Net income, which consisted of (1) wages and salaries (Appendix Table 32), (2) social security contributions by employers (Appendix Table 32), (3) farmers' income in cash and in kind (Table 1 B, entries 2.A.(1)c, and 2.A.(2)b), (4) agriculture tax (Table 2 B, entry 3.B.(2)), and (5) farm investment in kind and inventory changes (Table 2 B, entry 4.A), amounted to 18,431 and 19,136 million crowns in 1955 and 1956, respectively. Subtracting the nonlabor returns computed above, we obtained 14,240 and 14,421 million crowns for 1955 and 1956, respectively, our estimates of labor income.

3. Forestry

This item consists of the wage bill, social security contributions by employers (see Appendix Table 32), a proportionate share of "other cash payments to households" (see note to industry, 1.(c), above), plus income from forestry as given in Table 1 B, entry 2.A.(1)d.

4. Construction

This is the sum of (1) the wage bill (from Appendix Table 32), (2) social security contributions by employers (10 percent of the wage bill), (3) the value of labor supplied by households for private housing construction (from Table 1 B, entry 2.A.(5)), and (4) a proportionate share of "other cash payments" to households (see note to industry, 1.(c), above).

5. Transportation and communications

As under construction above, except for item (3) which does not apply here.

6. Trade, banking, and insurance

As under transportation and communications.

7. Housing

As under transportation and communications.

8. Government

This corresponds to the value added in the government sector (see Table 3 A).

9. Other sectors

As under transportation and communications, above. This category covers the remaining branches listed in Appendix Table 32 under II.B.(1)(f), (h), (i), (j), and II.B.(2), as well as services produced by the household sector (see Table 1 A).

Sources to column (3) of Appendix Table 39 are given in Appendix Table 42 and its supporting notes.

NOTES TO APPENDIX TABLE 42

In all four years the nonlabor returns were allocated in principle proportionately to the current value of fixed and working capital in individual branches. The total of nonlabor returns to be allocated in each year is the difference between the gross national product at market prices and the sum of labor returns and adjusted depreciation (see Appendix Tables 40, 41, 49, and 50). The distribution of capi-

APPENDIX TABLE 42

ALLOCATION OF RETURNS TO FACTORS OTHER THAN LABOR,
1947–48 AND 1955–56

(*Million crowns*)

(1)	(2) 1947	(3) 1948	(4) 1955	(5) 1956
1. Industry	10,673	10,781	15,469	17,110
2. Agriculture	7,111	7,485	8,465	9,353
3. Forestry	475	465	549	607
4. Construction	1,333	1,319	2,884	3,338
5. Transportation, communications	5,977	5,985	6,543	7,045
6. Trade, banking, insurance	3,061	3,012	4,145	4,643
7. Housing	8,457	8,390	9,401	10,382
8. Government	—	—	—	—
9. Other	1,108	1,086	1,161	1,266
Total	38,195	38,523	48,617	53,744

tal by individual branches used in making the allocations of nonlabor
returns is shown in Appendix Table 43. Improvements on land, such
as drainage systems and irrigation facilities, are included in the capital figures for agriculture, but the value of land per se is not included
in the basis for reallocating nonlabor returns. Working capital in agriculture, however, includes the value of unfinished production, and
this varies according to the value of the land.

APPENDIX TABLE 43

CAPITAL DISTRIBUTION BY ECONOMIC BRANCHES,
1947–48 AND 1955–56

(*Billion crowns, 1955 prices*)

	1947	1948	1955	1956
1. Industry	80.9	83.4	123.9	129.7
2. Agriculture	53.9	57.9	67.8	70.9
3. Forestry	3.6	3.6	4.4	4.6
4. Construction	10.1	10.2	23.1	25.3
5. Transportation, communications	45.3	46.3	52.4	53.4
6. Trade, banking, insurance	23.2	23.3	33.2	35.2
7. Housing	64.1	64.9	75.3	78.7
8. Other	8.4	8.4	9.3	9.6
Total	289.5	298.0	389.4	407.4

NOTES TO APPENDIX TABLE 43

1. Industry

This sector includes mining and manufacturing. The value of
capital broken down by types is shown in Appendix Table 44 and
is documented in the following remarks.

APPENDIX TABLE 44

VALUE OF INDUSTRIAL CAPITAL, 1947–48 AND 1955–56

(*Billion crowns, 1955 prices*)

	Fixed Capital		Working Capital				
Year	Full Replacement Value	Depreciated Value	Stocks of Raw Materials	Work in Progress	Stocks of Finished Products	Total	Total Capital
1947	107.9	59.3		21.6		21.6	80.9
1948	112.3	61.8		21.6		21.6	83.4
1955	158.3	87.1	21.7	11.5	3.6	36.8	123.9
1956	166.8	91.7	23.3	11.1	3.6	38.0	129.7

(a) Value of fixed capital. The full replacement value of fixed capital was obtained starting from the January, 1955, value, estimated in absolute terms (150.0 billion crowns as of January 1, 1955, see Appendix Table 23); values at the end of 1948, 1955, and 1956 were derived by means of an index of the value of fixed capital for the period 1949–58 (see State Statistical Office, *Statistická ročenka,* 1959, p. 39); the 1947 value was obtained by subtracting the 1948 value of investment (4,375 million crowns, *ibid.,* 1959, p. 109) from the 1948 value of fixed capital estimated previously. The current value of fixed capital after depreciation was estimated at 55 percent of the full reproduction value, assuming the same rate of cumulated past depreciation of existing fixed capital as that estimated officially for 1955 (see *Statistický obzor,* 1959, No. 1, p. 17). The two sets of figures are shown in columns 2 and 3.

(b) Value of working capital. In the definition used here working capital consists of stocks of raw materials, work in progress, and stocks of finished products. The total value of working capital in 1947 and 1948 was estimated from the 1955 total, on the assumption that from 1948 to 1955 it increased by 70 percent, that is, by the same percentage as national income in industry (see official index in State Statistical Office, *Statistická ročenka,* 1959, p. 35). The totals for 1955 and 1956 were obtained by estimating separately each component, as follows:

(i) Average stocks of raw materials: The total value of raw materials used up during the year was roughly estimated from the total value of industrial output (about 120 billion crowns in 1955 and 131 billion crowns in 1956, see Jaromír Dolanský in supplement to *Rudé právo,* March 6, 1957) and the cost structure in industry (see State Statistical Office, *Statistická ročenka*, 1957, p. 98); the total value of raw materials was then divided by the annual turnover coefficient, derived from data on the average length of turnover of raw materials in days (*ibid.*, 1959, p. 142).

(ii) Work in progress: The average value of work in progress was approximated as the total annual cost of gross production divided by the annual turnover coefficient, derived from data on the average length of turnover of work in progress (sources as under (i) above).

(iii) Average stock of finished products: This was approximated as the total annual value of finished products divided by the annual turnover coefficient derived from data on the average length of turnover of finished products in days (sources as under (i) above; cost of finished output was approximated from data on the cost pattern and the industrial wage bill from *ibid.*, 1959, p. 161).

2. Agriculture

The figures in Appendix Table 43 were obtained as sums of values, in 1956 prices, of the following elements:

1. Buildings, machinery and equipment amounting to 29.5, 29.5, 30.9, and 33.2 billion crowns for the respective years (calculated from data on quantities and prices given in Lazarcik, *Production and Productivity in Czechoslovak Agriculture,* Tables A-24, A-25, and A-26).

2. Livestock amounting to 13.4, 13.4, 17.3, and 17.4 billion crowns for the respective years (calculated from *ibid.;* prices from Table 6, livestock numbers from Table A-6, and average weights from Table A-8).

3. Other amounting to 11.0, 15.0, 19.6, and 20.3 billion crowns for the respective years. This element, which consists partly of fixed capital (for example, fruit trees) and partly of average working capital, was approximated as equal to the total annual value of intermediate products plus current operating expenses in 1956 (calculated from *ibid.*, Tables 7, 10, and 13). This method of approximation is based on the 1946 near-identity of the two magnitudes: the calculated 1946 value of "other capital" amounted to 39.8 billion crowns (see Institute for Agricultural Accounting and Management, *Zprávy,* 1949, No. 1, pp. 20, 21; 1946, No. 2–4, pp. 48–49), and the value of intermediate products plus current operating expenses to 40.9 billion crowns (see Lazarcik, *Production and Productivity in Czechoslovak Agriculture*).

3. Forestry

The figures in Appendix Table 43 represent an estimate of fixed capital, depreciated value, excluding the value of land and trees, and disregarding working capital as insignificant. The estimates were obtained starting from the total 1955 full replacement value at the beginning of the year (25.9 billion crowns, see Appendix Table 23); values for the required years (including 1955) were derived with the help of an index of fixed capital in agriculture and forestry (see *Statistický obzor*, No. 1, 1959, p. 12); the value net of the value of land and trees was estimated as 24.1 percent of the total value (see State Statistical Office, *Statistická ročenka*, 1957, p. 292); the rate of accumulated past depreciation was set, for all years, at one third of the full replacement value, the same as in transportation (see below).

4. Construction

The figures in Appendix Table 43 are the sums of estimates of fixed and working capital shown in Appendix Table 45. Fixed capi-

APPENDIX TABLE 45

CAPITAL IN CONSTRUCTION, 1947–48 AND 1955–56

(*Billion crowns, 1955 prices*)

Year	Fixed Capital	Working Capital	Total Capital
1947	2.1	8.0	10.1
1948	2.2	8.0	10.2
1955	3.1	20.0	23.1
1956	3.3	22.0	25.3

tal was estimated in a way analogous to that for industry. The full replacement value as of December 31, 1954, that is, 5.5 billion crowns (see Appendix Table 23), was extrapolated by means of the index of fixed capital (see *Statistický obzor*, No. 1, 1959, p. 12). Depreciated value was calculated at 55.2 percent of the full replacement value (see *Statistický obzor*, No. 1, 1959, p. 17). Working capital was approximated as roughly equal to the value of annual state-plan investments (see State Statistical Office, *Statistická ročenka*, 1957, p. 71; the 1948 value was used for 1947 as well), uncompleted construction being roughly equal to the annual volume of investments (*Plánované hospodářství*, 1959, No. 1, pp. 6–25). The annual volume of investment, however, contains some production of sectors other than construction. We assumed that the excess on this account roughly corresponds to the inventories of building materials of construction firms.

5. Transportation and Communications

The figures given in Appendix Table 43 are derived in Appendix Table 46. For fixed capital the method of estimation and sources

APPENDIX TABLE 46

CAPITAL IN TRANSPORTATION AND COMMUNICATIONS,
1947–48 AND 1955–56

(*Billion crowns, 1955 prices*)

Year	Fixed Capital	Working Capital (inventories)	Total Capital
1947	41.2	4.1	45.3
1948	42.1	4.2	46.3
1955	47.6	4.8	52.4
1956	48.5	4.9	53.4

were the same as for construction; the rate of accumulated past depreciation was set at 33.3 percent taking into consideration the available Czechoslovak estimates for industry, construction, and agriculture. Working capital, in the sense of inventories, was set very roughly at 10 percent of fixed capital.

6. Trade, banking, and insurance

Our figures in Appendix Table 43 are based on the detailed figures shown in Appendix Table 47. The value of fixed capital was

APPENDIX TABLE 47

CAPITAL IN TRADE, 1947–48 AND 1955–56

(*Billion crowns, 1955 prices*)

Year	Fixed Capital	Working Capital (inventories)	Total Capital
1947	6.0	17.2	23.2
1948	6.1	17.2	23.3
1955	7.3	25.9	33.2
1956	7.7	27.5	35.2

estimated in the same way as for transportation and communications. Trade here covers both material procurement and supply, and trade as given in Appendix Table 23; we assumed that official estimates for banking and insurance are also included under these titles. The value of working capital was approximated as that of trade inventories. The 1955 value is from *Statistický obzor*, 1957, No. 6, p. 257; our estimate for 1956 is the average of inventories as on June 30, 1956, and those as on December 31, 1956, given in *ibid.;* for the years

1947 and 1948 we used an estimate for 1949 derived from the 1955 estimate on the assumption that inventories changed at the same rate as the volume of retail trade turnover (State Statistical Office, *Statistická ročenka*, 1957, p. 17).

7. *Housing,* and 8. *Other*

The estimates shown in Appendix Table 43 were obtained in the same way and from the same sources as for industry (see Appendix Table 48). The rate of accumulated depreciation applied here was

APPENDIX TABLE 48

FIXED CAPITAL IN HOUSING AND OTHER SECTORS,
1947–48 AND 1955–56

(*Billion crowns, 1955 prices*)

Year	Fixed Capital in Housing	Fixed Capital in Other Sectors
1947	64.1	8.4
1948	64.9	8.4
1955	75.3	9.3
1956	78.7	9.6

also that of industry, the highest rate of all sectors, in view of the lack of expansion of housing since the beginning of World War II. Working capital was disregarded as relatively insignificant.

Our estimates of depreciation allowances shown in column (4) of Appendix Table 39 are derived in Appendix Tables 49 (for 1947 and 1948) and 50 (for 1955 and 1956).

APPENDIX TABLE 49

DEPRECIATION ALLOWANCES IN 1947–48, ADJUSTED ALLOCATION

(*Million crowns*)

(1)	(2)	(3)	(4)	(5)
	Corresponding to Capital Valuation in 1955 Prices		Corresponding to Valuation in Current Prices	
Economic Branch	1947	1948	1947	1948
1. Industry	5,288	5,501	9,936	12,631
2. Agriculture	1,062	1,062	1,995	2,438
3. Forestry	129	129	242	296
4. Construction	296	296	556	680
5. Transportation, communications	2,662	2,718	5,002	6,241
6. Trade, banking, insurance	356	356	669	817
7. Housing	2,833	2,833	5,323	6,505
8. Other	366	366	688	840

APPENDIX TABLE 50

DEPRECIATION ALLOWANCES IN 1955–56

(1)	(2)	(3)	(4)	(5)	(6)
	Fixed Capital Full Replacement Value (billion crowns)		Depreciation Rate (percent)	Depreciation Allowance (billion crowns)	
Economic Branch	1955	1956		1955	1956
1. Industry	158.3	166.8	4.9	7,757	8,229
2. Agriculture	30.9	33.2	3.6	1,112	1,195
3. Forestry	6.6	6.9	2.4	158	166
4. Construction	5.6	5.9	7.6	426	448
5. Transportation, communications	71.4	72.8	4.3	3,070	3,130
6. Trade	11.0	11.6	3.9	429	452
7. Housing	136.9	143.0	2.4	3,286	3,432
8. Government	—	—	—	—	—
9. Other	16.9	17.4	2.4	406	418

NOTES TO APPENDIX TABLE 49

In Appendix Table 49, columns 2 and 3, depreciation allowances corresponding to the estimated 1947 and 1948 values of fixed capital in 1955 prices were derived from the depreciation rates for 1955 shown in Appendix Table 50, column 4 for industry, agriculture, and transportation. The derivation of other sectors' depreciation is based on the assumption that "correct" depreciation allowances should change at the same rate as the full value of capital (that is, before deducting any capital consumption) in the individual branches. These rates of change are given in corresponding index series in State Statistical Office, *Statistická ročenka,* 1958, p. 32. We used the index for 1948 for 1947 as well.

To obtain depreciation allowances corresponding to the value of fixed capital in current prices in columns 4 and 5, which are required for Appendix Table 39, we applied to the depreciation allowances corresponding to 1955 prices a price index for investment goods calculated by Boris Pesek (see his Czechoslovak Monetary Policy, 1945–53, p. 55). The 1953 price relative of this index series was taken to represent the 1955 price relative, it being closest in time during a period of relative price stability in the producer goods sector.

NOTES TO APPENDIX TABLE 50

In Appendix Table 50, the "correct" depreciation allowances are calculated from the full replacement value of fixed capital (columns

2 and *3*) using the Czechoslovak estimates of the true rates of depreciation by individual branches (column *4*). The specific sources and details of estimation are given below.

Columns 2 and 3

These are 1954 year-end figures from Appendix Table 23, extrapolated by means of the index of the value of fixed capital (State Statistical Office, *Statistická ročenka,* 1958, p. 32; end-of-the-year values were used in place of annual average values).

Column 4

Depreciation rates for individual sectors (except industry and agriculture) were obtained as weighted averages of depreciation rates for buildings (2.4 percent), machinery (9.1 percent), and means of transportation (11.7 percent), given in *Statistický obzor,* 1956, No. 10, p. 437. The weights are the proportions of these three basic types of fixed capital in total fixed capital given separately for each economic branch in State Statistical Office, *Statistická ročenka,* 1957, p. 292. In most cases these three types of fixed capital account for about 80 percent of the total. The depreciation rate in industry was derived from figures on industry's capital consumption allowances and fixed capital, calculated in the note to entry 6 (for 1956) in Table 2 A. In the case of agriculture we calculated the depreciation rate with respect to the value of buildings and machinery only.

APPENDIX H: GROSS NATIONAL PRODUCT BY USE AT FACTOR COST

We show here the detailed calculations underlying Table 7 in Chapter III. In addition to Table 7, we presented there an alternative tabulation of GNP by end use at factor cost for 1955–56. The basic difference between the approach in Table 7 and that in the alternative calculation is that in the latter we explicitly take as the gross rent component of personal consumption at factor cost the gross value added by housing in the calculation of GNP by sector of origin offered as an alternative to Table 6 (see p. 61, above) plus the estimated current purchases by housing (at factor cost) from other sectors of production. Thus gross rent in 1955 and 1956, respectively, in millions of crowns was taken at 13,102 and 14,228; and within these figures the gross value added by housing was (in million crowns), respectively, 12,095 and 13,177. The balance represents current purchases by housing from other sectors. These purchases were derived from the estimates of gross rent at current established prices as shown in Table 1 B, items 3.B.(1)d and 3.B.(2)d by subtracting the house tax and the labor cost as given in Appendix Table 36, item A.2.d, and Appendix Table 41, item 7. The result was taken as more or less correct at factor cost since some of the purchases were presumably at prices including the turnover tax. In taking gross rent at factor cost at the values shown above we have in effect already allocated a part of the turnover tax; only the balance of the turnover tax is then redistributed among the eligible end uses proportionately to their values net of the tax. Here we followed precisely the same methodology as that employed for Table 7, whose documentation follows immediately.

1947–48

We assumed here that the incidence of indirect taxes, subsidies, and accounting profits was sufficiently random so that the structure of gross national product at market prices would be reasonably close to what it would be at factor cost. The tabulation below shows the values in million crowns from which the percentage distribution in Table 7 was derived.

	1947	1948
Personal consumption	179,060	186,325
Government	32,726	36,030
Defense and security	14,743	14,284
Gros investment	20,313	49,416
Gross national product	246,842	286,055

The figures for personal consumption were taken from Table 5 A, items 1 and 2.A; government and defense and security from Appendix Table 53; and gross investment from Table 5 C.

To check our assumption, we made rough adjustments of the values at market prices along the lines used below for 1955–56; these showed that only small changes in structure would result.

We noted first that 26,765 million crowns of indirect taxes, including the profits of state monopolies, impinged on household consumption expenditures in 1947 (see Dolanský, *Výklad k rozpočtu, 1948*, pp. 162–63). We deducted this amount of taxes from the value of household consumption (see Table 7) and assumed that the balance of the indirect taxes unaccounted for so far, namely 15,865 million crowns (see total in Table 2 A, item 5), affected all final uses in a more or less uniform manner. Then, considering the 26,765 million crowns of indirect tax as factor returns, we redistributed this sum to all the final uses—consumption, government, gross investment—in proportion to their values (consumption taken at the reduced value noted above), thus restoring the total gross national product to its value in crowns at market prices. The relatively small change in structure of the gross national product in 1947 after this adjustment is shown below in percentage terms.

	Before Adjustment	After Adjustment
Consumption	72.5	70.2
Government	19.2	20.4
Gross investment	8.2	9.4
Total	100.0	100.0

There is still present the divergence from factor cost due to subsidies (about 6.6 billion crowns in 1947; see Table 2 A). Since about 60 percent of the total subsidies were directed to agriculture and thus

served primarily to reduce the prices of consumer goods, and, since
other subsidies probably benefited consumption along with the other
uses, a correction for subsidies should raise the share of consumption somewhat. Profits in 1947–48 were relatively small (see Table
2 A) and probably did not cause a significant divergence from factor
cost, at least so far as structure by final use is concerned. On balance,
we concluded that at the level of aggregate final uses the market
price structure would be reasonably close to factor cost in 1947–48.

1955–56

As regards 1955–56, an adjustment to market prices was necessary to approximate factor cost in view of the large magnitude of
the turnover tax and its one-sided effect on the pattern of final uses.
For reasons given in Chapter III, we restricted our adjustment only
to indirect taxes.

Our adjustment for 1955–56 is presented in Appendix Tables 51
and 52. We first calculated in Appendix Table 51 the value of the
use categories net of indirect taxes. This was done by identifying

APPENDIX TABLE 51

TAXED COMPONENTS OF GROSS NATIONAL PRODUCT, 1955–56
(*Million crowns*)

(1)	(2)	(3)	(4)	(5)	(6)	(7)
	Value in Current Prices		Tax Incidence		Value excluding Tax	
	1955	1956	1955	1956	1955	1956
Consumer purchases	74,471	76,949	37,791	37,129	36,680	39,820
Military subsistence	850	700	431	338	419	362
Purchases by government	10,312	10,787	5,233	5,205	5,079	5,582
Inventory changes in trade	1,025	2,820	520	1,361	505	1,459
Private and cooperative investment	3,712	6,276	1,884	3,028	1,828	3,248
Total	90,370	97,532	45,859	47,061	44,511	50,471

the taxed components and their values in current market prices and
assuming that the tax impinged on all of them at the same rate.
To determine the average rate of tax, we divided the total indirect
tax receipts, 45,428 million crowns in 1955 and 46,724 million in
1956 (see Table 2 A) by the values subject to tax, excluding once
from the total the value of military subsistence and clothing to avoid
double counting (it appears both in consumer purchases and separately as an element of government services). The total tax incidence

in columns *4* and *5* is larger than the tax actually collected because of the necessary double inclusion of military subsistence and clothing in gross national product.

The list of components subject to tax and the sources of the figures follow.

Consumer purchases (components from Tables 1 A and 1 B, as itemized below):

1. Household sector services: compensation in kind plus current purchases by nonprofit organizations
2. Retail trade purchases
3. Purchases of services
4. Wages in kind, excluding agriculture
5. Military subsistence and clothing

Military subsistence and clothing (considered here as part of government services, see Table 1 B).

Current purchases by government, excluding military (see Appendix Table 53, column *3,* item 9 less item 8, less government purchases from abroad, given in Table 3 A).

Inventory changes in trade (estimated very roughly as part of total inventory changes given in Table 2 A in the same proportion as the share of trade in total working capital, that is, 24.2 percent in 1955 and 24.4 percent in 1956, based on figures given in Appendix G).

Private and cooperative investment (see State Statistical Office, *Statistická ročenka,* 1957, p. 71).

In Appendix Table 52 we redistributed the total of indirect taxes deducted in columns *4* and *5* of Appendix Table 51 among selected final use categories. At this stage the indirect tax total is regarded as consisting of nonlabor factor returns. All final use categories except those listed below were considered eligible to share in this redistribution in proportion to their values excluding indirect taxes; the average rate being determined by dividing the total to be distributed by the total of the eligible use categories. The value of excluded items listed below either consisted entirely of labor contributions or were considered already to include full returns to nonlabor factors:

In consumption: (i) cash wages, salaries, and social security contributions for household sector services, (ii) farm market purchases, and (iii) gifts from abroad (see Tables 1 A and 1 B).

GROSS NATIONAL PRODUCT AT MARKET PRICES AND AT FACTOR COST, 1955–56

(Million crowns)

(1)	(2)	(3)	(4)	(5)	(6)	(7)
	At Market Prices		Value excluding Indirect Taxes		At Factor Cost	
	1955	1956	1955	1956	1955	1956
Personal consumption	83,232	86,219			67,175	71,103
Consumer purchases	74,471	76,949	36,680	39,820	54,781	58,242
Gross rent	1,661	1,761	1,661	1,761	2,481	2,576
Farmers' income in kind	5,700	6,000	5,700	6,000	8,513	8,776
Other	1,400	1,509	(1,400)	(1,509)	1,400	1,509
Government	18,807	19,980			16,080	17,357
Purchases from abroad	50	50	(50)	(50)	50	50
Other purchases	10,312	10,787	5,079	5,582	7,585	8,164
Money compensation of employees	8,445	9,143	(8,445)	(9,143)	8,445	9,143
Defense and security	12,643	8,105			17,359	10,518
Military subsistence	850	700	419	362	626	529
Pay in money	1,782	1,819	(1,782)	(1,819)	1,782	1,819
Military purchases	10,011	5,586	10,011	5,586	14,951	8,170
Gross investment	36,555	47,937			50,622	63,263
Inventory changes of trade	1,025	2,820	505	1,459	754	2,134
Other inventory changes	3,210	8,736	3,210	8,736	4,794	12,778
Private and cooperative investment	3,712	6,276	1,828	3,248	2,730	4,751
Foreign investment	659	1,654	659	1,654	984	2,419
State investment	27,175	27,515	27,175	27,515	40,586	40,245
Unpaid labor	774	936	(774)	(936)	774	936
Gross national product	151,237	162,241			151,237	162,241

In government: (i) money compensation of employees (see Appendix Table 53, column 2, excluding defense) and (ii) government purchases from abroad (see Table 3 A).

In gross investment: (i) unpaid labor in farm investments in kind (see Appendix Table 24, items c, d, and e) and (ii) unpaid labor in community improvement projects (see Table 3 A).

These excluded items are indicated in parentheses in Appendix Table 52, columns 4 and 5. Other items in columns 2 and 3 of this table were found either in Appendix Table 51 or in the sources indicated below for specific items:

Gross rent, cash and imputed, and farmers' income in kind—Table 1 B; military cash pay—Appendix Table 53, item 8, column 2, less military subsistence and clothing given in Table 1 B; military purchases—Appendix Table 53; other inventory changes—Table 2 A, item 2, less the estimated inventory changes in trade in Appendix Table 51; foreign investment—Table 5 C; state investment—residual in gross investment in Table 5 C after subtracting the other investment components in Appendix Table 52.

APPENDIX I: RESOURCE ALLOCATION AMONG GOVERNMENT SECTOR SERVICES, 1947-48 AND 1955-56

Our estimates of the cost of government services are shown in detail in Appendix Table 53 and documented in the notes below.

Column 2. Labor cost

This item includes cash wages, wages in kind, and social security contributions by employers.

1947 and 1948. Cash wages and salaries are from Appendix Tables 29 and 31. The detailed breakdown of the data by sectors is from National Assembly, *Státní závěrečný účet,* 1947, p. 13, and 1948, p. 13. Wages in kind (military subsistence and clothing) and the total figure for the social security contributions are from Table 3 A, items 4.B and 4.C, respectively. The distribution of the total social security contributions among the sectors was made proportionately to the cash wages in each sector.

1955 and 1956. All data are from Appendix Table 32. The total for education and culture in 1955 was allocated between education on the one hand and culture on the other, in proportion to the corresponding budget outlays as given in Appendix Table 36. Outlays for 1956, given in one sum for education and culture, were assumed to be divided between the two in the same ratio as in 1955.

For the present purpose outlays in culture were reduced by the amount of subsidies to cultural institutions in the enterprise sector (150 million crowns in 1955 and 200 million crowns in 1956; see Appendix Table 32, notes to item II.B.(i)). The resulting budget figures used for allocation of labor cost were (in million crowns):

	1955	1956
Education	4,576	5,039
Culture	1,045	1,305

RESOURCE ALLOCATION AMONG GOVERNMENT SECTOR SERVICES, 1947–48 AND 1955–56

(Million crowns, unless otherwise indicated)

(1)	(2)	(3)	(4)	(5)	(6)	(7)
	Labor Cost	Purchases on Current Account	Value of Service at Current Prices	Column (4) as Percent of GNP	Value of Services at "Factor Cost"	Column (6) as Percent of GNP
1947						
1. Administration	10,443	5,477	15,920	6.4		
2. Education	5,638	2,733	8,371	3.4		
3. Culture	78	104	182	0.1		
4. Health	431	1,362	1,793	0.7		
5. Science and research	679	862	1,541	0.6		
6. Social welfare	1,092	2,677	3,769	1.5		
7. Quasi-governmental organizations	865	285	1,150	0.5		
8. Defense and security	7,722	7,021	14,743	6.0		
9. Total government	26,948	20,521	47,469	19.2		
1948						
1. Administration	10,888	5,722	16,610	5.8		
2. Education	6,041	3,371	9,412	3.3		
3. Culture	80	118	198	0.1		
4. Health	502	2,073	2,575	0.9		
5. Science and research	737	909	1,646	0.6		
6. Social welfare	1,379	3,003	4,382	1.5		
7. Quasi-governmental organizations	904	303	1,207	0.4		
8. Defense and security	7,837	6,447	14,284	5.0		
9. Total government	28,368	21,946	50,314	17.6		

APPENDIX TABLE 53 (continued)

(1)	(2)	(3)	(4)	(5)	(6)	(7)
	Labor Cost	Purchases on Current Account	Value of Service at Current Prices	Column (4) as Percent of GNP	Value of Services at "Factor Cost"	Column (6) as Percent of GNP
1955						
1. Administration	2,083	364	2,447	1.6	2,364	1.6
2. Education	2,280	2,900	5,180	3.5	4,413	2.9
3. Culture	521	662	1,183	0.8	1,008	0.7
4. Health	1,331	3,649	4,980	3.3	4,015	2.7
5. Science and research	1,128	1,439	2,567	1.7	2,186	1.4
6. Social welfare	782	998	1,780	1.2	1,516	1.0
7. Quasi-governmental organizations	320	350	670	0.5	578	0.4
8. Defense and security	2,632	10,011	12,643	8.5	17,359	11.5
9. Total government	11,077	20,373	31,450	21.0	33,439	22.1
1956						
1. Administration	2,049	224	2,273	1.4	2,231	1.4
2. Education	2,413	3,083	5,496	3.4	4,746	2.9
3. Culture	626	799	1,425	0.9	1,231	0.8
4. Health	1,482	3,593	5,075	3.2	4,201	2.6
5. Science and research	1,411	1,707	3,118	2.0	2,703	1.7
6. Social welfare	839	1,014	1,853	1.2	1,606	1.0
7. Quasi-governmental organizations	323	417	740	0.5	639	0.4
8. Defense and security	2,519	5,586	8,105	5.1	10,518	6.5
9. Total government	11,662	16,423	28,085	17.5	27,875	17.2

NOTE: Totals may not agree with the sums of indicated items because of rounding.

The totals for health and social welfare in Appendix Table 32 were allocated between the two services by calculating first the labor cost in the health services and then taking the residual as labor cost in social welfare. The labor cost in health was estimated by using employment data on health personnel in State Statistical Office, *Statistická ročenka,* 1957, p. 255 (97,605 persons in 1955, 102,769 persons in 1956), and average monthly wages in health and social welfare, *ibid.,* p. 69 (1,033 crowns in 1955 and 1,092 crowns in 1956). Social security contributions were taken at 10 percent of the wage totals.

Column 3. Purchases on current account

1947 and 1948. Purchases on current account by the central government by sector are from National Assembly, *Státní závěrečný účet,* 1947, p. 13, and 1948, p. 13, and from Appendix Table 13. Purchases on UNRRA account (see note to item 3 in Appendix Table 13) were allocated to social welfare. State debt service (see item 4 in Appendix Table 13) and purchase by the government from the foreign sector (see Table 3 A, item 3.B) were allocated to administration. Purchases by the trade unions and political parties on the one hand, and by social security institutions on the other (see items 7, 8, and 9 in Appendix Table 13) were allocated to quasi-governmental organizations and to social welfare, respectively. Other (unspecified) purchases by central government, as well as purchases by local government (see items 5 and 6 in Appendix Table 13, respectively) were allocated among the indicated service sectors in the same proportions as purchases by the central government, excluding defense, given in National Assembly, *Státní závěrečný účet,* 1947, p. 13, and 1948, p. 13.

1955 and 1956. Total purchases on current account made by the government (see Table 3 A, item 3) were allocated among the given categories as follows:

(1) Current purchases by administration, health, and defense and security services were obtained as the difference between, on the one hand, total budget outlays under administration, health, and defense, including internal security (see Appendix Table 36, item B.2.b, 3, and 4) and, on the other hand, the sum of labor cost (see above), purchases on capital account (see State Statistical Office, *Statistická ročenka,* 1957, p. 71), and capital repairs (see *ibid.,* 1959, p. 132). The value of capital repairs in this source, given in 1959 prices, was adjusted to 1957 current prices (and used for

1955 and 1956 values, see *ibid.*, 1958, p. 109, and *ibid.*, 1959, p. 132). The purchases on capital account and capital repairs by the health service, which were lumped together with social welfare in the original source, were estimated by allocating the totals between health and social welfare in the same proportion as the corresponding labor cost totals in column *1*.

(2) Current purchases of quasi-governmental organizations are taken from Table 2 A, item 1.C (see note thereto in Appendix B).

(3) The residual purchases on current account (5,999 million crowns in 1955 and 6,603 million crowns in 1956) were allocated among the remaining four categories (education, culture, social welfare, and science and research) in the same proportions as the corresponding total expenditures given in Appendix Table 36. The estimates are given below (in million crowns):

	1955		*1956*	
	Total Expenditures	*Current Account Expenditures*	*Total Expenditures*	*Current Account Expenditures*
Education	4,576	2,900	5,039	3,083
Culture	1,045	662	1,305	799
Science and research	2,271	1,439	2,789	1,707
Social welfare	1,574	998	1,658	1,014
Total	9,466	5,999	10,791	6,603

The figures for culture shown in Appendix Table 36 were reduced by subsidies to cultural institutions in the enterprise sector, just as in the allocation of labor cost in column *1*. Budget outlays available in Appendix Table 36 in one sum for social welfare and science and research (under the title "Unspecified") were allocated between science and research on one hand and social welfare on the other in proportion to the corresponding labor cost totals in column *1*. The original totals (3,945 million crowns in 1955 and 4,547 million crowns in 1956) were reduced, for the purpose of allocation, by 100 million crowns both in 1955 and in 1956, representing the estimated transfers to social organizations, taken as equivalent to the value of their purchases on capital account (see Appendix Table 17).

Column 4. Value of service at current prices
This is the sum of values in columns *2* and *3*.

Column 5. Column 4 as percent of GNP
The corresponding totals of GNP are from Table 5 A.

Column 6. Value of service at "factor cost"
1947 and 1948. Not applicable; we assumed that the market price values were sufficiently close to factor cost to make an adjustment unnecessary.

1955 and 1956. The total of government purchases on current account in adjusted prices, as well as those on defense and security, are from Appendix Table 52. The difference between these two was distributed among service categories 1 to 7 in proportion to the value of these purchases in current prices given in column *3*.

Column 7. Column 5 as percent of GNP
1947 and 1948. Not applicable.
1955 and 1956. The corresponding GNP totals are those given in Table 5 A (151,237 million crowns in 1955 and 162,241 million crowns in 1956).

One of the striking changes in the structure of resource allocation within government services is the reversal of the ratio between the relative shares of administration and education: while in 1947–48 this ratio was about 2:1, it changed to about 1:2 in 1955–56 (see column *5,* Appendix Table 53). However, not too much significance should be attached to these changes. They could result from a number of possible causes: changes in government organization following the Communist takeover in 1948; changes in the definition of administration expenditures; changes in the delimitation of current purchases as against investment expenditures and capital repairs; changes in the relative employment, as well as wage and salary rates, among government service categories; changes in the real level of material expenditures; changes in the ratios between labor and other current costs within individual service categories; changes in the relative prices of labor and material; defects in the applied method of allocating certain expenditures, for example, purchases by local government in 1947 and 1948. Information at our disposal does not make it possible to judge either which factors were responsible for the change in question or to what extent they were responsible.

BIBLIOGRAPHY

Alton, Thad Paul and associates. National Income and Product of Hungary in 1955. Unpublished MS, New York, 1960.
—— National Income and Product of Poland, 1954–56. Unpublished MS, New York, 1960.
Bača, Jan. *Za další rozvoj socialistické zemědělské družstevní velkovýroby v lidově demokratické ČSR* (For Further Expansion of the Socialist Large-Scale Agricultural Cooperative Production in the People's Democratic Republic of Czechoslovakia). Prague, 1958.
Baláž, Anton. *Chozrasčot priemyselných podnikov* (Economic Accounting of Industrial Enterprises). Bratislava, Slovenské vydavateľstvo technickej literatury, 1956.
Bergson, Abram. *Soviet National Income and Product in 1937*. New York, Columbia University Press, 1953.
Bergson, Abram, and Hans Heymann, Jr. *Soviet National Income and Product, 1940–48*. New York, Columbia University Press, 1954.
Blahušiak, Juraj. *Organisace práce a mezd. Mzdové fondy* (Organization of Labor and Wages. Wage Funds). Prague, Vydavatelstvo ROH, 1954.
Boreš, František, and others. *Problémy nové soustavy plánování a financování československého průmyslu* (Problems of the New System of Planning and Financing in Czechoslovak Industry). Prague, Státní nakladatelství technické literatury, 1957.
Busek, Vratislav, and Nicholas Spulber, eds. *Czechoslovakia*. New York, Frederick A. Praeger, 1957.
Československý přehled (Czechoslovak Survey). New York, Free Europe Committee, 1954.
Choděra, Otokar. *Domovní daň* (House Tax). Prague, Orbis, 1954.

Czechoslovakia. General Secretariat of the Economic Council. *Průběh plnění hospodářského plánu* (The Course of Fulfillment of the Economic Plan). 1947. Government Report to the National Assembly. Prague, 1948.

Czechoslovakia. Institute for Agricultural Accounting and Management. *Zprávy Zemědělského ústavu účetnicko-spravovědného republiky Československé* (Reports of the Institute for Agricultural Accounting and Management). 1946–49. Prague, 1946–49.

Czechoslovakia. Ministry of Finance. *Plnění a kontrola státního rozpočtu v roce 1953* (Fulfillment and Control of the State Budget in the Year 1953). Internal Handbook. Prague, 1953.

—— *Státní hospodaření za války a po revoluci* (State Management of the Economy During the War and After the Revolution). Prague, 1946.

Czechoslovakia. Ministry of Interior. *Úřední list republiky Československé* (Official Gazette of the Czechoslovak Republic). 1947–58. Prague, 1947–58.

Czechoslovakia. National Assembly. *Sbírka zákonů a nařízení republiky Československé* (Collection of Laws and Ordinances of the Czechoslovak Republic). 1946–53. Prague, 1946–53.

—— *Státní závěrečný účet republiky Československé* (State Closing Account of the Czechoslovak Republic). 1947–48. Prague, 1949–50.

—— *Těsnopisecké zprávy o schůzích Národního shromáždění republiky Československé* (Stenographic Reports on Sessions of the National Assembly of the Czechoslovak Republic). Third session, 1947; fourth session, March 21–23, 1955; tenth session, February 9–10, 1956; seventeenth session, April 17–18, 1957. Prague, 1947–57.

Czechoslovakia. State Statistical Office. *Annuaire statistique de la République Tchécoslovaque.* Prague, 1938.

—— *Cenové zprávy Státního úřadu statistického* (Price Reports of the State Statistical Office). 1947–48. Prague, 1947–48.

—— *Deset let rozvoje národního hospodářství a kultury Československé republiky 1945–1955* (Ten Years of Economic and Cultural Development of the Czechoslovak Republic, 1945–1955). F. Herbst, and others, eds. Prague, Rudé právo, 1956.

—— *Průmyslové zprávy Státního úřadu statistického* (Industrial Reports of the State Statistical Office). 1947–48. Prague, 1948–49.

—— *Statistical Bulletin of Czechoslovakia.* 1947–48. Prague.

—— *Statistical Digest of the Czechoslovak Republic, 1948.* Prague, 1948.

—— *Statistická ročenka republiky československé* (Statistical Yearbook of the Czechoslovak Republic). 1957–59. Prague, 1957–59.

—— *Zprávy Státního úřadu statistického* (Reports of the State Statistical Office). 1948–49. Prague, 1948–49.

Dolanský, Jaromír. *Výklad k rozpočtu* (Commentary on the Budget). 1948–49. Prague, Ministry of Finance, 1948–49.

Finance a úvěr (Finances and Credit). 1957–58. Prague.

General Secretariat of the Economic Council, *see* Czechoslovakia. General Secretariat of the Economic Council

Gilbert, Milton, and Irving G. Kravis. *An International Comparison of National Products and the Purchasing Power of Currencies.* Paris, Organization for European Economic Cooperation, 1954.

Hospodářské noviny (Economic News). 1957–58. Prague.

Hungary. Central Statistical Office. *Adatok és adalékok a népgazdaság fejlödésének tanulmányozásához, 1949–1955* (Data and Contributions to the Study of the People's Economy, 1949–1955). Budapest, 1957.

Institute for Agricultural Accounting and Management, *see* Czechoslovakia. Institute for Agricultural Accounting and Management

International Monetary Fund. *Balance of Payments Yearbook, 1948 and 1949.* Washington, D.C., 1950.

Lazarcik, Gregor. *Production and Productivity in Czechoslovak Agriculture, 1934–38 and 1946–57.* PH.D. dissertation, Columbia University, 1960. Microfilm edition.

Ministry of Finance, *see* Czechoslovakia. Ministry of Finance

Ministry of Interior, *see* Czechoslovakia. Ministry of Interior

Mladá fronta (Young Front). 1955. Prague.

National Assembly, *see* Czechoslovakia. National Assembly.

National Bank of Czechoslovakia. *Bulletin.* 1949. Prague.

Népszabadság (People's Liberty). 1956. Budapest.

Nová mysl (New Thought). 1956–58. Prague.

Noviny vnitřního obchodu (Domestic Trade News). 1957. Prague.

Odborář (The Trade-Unionist). 1957. Prague.

Organization for European Economic Cooperation. *A Standardized System of National Accounts.* 1958 edition. Paris, 1959.

Pesek, Boris. Czechoslovak Monetary Policy, 1945–53. Unpublished PH.D. dissertation, University of Chicago, 1956.

Plánované hospodářství (Planned Economy). 1955–56, 1959. Prague.

Podniková organisace (Enterprise Organization). 1958. Prague.

Poland. Central Statistical Office. *Dochód narodowy Polski 1956* (National Income of Poland, 1956). Warsaw, 1958.

—— *Rocznik statystyczny, 1957* (Statistical Yearbook, 1957). Warsaw, 1957.

Politická ekonomie (Political Economy). 1955, 1958. Prague.

Práce (Labor). 1953, 1955–57. Prague.

Pravda (Truth). 1953. Bratislava.

Presse, Die. 1955. Vienna.

Prouza, Bohumil. *Společné fondy v JZD* (Communal Funds in Agricultural Collectives). Prague, Státní zemědělské nakladatelství, 1957.

Rudé právo (Red Right). 1948, 1952–58. Prague.

Slovakia. State Planning and Statistical Office. *Statistická príručka Slovenska, 1948* (Statistical Handbook for Slovakia, 1948). Bratislava, 1948.

Slovenský včelár (Slovak Beekeeper). 1948. Bratislava.

Spáčil, Bedřich. *Veřejné hospodářství československé v roce 1947* (Czechoslovak Public Finances in the Year 1947). Prague, Ministry of Information, 1947.

Stádník, Miloš. *Czechoslovak National Income and the Methods of Its Assessment.* Prague, Ministry of Information, (194–?).

—— *Národní důchod a jeho rozdělení* (National Income and Its Distribution). Prague, 1946.

State Statistical Office, *see* Czechoslovakia. State Statistical Office

Statistické zprávy (Statistical News). 1956–58. Prague.

Statistický obzor (Statistical Review). 1956–58. Prague.

Statistický zpravodaj (Statistical Reporter). 1947–50. Prague.

Stone, Richard. "Functions and Criteria of a System of Social Accounting," in International Association for Research in Income and Wealth. *Income and Wealth, Series I.* Cambridge, 1951, pp. 1–74.

Sudetendeutsche Zeitung. 1957. Munich.

Süd-Ost Pressedienst. 1952. Salzburg.

Svoboda, Karol, *Prečo a ako hospodáriť podla vzorových stanov JRD* (The Why and How of Farming According to the Model Statute of Agricultural Collectives). Bratislava, 1957.

Tuček, Miroslav. *Vývoj československých financí v letech 1945–52* (Evolution of Czechoslovak Finances in the Years 1945–52). Prague, Státní pedagogické nakladatelství, 1953.

United Nations. *A System of National Accounts and Supporting Tables.* Studies in Methods, No. 2. New York, 1953.

—— *National Income Statistics of Various Countries, 1938–1948.* Lake Success, N.Y., 1950.

Veltruský, Ladislav, and others. *Československé finance* (Czechoslovak Finances). Prague, Orbis, 1958.

Zápotocký, Antonín. *Revoluční odborové hnutí po únoru 1948* (Revolutionary Trade-Union Movement after February 1948). Prague, Prace, 1952.

Zemědělské noviny (Agricultural News). 1957. Prague.

Životní úroveň v ČSR (Living Standards in Czechoslovakia). Supplement to Hospodářské noviny (Economic News), September, 1957.

KEY TO TABLE ITEMS

INDEX